BY MARTIN DUBERMAN

Charles Francis Adams, 1807–1886 (1961)
The Antislavery Vanguard: New Essays on the Abolitionists [Ed.] (1965)
James Russell Lowell (1966)
The Uncompleted Past (1969)
Black Mountain: An Exploration in Community (1972)

PLAYS:
In White America (1964)
The Memory Bank (1970)
Male Armor (1975)

MALE ARMOR

Selected Plays, 1968–1974

Martin Duberman

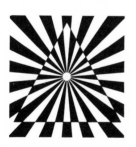

E. P. Dutton & Co. Inc.   ·   New York   ·   1975

Library of Congress Cataloging in Publication Data

Duberman, Martin
Male armor.

CONTENTS: Metaphors.—The colonial dudes.—The recorder. [etc.]
I. Title.
PS3554.U25M3   812'.5'4   75-6510

First Edition

10   9   8   7   6   5   4   3   2   1

Published simultaneously in Canada by Clarke, Irwin & Company Limited,
Toronto and Vancouver
ISBN: 0-525-47402-1
Designed by The Etheredges

For Leo Bersani

CONTENTS

INTRODUCTION

In looking over the various plays I've written during the past six years, I had to try to understand by what criteria I was deciding to include some in this volume and omit others. One criterion was obvious: I wanted to get work into print which I thought had deserved but hadn't been able to find production (and, thus, the inclusion of the two long plays, *Payments* and *Elagabalus,* which together make up the bulk of this volume). That much can be chalked up to the playwright's usual conviction that he or she has been doing major work unconscionably ignored (though—happily for the playwright's peace of mind—not work *inexplicably* ignored; we always have at hand the comforting "truism" that our commercial theater is inhospitable to material not immediately accessible to popular taste).

But there are some unproduced plays of mine that I chose not to publish in this collection. A few I no longer like. A few don't "fit." But fit *what?* As I looked over the total body of work I'd done since 1968, I felt that a significant part of it formed a unit. Only the *The Guttman Ordinary Scale* stuck out— neither an obvious reject nor an obvious choice; friends were divided in their advice, and I myself remained uneasy with a "cartoon" play that seemed at variance in tone with the other pieces I'd decided to include. Finally, I put *Guttman* in; its content, if not style, did seem to tie it authentically to what I had come to see as the dominant connecting theme.

A playwright discussing his "theme" can—aside from verging on parody—end with an exercise in self-sabotage, the reduction of various threads to a single machine-made line. (It's a habit we pick up from critics—or from being denied the right kind). If I had written these plays as self-conscious of "theme" as I've since become in reading them over, I doubt if they would have whatever theatrical vitality they do.

Having said that, I still feel the need (perhaps it's my academic training) to articulate my sense of what binds the plays in this volume together. The connection I've chosen to stress is best summarized in the title: *Male Armor*. Since 1968, when the first draft of the earliest play in this collection was written, I've been nagged by a question that has only recently become fully conscious (in me and in the culture): "What does it mean to be a 'man'?"

For many people concerned with that question, the writings of Wilhelm Reich have been of special importance; and "male armor" is deliberately meant to recall Reich's broader concept of "character armor"—meaning, the devices we use (which then use us) to protect ourselves from our own energy, and especially from our sexual energy: the strategies that help us grow a skin—and then keep us in it.

I don't mean to suggest that these plays were conceived to "illustrate" Reichian theory. Until the last few months, I'd never read a word of Reich. He was some distant figure I vaguely connected to a strange box in which people sat to regain their potency. Even now, knowing more of Reich's work, my feelings have progressed only to the level of fascinated ambivalence. Yet, his concept of "character armor" does beautifully fit the encased, immovable men who dominate these plays (not all the men; of the few exceptions, more in a minute).

The Reichian concept fits them because they're semi-automatons, men acting out roles they never designed and hardly notice, roles by their nature destructive because they keep the individuals from *themselves*—and thus from others. The men in *Metaphors* and *The Electric Map* are those most fully entrapped by their own defenses. But "armoring" also effectively describes the disabling limitations of Dr. Oates in *Guttman;* of all the secondary male figures in *Elagabalus;* and, in a less encompassing way, of Bob, the central character of *Payments.* (As well as accounting for—armor does serve its purposes—their narrowly concentrated strengths.) The same may be said of the two men in *The Recorder,* though in that play whimsical impulse, tricks of memory, a trace of sexual intrigue and the tape recorder's own independent life, all work to unsettle the characters' protective shells.

There are a few men in these plays who occupy less defended ground—Adrian in *Elagabalus* and Wayne and Foley in *The Colonial Dudes.* With them I was working to suggest some possibilities of "maleness" we've only recently begun to explore in our society (not working as self-consciously—I feel I have to say again—as this retrospective summary suggests; most of what I write here is theory after the fact—the fact of wanting to work out in dramatic terms a quirk of personality or situation which had somehow lodged itself in my head).

I'm certain that many readers will find Adrian merely tiresome, in no way more appealing than the more obviously armored men in the other plays. He may seem to choose and alternate his personae with greater freedom and from a far wider repertory than most people imagine is available to them, but his style, many may feel, is unfettered only in comparison with those around him. And perhaps not even then; for Adrian is driven by his own imperatives, ones derived from the newest social dicta about the necessity for androgyny, and profoundly reliant for their implementation on the privileges available to those with leisure and wealth.

Not only do I anticipate this distaste for Adrian, but to some extent share it. Yet I'm drawn to him, too—far more than to the evasive sparring partners in *Metaphors, The Electric Map,* and *The Recorder.* Adrian is playful and daring. His gaiety may be contaminated by petulance and willfulness, but he *is* moving toward an *un*-armored territory, moving out so far that finally he's left with no protection against the traditional weaponry brought to bear against him—none, that is, other than the ultimate defense of self-destruction; a choice *he* makes—in defiance, and in the conviction that Carthages will everywhere continue to rise against Rome.

The only men in these plays to whom I feel more warmly bound than to Adrian are Foley and Wayne in *The Colonial Dudes* (Jim, in *Guttman,* too, but there, the intentional cartoon stands in the way of any real affect). Foley and Wayne are my imagined versions of the "best" of their respective generations attempting to come together (just as Paul and the Interviewer in *Metaphors,* conversely, are resolutely destined to remain apart). Hesitantly, sometimes mistrustfully, Wayne and Foley prove willing to test whether their surface differences *need* to obscure their underlying sympathies. Both men manage a considerable passage—away from familiar and comfortable formulas, toward some painful but promising redefinitions. They end, shyly, caring for each other a great deal—and more aware of unsuspected resources for caring within themselves.

I want to conclude with a word about one of the few women in these plays: Nancy in *Payments.* More than with any of my other characters, I keep losing my sense of her; she goes out of focus—then comes back in obsessional detail. I feel defensive about her, as if some part of myself was going to be put under moral scrutiny and misunderstood. So much of what she does seems ugly, her behavior bizarre, her choices bitter and reckless. Perhaps my need to explain and defend her here is due to having over-elaborated her in my head and under-inventing her on the page. I prefer to think it's because of my fear that her unorthodoxy will be too easily equated with "man-hating," that the fierceness of her struggle to get to a *different place* will be misinterpreted as mere freakish destructiveness. Nancy doesn't know her destination—that's the essence of her daring—and the path she sets out on is surely unconventional. But it's conventions that have smothered her, that have narrowed her options to where she must choose between not moving at all and taking a bizarre gamble. She knows that *if* she gets to a new place, it won't be peaceful—but neither will it be hypocritical and sterile. Her initial hope is that she can help Bob get there, too (and her deepest impulses *are* generous)—a hope finally thwarted. But *Nancy,* in any case, is determined on change.

It may seem paradoxical that I should single out one of the few female characters in these plays as being for me the most poignant personification of the effort to pierce "male armor." But that armor isn't, after all, wholly confined to one gender. And as for the courage needed for the assault against it, it does seem to me that in the "real" world these days it *is* some few women who are doing the most to disclose the omnipresence of "armoring"—and to help us release the energy trapped within.

METAPHORS

PRODUCTION AND PUBLICATION HISTORY:

An earlier version of *Metaphors* was part of an omnibus of eleven plays, *Collision Course,* that opened at the Café Au Go Go, New York City, on May 8, 1968. That version has since been performed by various stock and amateur groups, and was published in *Collision Course,* Edward Parone, ed. (Random House: 1968).

This more recent, longer version of *Metaphors* has not previously been published. It was part of an evening of three of my one-act plays first performed (January 1972) in workshop at The New Dramatists, and then at The John Drew Theater, Easthampton (August 1972). Two of the three plays—*Metaphors* and *The Colonial Dudes*—were subsequently presented (fall 1973) at The Manhattan Theater Club.

The admissions office at Yale: an elegant room, complete with fireplace.

Behind the desk sits a middle-aged man—the INTERVIEWER. *As the curtain rises,* HE *is thumbing through a batch of papers.*

Seated in a chair at the side of the desk is a handsome young man, PAUL. *Both are conservatively dressed in jackets and ties.*

INTERVIEWER: How old are you, Paul?

PAUL: Nineteen, sir.

INTERVIEWER: That's a little older than most entering freshmen. But never mind. Is Yale your first choice?

PAUL: Yes, sir.

INTERVIEWER: Now tell me in your own words why you want to come to Yale.

PAUL: *(After a pause, in dreamy tone)* I want to develop my mind, sir.

INTERVIEWER: Your mind . . . ?

PAUL: I'm very concerned about my mind, sir.

3

INTERVIEWER: *(Perfunctory)* Yes. Well, that's fine. Every young man should be. *(Leafs through a batch of papers on the desk)* Frankly, Paul, your high school record is not distinguished.

PAUL: I know.

INTERVIEWER: I can't say that your chances of getting into Yale are very good. We only take the top men, you know.

PAUL: Yes, I know.

INTERVIEWER: *(Brightly)* How about extracurricular activities? They might improve your chances. We try to keep an eye out these days for the unusual boy, someone whose talent is not immediately apparent from his academic record. Do you follow my meaning?

PAUL: Mmm. I mean: yes, sir.

INTERVIEWER: How about summer jobs, for example? Done anything unusual during the summers?

PAUL: I worked for *Time* magazine one summer.

INTERVIEWER: *(Patronizing)* That's hardly unusual, Paul.

PAUL: Oh, I didn't mean in the office. I worked in the warehouse. You got to have smarts for that.

INTERVIEWER: Smarts?

PAUL: *(Pointing to his temple)* Up here. The gray matter.

INTERVIEWER: I see. Smarts. *(Makes a brief notation on his writing pad)*

PAUL: You know what a window is on an envelope?

INTERVIEWER: Yes, I think so. That's the transparent area where the address shows through.

PAUL: Absolutely! Well, at *Time* they got five different kinds of windows on their envelopes. When a call comes to the warehouse, you got to be able to pick out the right window just like *that!* One pause and you're dead.

INTERVIEWER: *(Sardonic)* Sounds very demanding.

PAUL: Let me tell you—it was rough! *(Pause)* You know the difference between six inches and eight inches?

INTERVIEWER: Two inches.

(HE smiles at his own joke. PAUL does not)

PAUL: *(Mysteriously)* Not to the touch. *(Change to bright-eyed tone)* In the warehouse you had to know on sight. And fast. "Six-inch envelope with the three-inch window." "Eight-inch envelope with the three-and-a-half-inch window." *(Points at INTERVIEWER)* You gotta choose! And quick!

INTERVIEWER: *(Prissy)* I think I have the picture. *(Makes another note on his pad)* Have you done any traveling during the summer vacation?

PAUL: Vacation?

INTERVIEWER: During summer recess, school break.

(PAUL laughs)

PAUL: Oh, yeah—the school break! I remember it well. *(Chuckles to himself)* Yeah, I've traveled. I think it cultures a person.

(INTERVIEWER frowns at the vulgarism)

But one world cruise is enough. If you see more, you lose your standards.

INTERVIEWER: *(Patronizing)* I'd never thought of it quite that way.

PAUL: What way have you thought of it?

INTERVIEWER: *(Startled)* Thought about travel?

PAUL: About cruising.

INTERVIEWER: I've never taken a cruise. I really can't say.

PAUL: Never cruised? Amazing! There aren't many of you guys left.

INTERVIEWER: *(A little edgy)* I assume then, Paul—to get back to my question—that your extracurricular activities have been limited, that you have no special talents, as we say.

PAUL: *(Shyly)* In fact I do have a special talent. But I don't like to talk about it.

INTERVIEWER: We appreciate modesty, Paul. But as I said, yours is a borderline case—at best.

PAUL: *(Hesitantly)* Well . . . it's my mind, sir. I have, what you might say, a supreme mind.

INTERVIEWER: *(Uncertain* HE *has heard correctly)* A supreme mind?

PAUL: Maybe not a supreme mind yet. That's what I'm working toward. But I have the talent for it. My friend says I do.

INTERVIEWER: You have a great many friends, I suppose.

PAUL: I have this friend. He already has a supreme mind. He's about your age. Forty-five. He says I can make it too.

INTERVIEWER: *(Impatiently)* I can't say I'm following any of this, Paul. You'll have to be a bit more precise.

PAUL: There's a door to every mind. And every door has a key. When you meet a stranger and can tell instantly what the key to his mind is, then you have a supreme mind.

INTERVIEWER: *(Patronizing)* Minds are complicated mechanisms, you know. There is no one key to a mind, or to a personality.

PAUL: People are very simple.

INTERVIEWER: On the contrary, Paul. People are very complicated.

PAUL: They get complicated. Because they can't satisfy that one need.

INTERVIEWER: There is no *one* need.

PAUL: It depends on the person. But each person has one. One need. One key. My friend knows what it is as soon as he meets you.

INTERVIEWER: You're talking gibberish.

PAUL: I felt the same way when my friend first told me. So he said I should put him to a test.

INTERVIEWER: This attitude of yours is not likely to—

PAUL: *(Interrupting)* —I put him to the test. I introduced him to a man I knew. Married, with two grown children. A doctor— Park Avenue specialist. Big in tropical diseases—

INTERVIEWER: *(Interrupting)* Mr. Wentworth—

PAUL: —they became lovers. My friend and the doctor became lovers.

INTERVIEWER: *(Outraged)* What in God's name are you talking about?!

PAUL: *(Hurt)* I'm sorry, sir. I thought you were interested. You asked if I had any special talent.

INTERVIEWER: And what does a homosexual scandal have to do with that?

PAUL: *(Indignant)* It was not homosexual. Nothing like that. He found the doctor's key, as he told me he would. He made that man happy. It's a beautiful story. *(Change to slightly menacing tone)* I wish you'd let me tell it without interruption.

INTERVIEWER: *(Startled, then apologetic)* I . . . uh . . . didn't mean to interrupt. I am interested, as you must know, in . . . in finding out what you're like. That, after all, is my job.

PAUL: *(More firmly)* Then try not to interrupt me again. You shouldn't spoil the beauty of the story by interrupting me.

INTERVIEWER: Very well. Let's—have your story. I won't interrupt.

PAUL: And don't rustle those papers, okay? It's disconcerting.

INTERVIEWER: Now, Paul, I really don't think—

PAUL: *(Ignoring* HIM *)* —they didn't become lovers right away. You see, the doctor didn't know his own key. My friend knew it. But it took time to get the doctor to see it. It happened in a very beautiful way. *(*HE *turns to* INTERVIEWER*)* You won't appreciate this story: you're not comfortable.

INTERVIEWER: I am comfortable.

PAUL: You look stiff behind that desk. Why don't you come sit on the floor.

INTERVIEWER: Don't be ridiculous. Go on with your story.

PAUL: My friend bought a small steel box. Airtight. A blue-gray metal box, almost black. It was a six-inch square. Airtight. *(Turns to* INTERVIEWER *)* Why don't you sit on the floor while I tell you the rest. You'll like it better that way.

INTERVIEWER: I'm fine right here.

PAUL: You might enjoy it. You ought to try everything.

INTERVIEWER: *(Uncertainly)* I would not enjoy it.

PAUL: *(Hurt)* Okay. But I'll have to stop the story. I can't tell you the rest the way you look.

INTERVIEWER: I look the way I always look.

PAUL: *(Sudden warmth)* Yeah, I know. *(Pause)* The trouble is, you're not appreciative.

INTERVIEWER: I beg your pardon?

PAUL: You won't accommodate yourself.

INTERVIEWER: I'm listening to you very closely. Indeed, I find you a most unusual young man.

PAUL: That's still outside in.

(Pause)

INTERVIEWER: I'm not fond of the floor.

PAUL: People have to make an effort. To understand. To unhinge. You got to see me with my eyes. Otherwise you're not doing your job. This is a story from the floor up, not the desk down.

(Pause; INTERVIEWER *sighs, then slowly gets out of his chair)*

INTERVIEWER: Oh, well. I don't suppose there's any dissuading you. *(Pause)* No, I think not. Well, if it'll amuse you, why not?

(PAUL smiles)

No one can say I'm not game.

PAUL: You're a groove, man. There should be more dudes like you.

(The INTERVIEWER *is now seated on the floor)*

INTERVIEWER: It is comfortable.

PAUL: It's great to be free. My friend wants everyone to be free. So they can't be hurt. But to be free you have to turn the key. *(Suddenly expansive)* You know what? I feel like singing. Have you ever heard Cat Stevens sing?

INTERVIEWER: Cat Stevens?

PAUL: He's very gentle with his music. Very tender. He speaks in messages that you have to put together and figure out. I'm saving my money. I want Cat to give a performance for me. He'll do it. I know he'll do it. *(Sudden shift)* Hey, man, I'm going to sing for you! Like you tell me if I got any special talent.

INTERVIEWER: I thought you were going to tell me about a steel box. The one your friend bought.

PAUL: *(Starts to sing)*

> When you walk through a storm,
> keep your chin up high,
> and don't be afraid of the dark.
> At the end of the road,
> there's a long, long—

Hell—I've forgotten that line! *(To* INTERVIEWER *)* What is it, huh? You know— *(Sings)*

> At the end of the road,
> there's a dum, dum, dum . . .

INTERVIEWER: I don't know. I don't sing.

PAUL: Oh. Well, what do you think? You think I got talent?

INTERVIEWER: Your voice has a nice rough texture to it. But I think it needs training.

PAUL: I know that.

INTERVIEWER: You're not inhibited. That's very important.

PAUL: For what?

INTERVIEWER: Entertaining.

PAUL: You gotta do what'll pleasure people. My dad—God bless his soul—he used to tell us—

INTERVIEWER: *(Interrupting)* —oh, is your father deceased? I'm sorry to hear that.

PAUL: Yes, he left us some time ago. He was tough on us. He used to whip our ass red. But a kid needs that. Makes him feel like somebody cares. *(Sudden shift)* Do you like rocks? I know someone who collects rocks. He's a millionaire, a darling man. He travels all over the world, looking for rocks.

INTERVIEWER: What do you mean by rocks?

PAUL: I mean rocks. Rocks. Why does everything have to be translated? Rocks are rocks.

INTERVIEWER: Oh. I thought you meant jewels. Or ice. *(Laughs nervously)* Or perhaps a sexual metaphor.

(PAUL smiles. The INTERVIEWER is embarrassed)

Rocks, you know, is a lower-class metaphor for the scrotum. *(Pause)* For balls.

PAUL: What's a metaphor?

INTERVIEWER: Using one word in place of another. To suggest their similarity. Like rocks and—balls.

PAUL: Are you lower class?

INTERVIEWER: Of course not. But one hears things. Around. You know.

PAUL: Mmm. I guess you keep up. Strange, you don't know Cat.

INTERVIEWER: If you're going to tell me about your friend and that box, I think you'd better.

PAUL: Do you know karate?

INTERVIEWER: *(Nervous)* Uh—no. That's like Yoga, isn't it? I don't keep up with that faddish sort of thing.

PAUL: Here, let me show you. *(Reaches over to the fireplace and grabs the poker resting in front of it)*

INTERVIEWER: Be careful of that!

PAUL: First I'll show you the Kata movements.

INTERVIEWER: The head is loose. It comes off.

(PAUL demonstrates the Kata movements, throwing the poker back and forth from hand to hand, shifting positions with energy and style; occasionally HE grunts or shouts. When HE finishes, HE stands over the INTERVIEWER, the poker still in his hand)

How'd you like it?

INTERVIEWER: Very good. Excellent.

PAUL: Okay. Now stand up. I'll show you the blocks.

INTERVIEWER: I'd really rather not. Thank you. I think perhaps—

(PAUL grabs him under the arms and forces him up)

PAUL: *(Cheerfully)* Come on! It'll only take a second. It's one of my special talents.

(INTERVIEWER is now on his feet)

Okay. Now come at me with your fists. Come on!

INTERVIEWER: *(Timidly)* Which fist?

PAUL: Either fist. Both. Surprise me!

INTERVIEWER: It's been years since I've . . . put on the gloves. Summer camp, I think it was. Back in—oh, Lord!—I got knocked out right in front of my parents! They were up for Visitors' Day—Week.

(HE makes a tentative jab at PAUL, who blocks the blow with a quick movement)

INTERVIEWER: Ow! You hurt my finger!

(PAUL *laughs*)

PAUL: You oughta toughen up those hands. You should start hitting a board. Before you know it, you'll have callouses as big as your finger. I once knew a guy who loved hitting the board so much, he'd have an orgasm.

INTERVIEWER: I don't approve of violence.

PAUL: You go to church a lot, I bet.

INTERVIEWER: No, now and then.

PAUL: I bet you go to church regular. What do you think about when you're there? Do you think about rocks? (*Without waiting for an answer*) I was brought up by the church. A priest had sex with me when I was nine years old.

INTERVIEWER: Terrible!

PAUL: There you go again. Man, you're a bad translator. You and those metaphors. It was *beautiful*, not terrible. *Beautiful*, man. The priest was very humble. You don't get anything straight, do you?

INTERVIEWER: What did your friend do with the box?

PAUL: Oh, you want to hear about the box. (*With a trace of menace*) You'll have to concentrate.

INTERVIEWER: I can—manage that.

PAUL: He filled it. Right to the top. *Right to the top*. Then he smoothed it down so that every corner was filled. If you had turned it upside down, a perfect six-inch square would have fallen out. Like wet sand out of a pail. Like a mud pie.

INTERVIEWER: He filled the box with mud?

PAUL: It looked like mud. Brown and dark. With streaks in it.

INTERVIEWER: (*Contentedly*) He filled the box with mud.

PAUL: *(Indignant)* You must be some kind of nut! What the hell would he fill a box with mud for? This is a grown man, baby. You're a very strange cat.

INTERVIEWER: *(Confused, upset)* Sorry. I must have misunderstood.

PAUL: You're good at that. *(HE pauses)* All right. We'll try again. It's really very simple. Like everything. When the box was filled, he sealed it. Then he took it—

INTERVIEWER: *(Interrupting timidly)* I'm terribly sorry but . . . I'm afraid I just do not—

PAUL: Now what?

INTERVIEWER: The inside . . . the . . . I don't understand what the box was filled with.

PAUL: You have to be kidding.

INTERVIEWER: No, truly, I . . . it wasn't mud, but I . . .

PAUL: *(With exaggerated slowness)* We'll go through it very slowly. First my friend took the empty, six-inch, steel box into the bathroom. He then took off his pants, carefully folded them over the towel rack . . .

INTERVIEWER: *(Alarmed and thrilled; audibly catches his breath)* I see! Of course! Yes, I see!

PAUL: You ought to stop thinking in metaphors. It blocks understanding. A is not like B. A is A.

INTERVIEWER: Quite right. A is A.

PAUL: Very good.

INTERVIEWER: So your friend sealed the box. Sealed it. And then . . . then I suppose he—

PAUL: *(Completing the INTERVIEWER's sentence)* —gave it to the doctor. *(Pauses; then with great feeling)* He said to him: "I know you want this more than anything else in the world, and I am giving it to you with the greatest feeling of tenderness." The doctor cried. He said it was the most beautiful gift he had ever received. They became lovers.

INTERVIEWER: *(Deeply moved)* The doctor cried. Aren't people wonderful? The doctor cried.

PAUL: He made that man happy. *(Pause)* That man smiles from morning till night. I visited him in the hospital the other day. He smiled the whole time. Like he was walking in a forest paradise, alone but not alone. He didn't even know I was there.

INTERVIEWER: *(Startled;* HE *begins to come out of his trance)* He didn't recognize you?

PAUL: He's alone with his lover. His lover is always with him. When he lies down on his cot, he puts out his arms as if cradling his lover. He even has an orgasm. He's completely happy. No cares. No pain. My friend turned the key for him. It's wonderful to make people that happy. I have the talent to do it. I can bring people that kind of happiness.

(The INTERVIEWER *slowly rises. It should be unclear whether what follows is hypocrisy or sincerity—the* INTERVIEWER *is himself unclear)*

INTERVIEWER: I believe you can, Paul. It's rare to meet a young man with your kind of talent and drive. I think you're going to make something of yourself. And I want to help.

PAUL: All I need is a place to develop my mind. Yale would be right for me.

(The INTERVIEWER *is now back at the desk;* HE *rustles through the papers)*

INTERVIEWER: *(Very serious)* The final decision is not mine alone, of course. But I can tell you this, Paul: It's clear to me that you're not the kind of student whose abilities are accurately represented by his academic record. Grades, after all, are a limited yardstick for measuring a limited kind of talent. Yours fall outside the usual range. *(With overwrought sincerity)* And I'm going to say as much to the admissions committee.

PAUL: Thank you, sir.

INTERVIEWER: I don't ask for thanks. Doing my job is its own reward. I like to help worthy young men get ahead. Now then, we understand each other.

PAUL: *(With just a trace of the sinister)* I think we do. If I come to Yale, sir, you won't regret it. I'm going to make you proud of me.

INTERVIEWER: I know you are. Well, my boy, it's goodbye for now.

*(*THEY *shake hands)*

PAUL: Goodbye, sir.

*(*HE *walks to the door, then turns to face the* INTERVIEWER*)*

I had an $18,000 painting in my last apartment. I had to take an axe to it. To everything. The important thing is freedom.

INTERVIEWER: Goodbye, my boy. *(Pause).* Till the fall.

PAUL: *(Scowling furiously)* More metaphors! I hate metaphors!

*(*PAUL *exits)*

CURTAIN

THE COLONIAL DUDES

PRODUCTION AND PUBLICATION HISTORY:

The Colonial Dudes was first performed in late 1969 at The Actors Studio, to reinaugurate its playwrights' unit. It was then done at the summer theater in Dorset, Vermont (1970); again at The Actors Studio in May 1971; as part of an evening of my short plays at The New Dramatists (May 1972); at The John Drew Theater, Easthampton (August 1972); and at The Manhattan Theater Club (fall 1973).

Stanley Richards chose *The Colonial Dudes* for his collection *The Best Short Plays 1973* (Chilton: 1973).

A wooden partition divides the stage into two parts.

One side of the partition is the office of ALEX FOLEY, *professor of English literature. On the other side is the corridor in front of his office.*

As the curtain rises, FOLEY *is at his desk, typing. He lights a cigarette, types some more, then sits back, looks disgustedly at his typewriter and mutters: "Von schmaky putz."* FOLEY *is about forty-five, burly, tough, bearded, dressed in the sort of informal, somewhat adventurous style that makes it clear* HE *is not a standard academic.*

In the corridor, upstage, sits WAYNE FROBER, *aged nineteen, long-haired, wearing a ratty leather jacket, blue jeans, no socks and sneakers.* HE *has bad skin. The neck of a pint bottle sticks out of his jacket pocket.* HE*'s sitting up against the wall of the corridor, eyes closed as if asleep.*

FOLEY *gets up from his desk, walks to the door of his office, opens it and steps into the corridor.* HE *begins to move purposefully down the hall when* HE *sees* WAYNE *and stops.* WAYNE *has not opened his eyes.*

FOLEY: Oh. Are you waiting to see me?

*(*WAYNE *barely opens his eyes)*

WAYNE: No.

FOLEY: *(Surprised)* You're not?

WAYNE: No.

FOLEY: Oh. *(Pause)* Mine's the only office up here, you know. There's no one else around.

*(*WAYNE *doesn't react)*

You're not waiting, then, for anyone else?

WAYNE: Yeah, I am.

FOLEY: *(Confused)* But as I said, mine is the only office up here.

WAYNE: Yeah, I know. I'm resting.

FOLEY: Okay. (HE *starts down the corridor)*

WAYNE: Hey!

*(*FOLEY *stops and turns around)*

FOLEY: Yes?

WAYNE: Where's Hale?

FOLEY: Hale who?

*(*WAYNE *laughs)*

WAYNE: Hale who. Oh, I like that. You made a poem: Hale who. Sounds like haiku. Hey—we can put the two together:
> Hale who
> Haiku.

FOLEY: That's not haiku. But not bad—at least for eight in the morning.

WAYNE: Man, is it that late!

FOLEY: Late? Nobody else has arrived in the building yet.

WAYNE: What are you doing here?

FOLEY: That's just what I was going to ask you.

WAYNE: I already told you. I'm waiting for Hale.

FOLEY: Hale who— *(Interrupts himself)* No, let's try it this way: Who is the Hale you're waiting for?

WAYNE: Shee—it! That's no poem.

FOLEY: Poems don't get answers.

WAYNE: Right! They get questions.

(Pause; FOLEY *waits for a second, shrugs, then starts down the corridor again)*

(Yelling after him) Hale Riker!

*(*FOLEY *stops, then turns around)*

FOLEY: Oh—Mr. Riker.

WAYNE: Is that what you call him—*Mr.* Riker?!

FOLEY: *(Embarrassed)* Well no, as a matter of fact. I call him Hale.

WAYNE: So do I.

FOLEY: Are you a student?

WAYNE: 'Course. Isn't everyone?

FOLEY: I mean, are you enrolled in the college?

WAYNE: I guess so.

FOLEY: You don't know?

WAYNE: Yeah. I'm a beginner, a freshman.

FOLEY: I see. And Mr. Riker—Hale—is your teacher.

WAYNE: No. He's a buddy. We shoot the shit together.

FOLEY: *(Staying cool)* That's nice. Where do you shoot it?

WAYNE: Oh man, I don't *shoot* nuthin'. I'm too young to shoot. I'm barely at the pill stage. *(Laughs at what* HE *thinks is a private joke)*

FOLEY: Shooting is bad news.

WAYNE: *(Impressed)* Oh—you know what shooting is?

FOLEY: Doesn't everybody? I'm sure Hale does.

WAYNE: Well Hale—he's a kid. Not much older than I am. But you —you're a, a . . .

FOLEY: Go ahead. I'm a what?

WAYNE: You're a regular Rip Van Winkle!

*(*WAYNE *laughs;* FOLEY *smiles)*

FOLEY: I guess I am pretty ancient.

WAYNE: Naw—that just came out. I often say things I don't mean. To hear how they sound: in case I ever really want to say them.

FOLEY: Why are you waiting for Hale here?

WAYNE: I don't like his corridor. It's got too many doors in it. I can't concentrate.

FOLEY: He probably won't be in for hours.

WAYNE: That's okay. It's nice up here. I like it. How come you get a corridor all to yourself?

FOLEY: *(Smiling)* It's what they call seniority.

WAYNE: Aha—you're a big shot.

FOLEY: No, just a survivor. *(Pause)* Well, I hope you find Hale all right. *(Starts to leave)*

WAYNE: Do you really?

FOLEY: *(A little exasperated)* There are things I care about more, it's true, but—

WAYNE: —I don't even know if *I* want to find him. I don't know if I'm in the mood for Hale. He can be a butternut.

FOLEY: What's a butternut?

WAYNE: *(Smiling broadly)* Gee, I don't know. Nice sound, though. *(Savoring the word)* B-U-T-T-E-R-N-U-T. Well, not that nice. It's got too many meanings already: butter, nut—all that stuff. You got to think of words that are brand new. Like—uh—stropel-dean!

FOLEY: The "dean" part means something. You know—dean of the College and all that.

WAYNE: *(Frowning)* Right. You see what happens? This atmosphere messes up your mind. I haven't been here two months and already I'm using words that mean something. *(Shakes his head)* It's a bummer. *(Looks dejected)*

FOLEY: *(Trying to cheer him up)* If all the words you use are new, nobody will understand you.

WAYNE: So?

FOLEY: You do want to communicate with people, don't you?

WAYNE: Oh sure. But that's not what words are for. Words are for disguise. Or for games. Disguise, when you're talking with someone. Games when you're alone. Now like here— (HE *reaches into his jacket and takes out three or four handwritten pages)* —here's a new game I wrote last night, while I was sitting here.

FOLEY: You've been here all night?

WAYNE: No. Since about four.

FOLEY: The building is locked at night.

WAYNE: Only the doors. *(Suddenly enthusiastic)* Hey, what are you doing?!

(FOLEY looks down at himself self-consciously)

FOLEY: Doing? Nothing.

WAYNE: I mean why'd you leave your office? Where are you going?

FOLEY: To get a drink.

(WAYNE *reaches into his jacket and takes out the pint of rum, which is almost empty*)

WAYNE: Here. Here's a drink. *(Holds out the bottle to* FOLEY*)*

FOLEY: Thanks. It's a little early for me. I was going to get a drink of water.

WAYNE: Suit yourself.

FOLEY: Is that rum?

WAYNE: Yup.

FOLEY: Seems a strange thing for you to be drinking. I think of rum as a skid row drink.

WAYNE: You can't drink rum on skid row. It's too expensive.

FOLEY: That's a point.

WAYNE: Rum is a colonial drink. Molasses Act of 1733 and all that. Very big in the history books.

FOLEY: *(Confused)* Rum?

WAYNE: *(Deadpan)* The Molasses Act. The British put a tax on molasses, which meant the colonists didn't have enough to make all the rum they needed. They needed a lot of rum. For corrupting the Indians and that sort of thing. So they got sore as hell at England and started dumping tea in the harbor. *(Pauses; scratches his head)* Seems to me I left something out. *(Shrugs)* Oh well. Anyway the British got scared and introduced salutary neglect. But that didn't work either: they didn't neglect enough. So the colonists finally said "the hell with it," and Paul Revere roused the Minute Men, who fired at a statue at Lexington. And before long we were the United States of America.

FOLEY: And that's why you drink rum.

WAYNE: Something like that.

FOLEY: You're one of the corrupted Indians.

WAYNE: *(Pleased)* Yeah! Here's to that! *(Hoists the bottle of rum, then uncorks it)* Here's to the Molasses Act! *(HE drinks)* Hey, you know?—you're a pretty good dude.

FOLEY: You're mixing the historical metaphor. No dudes in the eighteenth century.

WAYNE: Here's to the colonial dudes! *(Drinks again)*

FOLEY: It looks like you've finished most of that pint.

WAYNE: Yeah—well I'm sick of weed. Puts you too far out. You know what I mean? Makes you vague, foggy.

FOLEY: I don't much like pot, either. Once in a while, maybe, at a party.

WAYNE: That's when it's worst. You *think* you know where everybody's at. But you're miles away. *(Pause)* So what are you doing?

FOLEY: After my drink of water?

WAYNE: Right.

FOLEY: I came in early to finish a piece I'm writing.

WAYNE: A piece of what?

FOLEY: A book review.

WAYNE: Hey, I'll tell you what—I'll read yours if you'll read mine.

FOLEY: You mean *now?*

WAYNE: You don't wanna. I can tell.

FOLEY: My review isn't finished.

WAYNE: Oh. Too bad. When I stop, I'm finished. I get bored easy.

FOLEY: I'd be glad to read yours, if you'd like.

WAYNE: *(Pleased)* Far out!

FOLEY: Why don't you come in the office.

WAYNE: Sure thing, Mr. Foley.

FOLEY: *(Surprised)* So you know who I am.

WAYNE: Oh, yeah. You're the dude who digs Steppenwolf.

(FOLEY opens the door to his office. THEY walk in. WAYNE looks around at all the books)

Uh-huh! Is that how you got to be a survivor?

FOLEY: One way.

WAYNE: I like books.

FOLEY: So do I. The feel of them.

WAYNE: Yeah! They're neat little packages. I mean, to hold.

FOLEY: What's your name?

WAYNE: Wayne. Wayne Frober. What's yours?

FOLEY: I thought you knew mine?

WAYNE: No. All I know is Professor Foley.

FOLEY: Alex. Alex Foley.

WAYNE: Hi, Alex.

FOLEY: Hi, Wayne. *(FOLEY starts to sit down behind his desk)*

WAYNE: You gonna sit *there?!*

FOLEY: Why not? This is where I sit.

WAYNE: Aw c'mon, Alex. That'll make the vibes all wrong, man.

FOLEY: The vibes?

WAYNE: The vibrations.

FOLEY: Oh. All right. Then *you* sit there.

WAYNE: That's no better. It's *positions* I don't like.

FOLEY: Now look, Wayne: If I can't sit down, how am I going to read your story?

26

WAYNE: You sit when you read? Oh wow—that's a groove! I lie down when I read. Or if it's a poem, I walk around. But never sit; it bends me the wrong way.

FOLEY: Well we all have our peculiarities. And one of mine is that I like to sit when I read. *(Starts to sit)*

WAYNE: *(Casual)* Okay. If that's what turns you on—sure, why not? By the way, it's not a story, it's a poem. So you might want to walk around a little bit.

FOLEY: I sit when I read poems, too.

WAYNE: No kidding? I'll have to try that.

(As a concession, FOLEY takes the chair to the side of the desk)

FOLEY: I'm full of ideas.

WAYNE: *(Serious)* Yeah, you're terriffic.

(Hands FOLEY the poem. THEY smile at each other. FOLEY begins to read)

I don't like what we said about books.

(FOLEY looks up from reading)

FOLEY: We didn't say much.

WAYNE: That's just it. Superficial. We said we "liked" them. Now what does that mean?

FOLEY: You said you like the feel of them—you like to hold them.

WAYNE: Yeah, but what's to like? It's only cloth, or paper. You can get to feel that anywhere—like up a Spanish girl's skirt.

FOLEY: What?!

WAYNE: Yeah, Spanish girls put paper up their skirts so when they walk it swishes like silk.

FOLEY: Never knew that.

WAYNE: Only poor Spanish girls. The rich ones wear real silk. Anyway, it can't be the weight, either. I mean, books. Shit, if all you want to do is hold a couple pounds, you could grab two pounds of anything. Like hamburger meat.

FOLEY: *(Confused)* Uh-huh.

WAYNE: 'Course hamburger meat doesn't have a very nice texture —in the naked hand, that is. Especially if you mix it with egg yolk, which is how my mother makes it. She's a pretty good cook, even though she isn't Jewish. Are you Jewish?

FOLEY: No.

WAYNE: Imagine that!—two non-Jews talking about books.

FOLEY: What's strange about that?

WAYNE: Jews have got the book bag sewn up. That makes it weird for us to like books so much. You got any ideas on that?

FOLEY: *(A little arch)* Could it be we enjoy the *contents* of the book —what's inside of it?

WAYNE: Could be, but I doubt it. Because I like holding books I haven't read. In fact, I often like those more. Reading a book can ruin it. No, I think it's a symbol thing. Like you hold these books or you stare at 'em and you think: wow! there it is, the world all wrapped up and ready to be eaten. Like a hamburger to go. *(Pause)* That's the second time I mentioned hamburgers. Funny. I must be homesick. *(To FOLEY)* My mother, you know, and the egg yolk.

FOLEY: Miss the home cooking, huh? You're living in a dorm, I suppose.

WAYNE: No, I'm not livin' anywhere right now. Corridors; that kind of thing. The old man threw me out.

FOLEY: Oh? I'm sorry to hear that, Wayne.

WAYNE: Oh yeah?—well he'd throw you out, too. You know: HAIR. The big threat. It's so fucking boring—that's what *everybody* gets thrown out for. Why couldn't he come up with something original at least. Like getting pissed off because I forgot my orthodontia exercises. *(Bares his upper teeth, like a horse about to whinny)* You see, it's these two. They're buck for good. Too late now. And all because I forgot the exercises. *(Shrugs)* Oh well—I guess there are worse things. *(Pause)* Trouble is, I got those, too. *(Points to his face)* This acne. The chicks sure don't dig it. Guys, it's okay. Like it makes you approachable; I guess they figure they got one up on you in the competition for GIRLS and POWER. But chicks—forget it! They take one look at this eruption and run like it's Vesuvius. *(Pause)* That's what the poem's about. Chicks and acne. What we call the enduring adolescent themes.

FOLEY: You write only about the universal.

WAYNE: Dig it! I'm a kid for all seasons. *(THEY laugh)* Well why don't you read it?

FOLEY: Well why don't you give me a chance?

WAYNE: So, okay, here's a chance. *(HE puts his elbow on the desk, leans his chin on it and self-consciously stares in the direction away from FOLEY)*

FOLEY: *(Reading aloud to himself, almost inaudible)*
      Silent falls the tamarack,

(WAYNE jumps up with embarrassment and starts pacing)
      Out of reaches,
      Out of sorrows
      Nearer men than you must tell.

WAYNE: *(Mumbling to himself)* How could I ask the guy if he's Jewish, with a name like Foley. Stupid.

FOLEY: You talking to me?

WAYNE: No. Keep reading.

FOLEY: Yes, sir!

WAYNE: Oh, sorry—I didn't mean it like that.

FOLEY: *(Smiling)* I know. Anyway, I like the four lines I managed to read. A dramatic beginning.

WAYNE: *(Beaming)* Oh, yeah? You mean, like it catches your interest.

FOLEY: I could hardly put it down.

WAYNE: You're making fun of me.

FOLEY: I'm not! Look, Wayne: it's *very* good. I'm leveling with you. Come to think of it, I should be offended. You're suggesting I'd say it was good if I didn't think so. Why would I?

WAYNE: To be pleasant.

FOLEY: People are pleasant because they want to be liked. I don't give a damn if anybody likes me or not. Including you.

WAYNE: No shit?

FOLEY: No shit.

WAYNE: That's very impressive. *(Pause)* I think. *(Pause)* I want *you* to like *me*. I suppose that's a defect in my character.

FOLEY: It depends on what you're willing to do to get me to like you. You don't strike me as a person who'd prostitute himself.

(WAYNE looks shocked)

WAYNE: *(Softly)* Jesus!

FOLEY: What's the matter?

WAYNE: *(Hesitant)* Well, it's just that . . . it's . . . *(Blurts it out)* — are you queer?!

FOLEY: Good God! You move a little fast!

WAYNE: You want to build up to it slow, huh?

FOLEY: I mean: you can be hard to follow—the way you jump from one thing to another.

WAYNE: It was perfectly logical. You asked what I'd do to get you to like me; whether I'd prostitute myself.

FOLEY: Now look! I never thought I'd have to explain this, but let me be very clear: I'm a married man with—

WAYNE: —you married to a woman?

FOLEY: *(Exploding)* Of course I'm married to a woman, for Christ's sake!

WAYNE: Well lots of people aren't. I know lots of men who are married to men.

FOLEY: Is that so?

WAYNE: Sure. It's a big thing. Besides, some men who *are* married to women enjoy tricking once in a while with a man. It's a very "in" thing. You know: sample all the varieties of human experience, and all that jazz.

FOLEY: I wouldn't know.

WAYNE: You've never tricked with a man?!

FOLEY: What does "tricked" *mean?!*

WAYNE: Oh, wow—you're somethin' else! There aren't many of you guys left! *(Low whistle)* You're a real find!

FOLEY: Now who's making fun of whom?!

WAYNE: Okay. I'm putting you on.

FOLEY: Thank you. Now: What does "tricked" mean?

WAYNE: Ball. *(Pause)* Hit the sack. *(Pause)* FUCK.

FOLEY: I get it.

WAYNE: I think it's nice you've never made it with a man. I admire that.

FOLEY: You're putting me on again.

WAYNE: No—I mean it. You don't try to keep up, buddy-buddy it with the kids. That's good, man. You stay you.

FOLEY: Thanks.

WAYNE: I don't mean you're square either. No; I got a whole theory about that. I think the squarest thing somebody your age can do is try to keep up.

FOLEY: I do have a beard.

WAYNE: How long have you had it?

FOLEY: Only a year.

WAYNE: *(Subdued)* Hmm. Well, that is disappointing. *(Brightening)* But at least you haven't tricked with a man.

FOLEY: You have, I gather.

WAYNE: *(Disgusted)* Yeah—had to. I was fifteen. Still interested in the status bit—you know, following the crowd. So I hit the sack with a couple of buddies. Just to keep up. Never again. I proved all I'm gonna prove. Men are not my bag. It's against my nature. *(Pause)* But, you know, you ought to try it once.

FOLEY: You just said you admired me for not trying it.

WAYNE: Yeah, I know I did. Well, I'm of two minds about it, to tell you the truth. I'm worried you didn't make a real choice; that you were too paranoid to consider it.

FOLEY: I've been asked, if that's what you mean.

WAYNE: Shit, I know you've been asked. Everybody knows the faculty is full of fags.

FOLEY: Now look, Wayne!

WAYNE: Don't faint. I won't name names. You probably know 'em all anyway.

FOLEY: It happens I don't. And I don't want to.

WAYNE: Bullshit. You're dying to know if *Mr.* Riker and I are making it.

FOLEY: I am not! Besides I already know. You said you only tricked once with a man—when you were fifteen.

WAYNE: I might have been lying. To spare you. You gotta go slow with the oldsters on the unisex theme.

FOLEY: You weren't lying. I think you tell the truth most of the time. And what's more, I'm not sure that's a virtue.

WAYNE: *(Interested)* No kidding? I thought the one thing you types liked about us was our "truth-telling."

32

FOLEY: Only very young children and very old people always tell the truth—because they can't help it.

WAYNE: Hey, I dig that! It's almost an epigram. *(Pause)* But I'm not sure what it means.

FOLEY: It means if you tell the truth all the time, you're either infantile or senile. Everybody else knows "truth-telling" is usually an excuse for cruelty.

WAYNE: Hmm. I'll have to think about that. *(Pause)* You don't mean I should go around telling lies?

FOLEY: Sometimes. White ones. Not out of deceit; out of kindness.

WAYNE: I need an example. I have a very concrete mind. *(Pause)*

FOLEY: Wayne: I think you have a mild case of acne.

WAYNE: You *what?!*

FOLEY: That's a white lie. Your acne is not so mild. But I like you. I don't want to hurt you.

WAYNE: Well you have.

FOLEY: See: you tricked me into telling the truth and now you're angry.

WAYNE: You're getting fond of that word.

FOLEY: What word?

WAYNE: Tricked. So you don't like my acne.

FOLEY: I did not say that.

WAYNE: So you like it.

FOLEY: I don't have a strong opinion one way or the other. I merely *described* your acne.

WAYNE: Oh, boy—there it is! The classic liberal remark! "I don't have a strong opinion one way or the other, I merely described an objective situation, my dear fellow—i.e., your acne." You know damn well you have an opinion of my acne, so let's have it! *(Pause)*

FOLEY: *(Accentuating each word)* I don't like your acne.

(WAYNE slumps dejectedly in his chair)

WAYNE: *(After a pause)* I knew it. I knew it the minute you invited me into your office. You wanted to stare at my pimples.

FOLEY: Well that's an improvement. Ten minutes ago you thought I wanted to sleep with you.

WAYNE: My genius, my art—what does it all matter? It always comes down to the same thing: they want to freak out over my blemished pores.

FOLEY: Wayne, you're putting me on again.

WAYNE: I'm not sure. It's a very depressing topic. I mean I get genuinely depressed about my acne. But I don't know if I'm depressed now. I thought I should go into my routine anyway —my Sorrows of Werther bit. If you don't keep practicing a role, you forget it. And that role I need. It's the only one that brings the chicks back after they go "ecch" at my face. You see they feel guilty for going "ecch." And that leaves 'em wide open. So you got to be sorrowful. You got to play hurt young genius. Then they can comfort you. It makes them feel like Florence Nightingale among the Zulus. It can lead to some beautiful things. Like miscegenation.

FOLEY: Sounds like acne has its advantages.

WAYNE: Only if the girl is nice—capable of guilt. But there aren't many of those any more. It's a new generation: without guilt. *(Depressed)* It's what we call progress. It's all in the poem, if you'd only read it.

FOLEY: It's not in the first four lines.

WAYNE: Of course not. I'm a subtle cat. I don't telegraph my moves. A slow cadenza in the beginning—like the beach at dawn, or—

FOLEY: *(Interrupting)* —a cadenza is a flourish that comes at the *end*, not in the beginning.

WAYNE: You're a pedant.

(FOLEY *jumps up*)

FOLEY: *(Half serious)* Now you've gone too far!

WAYNE: *(Delighted)* Oh yeah?! Terrific! So that's where you live—huh? You hate being called a pedant!

FOLEY: Especially for the wrong reason. Someone who uses words with accuracy is *not* a pedant.

WAYNE: Who says the way you use "cadenza" is accurate?

FOLEY: The dictionary.

WAYNE: The *DICTIONARY!!* Oh, you're too much!

FOLEY: *(Formal)* The dictionary tells us what a particular collection of sounds—like CA-DEN-ZA—means to most people. In other words, how you can make yourself understood.

WAYNE: Most people never heard of CA-DEN-ZA.

FOLEY: That's not the point.

WAYNE: I don't care what most people think.

FOLEY: Don't you want them to understand you?

WAYNE: They can't.

FOLEY: Wayne; *you're* an élitest.

WAYNE: Hey—watch that!

FOLEY: Aha!—so now we know where *you* live! Well you better face it: you want to create a private language accessible only to the few. That, my boy, is the sign of an undemocratic mind.

WAYNE: Don't call me "my boy."

FOLEY: Did I?

WAYNE: Yes. And it's not the racial overtones I object to.

FOLEY: You're creating a diversion. Deal with my main point.

WAYNE: Words change their meaning. People who use words in a new way keep the language alive.

FOLEY: People like you.

WAYNE: Yeah. *(Smiling broadly)* Maybe even you. Like take the word "dig." Ten years ago most people used "dig" to mean shovel a hole. Then a few people started using it to mean "like" or "understand." "I dig you, baby" now means "I like you, baby, and I get what you're saying." Now if we'd stuck to the dictionary—to the majority's authority *(Suddenly struck by his own phrase)* Hmm—the "majority's authority." That's rather nice. Haiku again. (*To* FOLEY) What was the first haiku we thought of?

FOLEY: *Neither* was haiku. Stick to the argument.

WAYNE: I'm getting tired. Too much logic depresses me.

FOLEY: You're copping out.

WAYNE: Cop-out!—there's another example! Now what did "cop-out" mean ten years ago? Nothing!

FOLEY: If it had meant nothing, it could never have come into common usage. "Cop" and "out" already had meanings; they were combined in a new way, that's all. You cannot talk gibberish and think you're being inventive. *(Pause)* Von schmaky putz.

WAYNE: What?!

FOLEY: See—it's gibberish. Doesn't mean a thing.

WAYNE: Say it again.

FOLEY: Von schmaky putz.

WAYNE: *(Belligerently)* Is that so! You think I'm some kind of dope? I know when I'm being cursed at.

FOLEY: Wayne—for God's sake!

WAYNE: Don't tell me! I heard it! PUTZ! Just like that he calls me a putz, and then says "For God's sake, Wayne"—like he'd never meant it. What really hurts is that you're not even Jewish. I call that underhanded.

FOLEY: Wayne—

WAYNE: —don't Wayne me.

FOLEY: Are you really angry?

(Pause)

WAYNE: *(Quietly)* Yes. *(Louder)* I will not be called a putz. That's worse than "boy"—I mean, since I'm white.

FOLEY: I don't even know what putz means!

WAYNE: Sure, sure.

FOLEY: I swear!

WAYNE: Listen, you people may not know much, but putz you've got to know: it's a literary convention.

(FOLEY bursts out laughing)

FOLEY: You've picked up a lot in two months!

WAYNE: That's the only thing I've heard since I got here. Everything's a "literary convention." *(Brandishes his bottle of rum)* This bottle! *(Waves it around his head)* This office! Your desk! Your name! Literary conventions. Agreed-upon symbols—that's all! Should we fail to sign the convention, we wouldn't know what to call anything. Everything would be a cop-out. Or a cadenza. Well, I've decided not to sign. I will not agree to the symbols. You are no longer Alex. You are Cadenza!

(The telephone on FOLEY'S desk rings)

FOLEY: Excuse me. The day seems to have begun.

WAYNE: Now there's a good phrase. I'm sure we can make a literary convention out of it.

(FOLEY picks up the receiver)

FOLEY: *(Into phone)* Hello . . . Oh, it's you . . . Yes, I *am* surprised. You're usually not in this early, are you? . . . Oh really? What's wrong? . . . *(Looks furtively at* WAYNE, *who starts wandering aimlessly around the office)* Yes, it happens I do know him . . .

*(*WAYNE *takes a cigarette from the pack on* FOLEY'S *desk)*

(To WAYNE, *sarcastically)* Help yourself. *(Into the phone)* Not well, no. But well enough to understand what you're saying . . . Uh-huh . . . Yes . . . Uh-huh . . . That's right. It's difficult for me to talk . . .

*(*WAYNE *stuffs his fingers into his ears)*

. . . Can you hang on a minute? *(*FOLEY *puts his hand over the receiver)* Will you please take your elbows out of your ears. There's nothing I have to say that you can't hear.

*(*WAYNE *removes his fingers)*

WAYNE: Meaning you won't say anything.

FOLEY: *(Responding to the challenge)* Is that so? *(Takes his hand off the receiver and talks into it)* Sorry . . . No, it's all right: I can talk. Now what is it you're worried about exactly? . . . *You're* worried, or his family is? . . . Yes I know about his father . . .

*(*WAYNE *reacts)*

. . . Yes, his hair . . . All right, then: his general appearance . . . I agree with you—

WAYNE: *(Interrupting)*—what do you agree with?

FOLEY: *(His hand over the receiver)* If you wait a second, you'll find out. *(Into the receiver)* As I started to say, I agree with you. There's nothing wrong with his appearance. Sure it's different. But I happen to like it. . . . Well that's his father's problem . . .

*(*WAYNE *sits)*

What else did he have to say? . . . *(Suddenly looks concerned, even frightened)* Oh? . . . No, no, I didn't know that . . . Yes . . . uh-huh . . . Right.

WAYNE: Should I put my fingers back in my ears?

FOLEY: *(Going on with the phone conversation)* I'll talk to you later about it . . . I'll call you when I get free . . . No, it shouldn't be long . . . Yes . . . Right. Goodbye. *(Hangs up receiver. Trying to sound expansive, jolly)* Well! Guess who?

WAYNE: Hale who.

FOLEY: *(Surprised)* That's right. How'd you know?

WAYNE: His voice has resonance. It carries.

FOLEY: *(Worried)* Oh, does it?

WAYNE: Don't panic. I couldn't hear the words, only the tone.

FOLEY: He's worried about you. Been looking for you half the night.

WAYNE: And I've been looking for him half the night. So we're both nuts. Hey—why did he call you? You're not supposed to know me. I'm a lowly freshman.

FOLEY: He didn't think I knew you. He wanted my advice. In general.

WAYNE: Must have been surprised.

FOLEY: He was.

WAYNE: He thinks I'm his discovery. His protégé. He's probably pissed off at you. No one else is supposed to know the Child Genius.

FOLEY: Meaning you, I gather.

WAYNE: 'Fraid so. It's my cross.

FOLEY: *(Glancing at WAYNE'S poem on his desk)* Well the first four lines are good.

WAYNE: Which is more than I can say for your book review. You know, that was pretty rotten of you, not letting me read it.

FOLEY: It isn't finished.

WAYNE: Neither is my poem. You're too self-protective.

FOLEY: Could be.

WAYNE: That's the easiest way to get hurt.

(WAYNE suddenly gets out of his chair. FOLEY involuntarily jumps)

Wow, man! Those coffee nerves! I was just reaching for my poem. I gotta split.

(Holds out his hand for the poem. FOLEY doesn't offer it)

FOLEY: Wayne, I want to talk to you.

WAYNE: Man, we been rapping for three days! It makes me nervous to talk so much. I worry about becoming too verbal. I'll end up like you: an expounder.

FOLEY: Look, I'm worried about you.

WAYNE: *(Embarrassed; pleased)* Oh, boy, another daddy. Just what I need. I hope you're better than the original.

FOLEY: Cut the sarcasm. I want to talk straight to you.

WAYNE: Who ever heard of a straight Cadenza?

FOLEY: The name is Alex.

(WAYNE hesitates, then shakes his head in mock self-disgust)

WAYNE: A man of my sophistication should be beyond the appeal of brute sincerity. *(Shakes his head again)* But—what can I tell you. *(Sits in chair)* I know why you're worried. I also know why you jumped. I'm a smart kid. I'm also storybook gentle. So don't worry. *(Pause)* You're still worrying.

FOLEY: Umm.

WAYNE: Will you feel better if you look at it, if you actually see it?

FOLEY: *(Nervously)* I don't think so.

(WAYNE digs in his pocket and takes out a switchblade. HE throws it, unopened, on the desk)

WAYNE: Here. Look at it. Big deal.

(FOLEY gingerly picks up the knife and examines it)

Not much to see, right? Standard brand. *(Pause)* Except for one little thing.

FOLEY: What's that?

(WAYNE leans across the desk)

WAYNE: Gimme. I'll show you.

(FOLEY, uncertainly, hands him the knife. WAYNE flicks it open, leans close to FOLEY, while pointing to the bottom of the blade)

Here. See this?

FOLEY: *(Apprehensive)* No. See what?

WAYNE: Jesus, man, if you'd stop shaking, you'd be able to focus your eyeballs!

FOLEY: I am not shaking.

WAYNE: I mean, I'm very hurt! What do you think I am, a *killer?*

FOLEY: I don't like knives.

WAYNE: Neither do I.

FOLEY: Then why do you carry one?

WAYNE: You make it sound like a papoose, like my lifetime companion. I've been "carrying" this knife for a big eight hours.

FOLEY: You shouldn't carry it at all.

WAYNE: *(Pointing to the bottom of the blade)* You want to see these initials or not? I mean, don't do me any favors. I'll take my blade and go. *(Pause)* And my poem, too.

41

FOLEY: *(Leaning forward)* I can't see any initials.

WAYNE: They're here—way down in the corner—real tiny. Like he was ashamed of them.

FOLEY: *(Squinting)* F.F., right?

WAYNE: Good man. It's always a comfort to find a professor who can read.

FOLEY: Who is F.F.?

WAYNE: Who do you think?

FOLEY: Franz Ferdinand.

WAYNE: What?

FOLEY: Franz Ferdinand, Archduke of the Austro-Hungarian Empire, was assassinated at Sarajevo in 1914—thereby precipitating the First World War.

WAYNE: *(Impressed)* That's a pretty good guess. Try again.

FOLEY: Frost.

WAYNE: It's a *real* person.

FOLEY: ROBERT FROST was a *real* person!

WAYNE: Oh—*Robert* Frost! I thought you meant Jack. *(Pause)* No, dummy, it's—FROBER!

FOLEY: What?

WAYNE: ME! Wayne Frober, remember?

FOLEY: Wayne does not begin with an F.

WAYNE: *Fred* Frober. The old man. It's Fred Frober's fucking knife. Fucking Fred Frober's fucking war knife.

FOLEY: He gave it to you as a going away present.

WAYNE: Fat chance! I took it.

FOLEY: Why?

WAYNE: I hate knives.

FOLEY: I see: you took it because you hate it.

WAYNE: I took it because the old man's crazy about it. It's like a voodoo thing with him. He takes it out and stares at it. Remembers the good old days—zapping it to the Japs.

FOLEY: I was in the Second World War, and the army did not issue switchblades as standard equipment.

WAYNE: He bought it himself. Had some deep American thing about sticking it in the belly of the Orient. Claims he did, too. Says he gave it to some Jap on Okinawa. I'll bet it was after the guy was dead. He's a mean bastard, my old man. He should be in Washington.

FOLEY: How did Hale know you had the knife?

WAYNE: I told him. I called him yesterday after I left home. Said I was in possession of a death weapon, and felt very strange.

FOLEY: That was thoughtful. You have him pretty worried.

WAYNE: He loves to worry about me. He gets bored with Jane Austen. *(Pause)* You think he's in his office?

FOLEY: He's waiting for me to call him back.

WAYNE: I can see him down there, fingering his *Pride and Prejudice.* Just another colonial dude. *(Starts to leave)* I guess I'll go see him. Tell him I've been talking the higher metaphysics with a full professor.

(FOLEY laughs. WAYNE leans over, takes the knife off the desk and picks up the pages of his poem)

FOLEY: Hey, aren't you going to let me finish it?

WAYNE: I figured I'd quit while I was ahead. You might not like the fifth line.

FOLEY: Then you can make a four-line poem out of it.

(WAYNE grins)

WAYNE: Yeah—maybe I'll get lots of little poems out of it. Lots of haiku. Then we'll publish 'em as a slim volume, and two weeks later I'll commit suicide.

(Pause; FOLEY frowns)

(Cheerfully) That way I'll be a legend. "Brilliant young man falls on sword," et cetera, et cetera. If you wait too long, then they can't say you were a "promising young poet." I think twenty —maybe twenty-two—is the cut-off point. *(Pause)* Anyway, you can read it, if you like.

FOLEY: I would like.

WAYNE: *(Pleased)* Okay. *(HE hands FOLEY the poem, then starts toward the office door, the knife still in his hand)*

FOLEY: Why don't you come by tomorrow, and I'll tell you what I think of it?

WAYNE: Sure. About eight A.M.?

FOLEY: Uh-no. It's not when I'm at my best.

WAYNE: I thought you were pretty good.

FOLEY: Thanks.

WAYNE: I mean—I'm a handful.

FOLEY: *(Sincere)* I think you're a delight.

WAYNE: *(Embarrassed; boyish)* Gee, thanks, Mr. Foley.

FOLEY: *Mr.* Foley! Now where did that come from?! Suddenly I'm back in your old man's generation!

WAYNE: *(Quietly)* I wish you were. *(WAYNE starts to open the office door, then turns back toward FOLEY)* You gonna let me read your book review?

FOLEY: Definitely.

WAYNE: Tomorrow?

FOLEY: I'll have a carbon waiting for you in the morning. *(Consulting his schedule pad on the desk)* How's eleven?

WAYNE: Beautiful.

FOLEY: Good. See you at eleven.

(WAYNE again starts to leave, hesitates for a moment, then turns back toward FOLEY and casually tosses him the closed knife)

WAYNE: Hang on to this for me, too, will you? I can pick it up some time.

(FOLEY catches the knife)

FOLEY: Sure. *(Pause; FOLEY opens the top drawer of his desk)* Look, I'll put it in here. Then if you ever want it, you can come get it. Okay?

WAYNE: Far out. *(Opens the office door and steps into the corridor)* See you tomorrow, man.

FOLEY: Say hello to Hale for me.

WAYNE: Aw—he'll probably give me up after this. I'm losing all my mystery. *(Pause)* Does that drawer have a lock on it?

FOLEY: No.

WAYNE: *(Sadly, shaking his head)* Good. Good. *(Pause)* Well, so long, Alex.

FOLEY: See you tomorrow, Wayne. *(As WAYNE leaves)*

THE CURTAIN FALLS

THE GUTTMAN ORDINARY SCALE

PRODUCTION AND PUBLICATION HISTORY:

   The Guttman Ordinary Scale was the second in an evening
of three of my one-act plays performed in workshop at The
New Dramatists (January 1972) and then at The John Drew
Theater, Easthampton (August 1972).

   It was published in Issue #9 (1975) of *The Gay Alternative.*

DR. OATES's office. *Typical clinical setting, except backstage left, a portable film screen and, on the other side of the room, a sixteen-millimeter slide projector.* DR. OATES, *a nondescript middle-aged man, is at the door saying goodbye to a young man,* ALLAN BOTS.

OATES: You have all your instructions straight, Mr. Bots?

ALLAN: Yes, I think so.

OATES: *(Severely)* Are you *sure*? We can't afford errors.

ALLAN: Yes.

OATES: The stilboestrol?

(ALLAN *reaches in his pocket and pulls out a small container of pills*)

ALLAN: Uh-huh. Right here.

OATES: One every six hours. If the vomiting becomes severe, shift for twenty-four hours to the emetine hydrochloride. Then to *renew* vomiting, two dessert-spoonfuls of mustard in a tumbler of warm water.

49

ALLAN: Got it.

(OATES *notices* ALLAN *looking at his crotch*)

OATES: Is the strain gauge comfortable?

ALLAN: *(Shy)* Yeah, kind of.

OATES: *(Annoyed)* Miss Fisher placed it snugly on the shaft. You must keep your hands *off* it.

ALLAN: I haven't touched it!

OATES: Then what *is* the trouble?

ALLAN: *(Embarrassed)* Well, I mean . . . maybe it shows . . .

OATES: *(Haughty)* The mercury strain gauge, Mr. Bots, was designed by the Physics Department.

ALLAN: Oh.

OATES: The rubber tubing is so fine-bore that only *your* manipulations can produce visibility.

ALLAN: *(Intimidated)* Sorry. It *feels* embarrassing.

OATES: *(Patronizing)* I understand. You'll adjust. *(Ushering him out the door)* Now then . . . one week from today, the same time.

ALLAN: *(Hesitating)* . . . uh . . . Dr. Oates . . . there's one other thing I . . .

OATES: Yes?

ALLAN: Well, it's, uh . . .

OATES: Come, come, speak up. It's important to express your feelings. That's the only way to guarantee value-free procedure.

ALLAN: I was hoping I could collect part of the fee now.

OATES: *(Severely)* The fee is paid at the *completion* of the experiment. That's stated explicitly in your contract.

ALLAN: Wow, I'm really hurting, man.

OATES: *(Looking at* ALLAN's *crotch)* Let's not be histrionic, Bots. It throws off the M factor.

ALLAN: The university's raised the library fee, and it's due this week.

OATES: We can't make exceptions.

ALLAN: But I am an exception. You said yourself ephebophiliacs are hard to find.

OATES: In *combination* with vagina dentata.

ALLAN: The university's going to get my ass. And my library card. And my M factor.

(Disgruntled, ALLAN *starts to leave)*

OATES: *(Relenting)* —Bots. Just a moment . . . sit down.

*(*OATES *goes over to his desk and pushes a button.* A FEMALE VOICE *comes over the intercom)*

FEMALE VOICE: Yes, Dr. Oates?

OATES: Please come in, Miss Fisher. *(To* ALLAN*)* I consider this unethical behavior on your part. However, we'll let it pass this once.

*(*MISS FISHER, *a dumpy, middle-aged woman, enters the office)*

MISS FISHER: Yes, doctor?

OATES: Miss Fisher—

Miss Fisher: *(Superefficient)* —yes, Dr. Oates!

OATES: —give Mr. Bots his first payment of twenty-five dollars.

MISS FISHER: In *cash?*

OATES: Yes. *(To* ALLAN*)* Let's not make a habit of this, Bots.

ALLAN: No, sir. *(Slyly)* No habits, I promise. Thanks very much, sir. See you next week. *(Exits)*

*(*MISS FISHER *starts to follow him out)*

OATES: *Miss* Fisher! *(*SHE *comes back)* Show in the next volunteer, Miss Fisher.

MISS FISHER: Yes, doctor. *(Calling offstage)* The doctor is ready for you, Mr. Cole.

(JIM COLE, a pleasant-looking young man, enters the office. HE's affable and expansive. DR. OATES goes forward to greet him)

OATES: *(Offering his hand)* How do you do, Mr. Cole.

JIM: How are ya?

(MISS FISHER exits, closing the door behind her)

OATES: Hope we didn't keep you waiting too long.

JIM: Oh, that's awright. I got a free day.

OATES: No classes at the university, eh?

JIM: Huh? Oh yeah—the university.

OATES: You are a student here?

JIM: Sure, that's right. Saw your ad in the *Tigertone.* Sounds like a good deal. I'm into all this, you know what I mean?

OATES: No.

JIM: I'm into what you people are doing. *(Boastful smile)* I turn on real easy.

OATES: That may not be a virtue—scientifically speaking. To study the physiological concomitants of sexual behavior, one needs *objective* indicators.

JIM: You just wait and see.

OATES: On the other hand, we're not interested in patients with impaired potency.

JIM: That's got a lovely sound.

OATES: I beg your pardon?

JIM: *(Savoring the words)* "Patients with impaired potency." It's music.

OATES: Not to the patients. *(Goes to his desk)* Miss Fisher took the preliminary information?

JIM: She's not very pretty.

OATES: Miss Fisher is a neutral indicator. Your response to her is within the normal range.

JIM: I like older women. But I don't think she's pure of her type.

OATES: You know the financial arrangements?

JIM: One hundred bucks for six sessions.

OATES: *If* we find you a suitable subject. If not, you'll be terminated promptly and paid twenty-five dollars.

JIM: Cash?

OATES: Check.

JIM: I could use the bread, man. How do I get to be "suitable"?

OATES: Suitability is a function of several variables. Rarity of type is one. Range of susceptibility another.

JIM: You've got a wonderful vocabulary.

(OATES *looks momentarily confused*)

I could listen to you all day.

OATES: Every science invents its language. New words for new phenomena.

JIM: I'm hip, baby. I'm in your groove tube.

OATES: Science and frivolity, *Mr.* Cole, do not cohabit.

JIM: I'm into just about everything.

OATES: *(Warning)* Some subjects are so special as to be useless to us. Just last week we had a boy in here who could be aroused by only a single fantasy.

JIM: Poor kid. Poverty-stricken.

OATES: He wanted to be run down by a girl with painted nails driving a Maserati-200.

JIM: *(Lighting up at the car's name)* A Maserati?! Oh *sure*! I once knew a zoophilic girl—you know, *partialismus* concerning the male horse genital.

OATES: Really! Could you introduce us? I mean, perhaps she'd like to volunteer for our study.

JIM: Nah, don't know where she's crashin' these days. *(HE beats out hoofbeat sounds on his pants)* I think she's in bluegrass country.

OATES: *(Sadly)* I see. *(Pause)* Where'd you learn the word "zoophilic"?

JIM: *(Enigmatic)* You know—hangin' around the track.

(OATES presses the intercom)

OATES: Come in, Miss Fisher.

MISS FISHER: Yes, doctor.

OATES: *(To JIM)* Behavioral science is concerned with two areas of human sexuality, Mr. Cole. One: diagnostic—perfecting techniques for identifying sexual preferences. Two: therapeutic—perfecting treatment for sexual deviation. *Our* study is concerned with perfecting diagnostic techniques.

(MISS FISHER enters)

The screen, Miss Fisher.

(MISS FISHER unfurls the screen against backstage wall, then prepares slides)

You understand then, Mr. Cole: we are concerned with identifying sexual preferences.

JIM: *(Earnest) Yeah.* A lot of people are concerned with that.

OATES: Miss Fisher will project slides on the screen one at a time in fixed random order.

JIM: *(Enthused)* Hey, that's good! "Fixed random order." That's what the prof in Lit. I must mean by "paradox."

OATES: *(Ignoring him)* Your galvanic skin response will be recorded in sten units on a plethysmograph and then evaluated against the IPAT Anxiety Scale ratings, thereby measuring your "choices" in physiological terms.

JIM: —excuse me, Dr. Oates.

OATES: Yes?

(JIM points to a doctor's white jacket hanging on the coat rack)

JIM: That's yours, isn't it?

OATES: Yes.

JIM: How come you don't wear it?

OATES: *(Intrigued)* Does it matter to you?

JIM: Well, if we're going to do it, we might as well do it right.

OATES: I see. By all means, if that's your preference. *(HE makes some quick jottings on his notepad, then goes to the coat rack. To MISS FISHER as HE passes her; stage whisper)* Finger plethysmography. *(HE puts on jacket. To JIM)* That better?

JIM: *(Grinning)* Oh, wow—fabulous! That's my color, man.

OATES: *(Probing)* White is your favorite color.

JIM: Only when it's moving. I hate it on a wall. For standing-still-color there's nothing like purple.

(OATES jots down another note)

OATES: I'm glad you saw that ad, Mr. Cole.

JIM: I dig you, too, man.

(OATES picks up an instrument from his desk, then goes to JIM)

OATES: Please hold up the middle finger of your left hand. *(Machine comes down from ceiling. JIM reacts with alarm)*

JIM: What's that?

OATES: This is a Guttman Ordinary Scale electrode. It will record your responses as you view the slides.

JIM: It won't hurt, will it? I'm not into pain at all, man. One of my buddies tells me it's a dynamite trip, but I'm not too sure about him.

OATES: Any fluctuation in sensitivity will be presignaled during the procedure. *(JIM is now wired to machine)* Are we ready, Miss Fisher?

MISS FISHER: Ready, doctor.

(OATES suddenly does a double take)

OATES: Miss Fisher!! That screen is *not* five feet from the subject's digital responder!

MISS FISHER: Oh—I am sorry, doctor! *(SHE moves the screen back two inches)*

OATES: Very well, then. The first slide.

(The lights dim. The figure of a beautiful nude female comes on the screen. JIM lets out a low whistle)

No audio responses, please, Mr. Cole. Stay with your feelings. The electrode will measure them more accurately than your vocal cords possibly could. *(Checks the recording graph)* Seven seconds. *(To JIM, pleased)* A vivid tracing, Mr. Cole! Maximum amplitude on the vertical axis.

JIM: *(Blushing)* Gee, doc, compliments go to my head.

(A buzzer sounds in the background)

OATES: The quiet buzzer has sounded. *(Pause; then to JIM)* You seem to be having some trouble with spontaneous recovery.

JIM: *(Grinning)* Isn't it something?

(OATES rechecks the graph)

OATES: Ah, there we are; initial value restored. Next slide, Miss Fisher.

(A beautiful male nude comes on the screen. JIM *jumps)*

JIM: Ow!

OATES: Mr. Cole—

JIM: —ow!!

OATES: —I asked you to—

JIM: —ow!! Ow!!

OATES:—restrain your verbal responses.

JIM: *(Holding up the electrode)* I got a shock! Shock*s!*

OATES: *("Patiently")* I assure you, the electrode is wired only for recording, not for conditioning.

JIM: Something hurt me!

OATES: *(Significantly)* The L score, Miss Fisher.

*(*MISS FISHER *consults a wall chart)*

MISS FISHER: *(Raised eyes)* Forty-seven *point* seven, doctor.

JIM: "L score"? What's an L score?

OATES: It purports to measure paranoid tendencies. *(Sternly)* I should tell you, Mr. Cole, that any attempt at crude artifact is readily identified.

JIM: *Me,* crude?!

OATES: "Crude artifact" means *faking* responses.

JIM: Why would anyone do that?

OATES: Well you might ask. Initially we had to use sex offenders as subjects in our study.

JIM: Before the new permissiveness.

OATES: Exactly. Now we employ university students.

JIM: *(Laconic)* Very different type thing.

OATES: The sex offenders, of course, were eager to conceal their real proclivities in order to avoid prosecution. *(Smug)* Our machinery became quite sensitive to subterfuge. *(Waxing eloquent)* The real breakthrough came two years ago with a pedophiliac who did everything he could in the routine verbal explorations to convince us that he was attracted to adult women. *(Triumphant)* But the plethysmograph proved conclusively that his strongest desire was evoked by the sight of the hairless vulva.

JIM: Why didn't he just buy his girlfriend a razor?

OATES: *(Shocked)* As I said, Mr. Cole, ours is a diagnostic, not a therapeutic enterprise.

MISS FISHER: *(Interrupting)* —Doctor, should I leave the slide on?

OATES: Are you prepared to continue, Mr. Cole?

JIM: *(Looking at the slide)* Is that guy a student, too?

OATES: He's a professional model.

(JIM looks at the screen again, chuckles)

JIM: It's like the Chinese say, "Thin in calf, thick in cock." And vice versa. *(HE glances pointedly at OATES's thick calves)*

OATES: *(Severely; starting to stutter)* I suggest we pro-proceed.

JIM: *("Hurt")* Well you said you were interested in physiology.

OATES: Shift to the neutral stimuli, Miss Fisher.

(A slide of geometric patterns comes on the screen. JIM giggles)

JIM: *(To OATES)* When you said "neutral stimuli," I thought you meant . . . *(Nods toward MISS FISHER; gesturing toward the screen)* Those are okay, too. I mean, if you're into neutral stimuli . . .

(OATES checks the graph readings)

OATES: *(Studying graphs; suspiciously)* Autonomic response identical to slide one. *(To MISS FISHER)* Return to slide two, Miss Fisher.

(The picture of the nude man comes back on the screen)

JIM: Hey, Doc, . . . Oh Doc . . . *Doc*! I know I'm not supposed to talk. But *(Holds up the electrode)* this thing makes me nervous.

OATES: Concentrate on the slide, Mr. Cole.

JIM: I can't. I'm afraid of another shock.

OATES: *(Still studying graph)* I say. Responses identical to female stimuli.

JIM: That's not my sex responding, it's my anxiety! *(Suddenly bemused)* Or are they one and the same? *(To* OATES*)* Can you tell the difference between anxiety arousal and sexual arousal? *(Smiles)* I got a pretty good vocabulary, too. *(*OATES *twitches slightly)*

OATES: Turn up the lights, Miss Fisher. *(To* JIM*)* Mr. Cole, your psychophysiological responses raise some doubt as to your clinical soundness.

JIM: You mean 'cause they're all the same, right?

OATES: Your reactions are not sexually specific.

JIM: I told you: I turn on real easy. Highly susceptible. As you can see from my pain threshold.

OATES: I think we'd better switch to the Semantic Differential Test, given your inclinations.

JIM: You mean 'cause I got so many.

OATES: I *mean*, your verbal orientation. Please take this card, Mr. Cole. *(Hands him a small chart)* On the left-hand side you'll find three adjectives, with ascending sexual implications, for describing males: *Interesting, Attractive, Handsome.* On the right-hand side you'll find three adjectives, with ascending sexual implications, for describing females: *Pleasurable, Exciting, Hot.* As Miss Fisher flashes a slide on the screen, use the adjective which best expresses your *immediate* reaction. Are you clear?

JIM: I have to stick to these six adjectives?

OATES: That is correct. Three for males, three for females.

JIM: How about a few adverbial modifiers—like "very" or "quite"?

(OATES *twitches again*)

OATES: This is a standardized test, Mr. Cole. If everyone used his own words, there'd be no basis for comparison, no possibility of science.

JIM: *Dig*, baby! That's my point.

OATES: There's a long list of volunteers waiting, Mr. Cole—people who have no problem following instructions.

JIM: When a woman turns you on, do you really say it's "pleasurable"—I mean, assuming you don't find her "exciting" or "hot"?

OATES: This test is not designed to evaluate *my* responses.

JIM: Which test do *you* use?

OATES: I am a *(Stuttering)* te-test*or*, not a te-test*ee*.

JIM: *("Sincere")* You really have a fantastic vocabulary.

OATES: *Shall* we proceed?!

JIM: Yeah! I hope I do well. I'd like to become a test*or* some day.

OATES: The first s-slide, Miss Fisher.

(*Slide of a nude reclining female comes on*)

JIM: Oh, wow—those feet!

OATES: The *adjectives*, Mr. Cole.

(JIM *fumbles, consults the chart*)

JIM: Oh yeah, . . . now let's see . . . uh—"interesting"!

OATES: You're using a *male* adjective.

JIM: Sorry!—I guess I misunderstood. I thought since *I'm* male, I was supposed to use the three male words. (OATES *twitches again*)

OATES: Male adjectives to describe male subjects; female adjectives to describe female subjects.

JIM: I *get* it! I'm a male subject, so I use male adjectives.

OATES: The subject of the slides, not the subject of the test.

JIM: *("Puzzled")* Are they different?

OATES: Mr. Cole: Is that you on the screen? *(JIM earnestly searches for his image on the screen)*

JIM: *(Matter-of-fact; serious)* No . . . no. I'm nowhere in the picture.

OATES: Precisely. The person on the slide, and you, are separate subjects.

JIM: Gotcha. *(Pause)* Except my *feelings* get projected onto the slide. So in a manner of speaking, we become one.

OATES: You become interrelated, not interchangeable.

JIM: Hey, that's cool, man. Heavy! When you become involved with a person, you don't become that person.

OATES: *(Patronizing)* A succinct definition of a "mature" relationship.

JIM: *(Enthused)* We're really getting somewhere, aren't we! So the point, then, is for me and the slides to come together in a mature way.

OATES: *(Hesitant)* That's . . . one way of putting it.

JIM: *(Pleased)* A *new* way, right? See, I'm not so dumb.

OATES: *(Patronizing)* The correlation between mental *(Twitches again)* and emotional maturity is slight.

JIM: Oh yeah—we had that in Philosophy I. The "mind-body problem."

OATES: I beg your pardon?

JIM: The duality bit. Descartes. Or Mani. Splitting experience into either/or categories. *(Smiles)* We're all done with that. *(Slyly)*

Finished with it in freshman year. Now we're into Philosophy II: the interconnection of practically everything. Man at one with himself and nature. Organic gardening and student rights in the high schools. Karma and Bill Graham. Graham crackers and Kropotkin. Abbey Road and Abby Hoffman. Hoffman Root Beer and—

MISS FISHER: *(Interrupting)* —Doctor Oates, my arm is getting tired.

JIM: *(Concerned) Sorry*! Are you arthritic or something?

MISS FISHER: Arthritis comes on rather late in life.

JIM: Dig. My grandfather had arthritis. *In* his hernia. That's how come it got strangulated.

MISS FISHER: Sounds like an interesting case.

JIM: Oh, he was a very interesting case. A butcher by trade. Looked like Buddha. *(Laughs)* There you go, see. Butchers and buddhas. There's no telling these days.

(OATES twitches)

OATES: Are you r-ready for the next slide, Mr. Cole?

JIM: Oh my, yes.

OATES: And this time we're going to stick to the adjectives, aren't we?

JIM: It's a pretty impoverished list.

OATES: It's adequate for the experiment.

JIM: What's the experiment adequate for?

OATES: *(Sighs; attempted irony)* You seem somewhat lacking in conceptual ability. *("Patiently")* However . . . we are applying the new techniques of behavioral science, Mr. Cole, to diagnose sexual preference.

*(*JIM *hits his head, as if remembering)*

JIM: Ah—right!—gotcha! Ha!

OATES: One question before we proceed . . .

JIM: *(All excited)* Shoot!

> (MISS FISHER *giggles.* OATES, *astonished, silences her with a stern look)*

OATES: Your initial response to the previous slide was *(Overarticulating)* "*Oh wow—those feet!*"

JIM: *(Smiling)* Right!

OATES: Did you mean to say "Oh wow—those *legs!*"

JIM: No, man—feet.

OATES: *(Ponderously)* I see. I wanted to be sure your reaction was not one of inadvertence.

JIM: *(Offended)* Now hang on! I got feelings, too!

OATES: *(Smug, as if* HE's *solved the riddle. To* MISS FISHER) Prepare the Rachman CS series to follow the next slide.

MISS FISHER: Yes, doctor.

OATES: *(Broad, self-satisfied smile)* Off we go! *(To* JIM, *expansively)* All things considered, I'd say you were quite an interesting subject.

JIM: "Interesting" or "pleasurable"?

OATES: *(Phony camaraderie)* Oh no you don't! I know my male adjectives!

> (THEY *laugh together like schoolboys over a dirty joke.* MISS FISHER *shifts the slides. The picture of a large, magnificently proportioned black male, stark naked, comes on the screen)*

OATES: Miss Fisher! *(SHE continues to stare entranced at the slide)*

OATES: *Miss Fisher!!*

MISS FISHER: Oh—is something wrong, doctor?

OATES: That slide is *not* part of the Semantic Differential Test!

MISS FISHER: Heavens—how did that happen?!

JIM: *(Abruptly)* Doctor, I have to void water.

OATES: Deflate the tra-traducer cuff, Miss Fisher.

(SHE *goes over to* JIM *and disconnects the electrode.* THEY *exchange a flirtatious look*)

MISS FISHER: There you are.

OATES: *(Pointing offstage)* First door to the right.

(JIM *exits, then immediately returns*)

OATES: To the *right!* (JIM *exits again*) Quick, the one-way window, Miss Fisher!

(MISS FISHER *hurries to the side wall, draws a curtain revealing the window, and stares through it.* OATES *paces*)

Did you note the way he stared at your legs when you deflated the cuff?

(MISS FISHER *is absorbed at the window*)

The Rachman Series will soon show his game.

(MISS FISHER *lets out a tiny shriek.* OATES *grabs his pen, ready to take notes*)

OATES: *(Impatiently)* Well? Well?

(MISS FISHER *sighs deeply*)

MISS FISHER: *(Love-struck tone)* Oh, my!

OATES: "Oh my" *what?!*

MISS FISHER: Oh my, what a remarkable perpendicular deviation!

OATES: Is he or is he not voiding?

MISS FISHER: Oh yes, he's voiding! Oh my, yes! *(Pause)* Oops— finished! (SHE *hurriedly closes the curtain*)

OATES: The slides, Miss Fisher. (MISS FISHER *takes out a fan*)

MISS FISHER: I don't know if I can take any more.

(JIM *comes back into the room*)

JIM: Hey, man, those velvet drapes in there are somethin' else! (HE *snuggles comfortably into chair and holds up his finger to be reattached to the machine*)

OATES: *No*, Mr. Cole. We're going to skip directly to the Rachman Series. *This* series, Mr. Cole, investigates a *(Portentous) somewhat different subject.*

JIM: I hope it doesn't have anything to do with kids, man, because if there's one thing—I mean, aside from pain—that I can't take, it's a bunch of those soft, hairless, little—

OATES: *(Interrupting)* —the series is concerned with what we call "movement artifacts."

JIM: You mean those "crude artifacts" we—

OATES: —*no* further questions, *please!* There's danger of contaminating your responses with informational preconditioning. Begin, Miss Fisher.

(In rapid-fire succession, a series of shoes and boots—knee-length, high-heeled, square-toed, etc.—flash on the screen. A brief pause after the series ends)

OATES: *(Beaming; smug)* Well?

JIM: You're really into leather, aren't you, man?! Got anything in cordovan?

(OATES, nonplussed, twitches violently)

Cordovan was the big thing in grade school. We were between the white-buck and sneaker generations.

MISS FISHER: *(Like a shy teen-ager)* You don't mean corfam, do you?

JIM: *(Good-natured teasing)* C'mon, Miss Fisher, you remember cordovan.

MISS FISHER: Not *really*. But I *think* that knee-length black boot in the fourth slide—

OATES: *(Interrupting)* —just a moment! *Just a moment!* Miss Fi-Fisher, may I remind you that you're a *N-Nurse?!* (JIM *jumps up*)

JIM: You *are?!* I thought you were a slide projectionist.

MISS FISHER: *(Proudly)* I have a master's degree in psychometrics.

JIM: Wow! You must have some brain on you. How come you sit back there?

OATES: Because *that* is where the sl-slides are projected from. Would you *kindly* be seated, Mr. Cole! *(Pause)* (JIM *sits*) The series you have just seen co-concern fetishistic objects frequently sought after and—

MISS FISHER: *(Interrupting; giggling)*—and frequently obtained.

JIM: *(To* OATES, *accusatory)* You didn't even look at the preliminary information on me that Miss Fisher so expertly took down.

MISS FISHER: It was a very interesting form.

JIM: Thank you.

OATES: The preliminary information is evaluated *at the appropriate time*.

JIM: After you've already made up your mind about me.

OATES: Mr. Co-Cole, I don't ju-justify my procedures to *undergraduates*.

JIM: Miss Fisher has a master's degree.

MISS FISHER: I worked with Tinker and Masturbation on Evans— I mean, with Tinker and Evans on masturbation!

JIM: Outasight! What role did Chance play?

(OATES slumps into his chair)

MISS FISHER: We've almost proved that masturbation is *the* crucial factor in producing deviant behavior. You see, ejaculation is critical in reinforcing fantasies that accompany masturbation. So if your first masturbation fantasy is about petrol, say—

JIM: *(Interrupting)*—petrol?!

MISS FISHER: Oh, yes! We worked for quite some time with a fifteen-year-old petrol addict. Very even-tempered youth. *(Giggles)* Sturdily built, too. Not a very intellectual family, though; that was part of the trouble. Would you believe that after only twenty half-hour sessions of aversion therapy, that boy was completely cured of petrol-sniffing?! Well . . . a little lighter-fluid now and then, but essentially, cured . . .

JIM: *(To* OATES; *indignant)* Did you know all this?! This woman is overqualified!

OATES: *(Weakly)* We are discussing the physiological con-concomitants of sexual behavior.

JIM: And what do you think that boy *did* when under the influence of petrol?

MISS FISHER: *(To* JIM) Oh my, that is astute of you. *(Lowering her eyes to the floor)* I wasn't going to say.

JIM: *(Overwrought sincerity)* I think you're *terrific,* Miss Fisher!

OATES: I am well aware of Tinker and Evans. Their work has yet to be replicated by an independent—

JIM:—it's Delgado and the rhesus monkeys all over again!

OATES: *(Continuing faintly)* . . . if they *are* proven right, that would mean there is no such thing as innate sexual preference. *All* would hinge on the accident of that first masturbation fantasy.

MISS FISHER: Only if accompanied by ejaculation.

JIM: *(To* OATES) Do you or do you not know Delgado's work with rhesus monkeys?

OATES: Of course.

JIM: The rhinal fissure experiment?

67

MISS FISHER: Yes!

(OATES looks uncertain)

JIM: One monkey, electrically prodded in his rhinal fissure, smiled upon 400,000 consecutive stimulations!

OATES: *(Defensive)* So?

JIM: So?! Delgado and his monkeys have conclusively shown that man is free to construct his identity. Human beings are born without minds, cannot develop minds without sensory input, and rely for sensory input on *all* experience. And here you are, trying to sell me a pair of cordovan boots. You should be ashamed.

(OATES looks sheepish. JIM gets down on one knee)

Will you marry me, Miss Fisher?

MISS FISHER: Oh, I'd like to, but—

JIM: —I know—your career.

MISS FISHER: No, it's not that. I'm about finished with masturbation. It's—well, I'm already engaged. To Bots, the mercury-strain boy. It happened while I was fitting him.

OATES: So much for free will.

(ALLAN BOTS falls into the room)

MISS FISHER: *Mr.* Bots! You were eavesdropping!

ALLAN: *(Embarrassed)* Not really. I mean, I came back to get refitted, and as I started to knock I couldn't help but hear . . .

MISS FISHER: *(Indignant)* You're not due for a refitting till next week.

ALLAN: I know but . . . *(Sheepish)* well, I kinda got to like it.

MISS FISHER: Disgusting!

JIM: *(To OATES)* O Physician! Look on thy handiwork and blush!

OATES: *(To MISS FISHER)* You're a disgrace to medical science!

68

(Including JIM*)* Both of you! *(Including* ALLAN*) All* of you!

MISS FISHER: *(To* JIM*)* Take me away from all this.

JIM: Now?

MISS FISHER: We can go see the rhesus monkeys together.

JIM: Do you mean it? I can't be trifled with.

MISS FISHER: I know Delgado personally.

JIM: Oh, my God!

*(*THEY *embrace passionately.* JIM *sweeps* MISS FISHER *into his arms)*

JIM: *(To* OATES*)* I'll never be able to thank you. *(*THEY *exit)*

OATES: *(Grumpily)* Everybody's a scientist. Let me see that strain gauge, Bots.

*(*ALLAN *starts to unzip his pants)*

ALLAN: Gee, that's awfully nice of you. I know you don't usually do this sort of thing.

OATES: Contrary to popular impression, Bots, scientists are not without compassion. When a fellow human being is in need . . .

ALLAN: Do you think Miss Fisher will come back?

OATES: Progress doesn't wait on individuals.

ALLAN: Mmm. That sounds right to me. *(*HE *is now stripped to his underpants)*

OATES: Before we go any further, Bots, I have something to ask you.

ALLAN: Yes sir?

OATES: What does the word "cordovan" mean to you?

BLACKOUT

THE RECORDER

PRODUCTION AND PUBLICATION HISTORY:

The Recorder was the first half of a double bill of my short plays (*The Electric Map* was the other) that opened in January 1970 at the off-Broadway Gate Theater under the collective title *The Memory Bank*. The Wakefield Tricycle Company and Basement Theatre presented *The Recorder* in London, February-March 1974.

The Recorder was first published in the *Evergreen Review,* April 1969, then (as part of *The Memory Bank*) by The Dial Press (1970). Stanley Richards chose *The Recorder* for his collection *The Best Short Plays 1970* (Chilton: 1970).

A play for TWO MEN *and a* TAPE RECORDER. *The* RECORDER
is on the table. SMYTH *is fiddling with it as the curtain rises.*

SMYTH: Huh! You'd think after a couple of hundred times I'd be
able to thread the damn thing.

ANDREWS: Take your time.

SMYTH: To tell you the truth, I'd just about given up hope that you'd
see me. I'm grateful to you for letting me come by.

ANDREWS: I admire persistence.

SMYTH: I didn't mean to plague you.

ANDREWS: It was my secretaries you plagued. But eventually word
does filter through to me.

SMYTH: When you didn't answer my third letter, I got a bit rattled.

ANDREWS: I was making enquiries.

SMYTH: I understand. You must get all kinds of requests.

ANDREWS: All kinds.

73

SMYTH: *(Still fiddling with the* MACHINE*)* Damn! I seem to be all thumbs today.

ANDREWS: You have quite a reputation for one so young.

SMYTH: Thank you.

ANDREWS: This book, of course, will boost it still further.

SMYTH: I hadn't thought of it that way.

ANDREWS: Oh my. Pure as well as accomplished.

SMYTH: I think the book will be timely.

ANDREWS: You've talked to many others, have you?

SMYTH: Oh literally hundreds, sir. You're the last.

ANDREWS: *(Pointing to the* TAPE RECORDER*)* And did you cart *that* with you everywhere?

SMYTH: Yes. It's not very heavy . . . Ah! There. That does it.

*(*HE *looks up at* ANDREWS*)* I hope this isn't going to bother you too much.

ANDREWS: Can't really tell. I've never used one before. I do feel self-conscious.

SMYTH: You'll forget it's there after a few minutes. That's the theory anyway. Frankly, I've never gotten used to it.

ANDREWS: Then why do you use it?

SMYTH: I want to get what you say straight. I've got a rotten memory. Funny in a historian, isn't it? Can't keep a fact in my head. It's safer using the machine. That way I'll be sure it's accurate.

ANDREWS: But it might not come out right. I *am* a little nervous.

SMYTH: About the machine?

ANDREWS: No, about it coming out right. I've forgotten a lot. I hope that the *(Pause)* talking *(Pause)* will bring back—

SMYTH: —don't worry. You'll relax once we get started.

(Strained pause)

ANDREWS: Shall I talk now?

SMYTH: I haven't turned it on. All set?

ANDREWS: I suppose.

SMYTH: Let's start right in then.

ANDREWS: Fine.

SMYTH: I'll stop it after a minute just to be sure we're recording. (HE *turns the* RECORDER *on, then returns to his seat*) Any time you're ready.

ANDREWS: Should I just talk?

SMYTH: Whatever makes you most comfortable.

ANDREWS: Is it recording?

SMYTH: Should be. Would it help if I asked direct questions?

ANDREWS: What do you particularly want to know?

SMYTH: Well, I guess most crucial would be—it's so hard to know what's finally going to be important . . . Why not just start talking about him. Anything you happen to remember.

ANDREWS: I remember next to nothing about his early life.

SMYTH: Anything. It might be important.

ANDREWS: You mean like his schooling?

SMYTH: If that's as far back as you can go.

ANDREWS: *(After a pause)* I can see him on a beach. He was three or four. Beautiful baby. Snow-white hair.

SMYTH: With his family?

ANDREWS: I suppose so. There's something about his sister. Probably not true. I shouldn't say it.

SMYTH: Please. You have my promise. This is strictly for my own information. Not a word will go into print, without your permission.

ANDREWS: I believe you. Still, one can't be sure. I do feel a responsibility.

75

SMYTH: I know what you mean. It's important to get everything as accurate as possible. That's why I use the machine. I don't want to have to rely on memory.

ANDREWS: Well. There was some story about his sister at the beach. They loved each other very much, you know. Everyone in the family said so; always. She was left to take care of him for a while. I don't think she was more than eight. He was very fair-skinned. She kept pouring water over his little body. To keep him cool, you know. She'd go back and forth to the ocean, filling her pail. Kept pouring it over him. He got a very nasty burn. Second-degree, I think they said. She was only trying to keep him cool. Poor child.

SMYTH: Who?

ANDREWS: Who?

SMYTH: You said "poor child." I wasn't sure who you meant.

ANDREWS: Oh. Him. I suppose. I did say "poor child"?

SMYTH: Yes. I'm quite sure.

ANDREWS: Curious. *(Brightening)* Well, if I did, it'll be on the machine.

SMYTH: Oh, Christ! I forgot to check if we're recording! *(Jumps up and goes to the* MACHINE. HE *clicks it off)* I'll just go back a bit. To be sure we're recording. This machine is bad on reproducing voices. You won't sound a bit like yourself.

ANDREWS: I've never heard myself.

SMYTH: Then you won't know how differently you sound.

ANDREWS: You'll be able to tell, though.

*(*SMYTH *starts to rewind the* MACHINE*)*

SMYTH: When I bought this machine I looked for one with a sensitive pickup. So that people wouldn't have to hold the mike in front of them. This one's very good. You can put it in the corner of a room and speak in your normal voice and it picks it right up. But the quality of the sound isn't so hot. Since I'm not recording music, though, I don't care. As long as the typist can hear the words.

ANDREWS: It must have been expensive.

SMYTH: *(Stopping the* RECORDER*)* That's more than enough. Remember—it won't sound like you. I mean the quality. Your voice has a lot more resonance.

*(*HE *turns on the* MACHINE*)*

MACHINE: "She'd go back and forth to the ocean, filling her pail. Kept pouring it over him. He got a very nasty burn. Second-degree, I think they said. She was only trying to keep him cool. Poor child."

*(*SMYTH *clicks off the* MACHINE*)*

SMYTH: There's the "poor child."

ANDREWS: Yes. You were right. It didn't sound like me.

SMYTH: But you'd never heard yourself.

ANDREWS: You know: what I thought I'd sound like. *(Pause)* It's working then?

SMYTH: Yes. We'll be able to relax now. I won't stop it again. *(*HE *clicks the* MACHINE *back on and returns to his seat)* Now let's see . . . where were we?

ANDREWS: I'm not happy about that.

SMYTH: But that's not the way you really sound.

ANDREWS: Not my voice. The story about the beach. I'm not at all sure it's true.

SMYTH: Can you recall when you first heard it?

ANDREWS: Heard it? I was there.

SMYTH: On the beach?!

ANDREWS: No, of course not. But it was retold in his family a thousand times. You must have heard it yourself.

SMYTH: I have, in fact. But your version is different. My accounts involved his mother, not the sister.

ANDREWS: That's absurd. A grown woman would never have done such a thing.

SMYTH: It does seem improbable. How did the mother strike you?

ANDREWS: Certainly not cruel. Far from cruel. She adored the boy. She was very beautiful.

SMYTH: What's your first memory of her?

(ANDREWS *thinks; then becomes agitated*)

ANDREWS: This kind of raking up. I really have my doubts, you know. What's the point?

SMYTH: I'm trying to understand what made him tick. I want to find out everything I can.

(*Pause*)

ANDREWS: I only remember a few things. Without all the rest, they can't be trusted. They'll loom too large.

SMYTH: Each person remembers a little. I put it all together.

(*The* MACHINE *squeaks*)

Hmm. I can't figure that out. It happens at the damnedest times. No pattern to it.

ANDREWS: Maybe it needs oil.

SMYTH: Oh, no! The manual says never to oil it. It has a sealed lubrication system.

(*The* MACHINE *squeaks again*)

ANDREWS: Then maybe it isn't level. The least thing throws them off. Maybe you'd better take notes instead.

(SMYTH *gets up*)

SMYTH: Let's try moving it. (HE *clicks the* MACHINE *off and starts to move it*)

ANDREWS: Watch the cord! It's going to pull the microphone out.

SMYTH: Oh, yes. Thank you. (HE *readjusts the cord, then turns the* MACHINE *back on.* HE *listens a few seconds*) Seems okay. You were right about leveling. Seems to have done it. (HE *goes back to his seat*) You were going to tell me your first recollections of the mother.

ANDREWS: I think I was not going to tell you.

SMYTH: I give you my word this is all strictly confidential.

ANDREWS: *(Looking at the* MACHINE*)* Notes are better. That's all they are, and everyone knows it: traces. They can be denied, destroyed.

SMYTH: The tape is yours. I'll have it typed up, and then I'll send you both the tape and the typescript.

ANDREWS: How will I know there isn't a carbon?

SMYTH: *(Embarrassed)* I guess you'll have to take my word.

ANDREWS: I don't even know you. Not really, that is.

SMYTH: It does come down to trust.

(Pause)

ANDREWS: You *will* ask my permission if you want to quote something from your carbon?

SMYTH: You have my word.

ANDREWS: Mm-hmm. *(Pause)* Well. The boy was a good deal older. Thirteen or fourteen. He got the idea one day to write a story.

SMYTH: Excuse me, I had hoped you would tell me about his mother.

ANDREWS: *(Sternly)* I'm about to.

SMYTH: Oh, I'm sorry.

ANDREWS: It was a moralistic little tale. About a girl named Jane who tried to be good but couldn't. He was very excited when he finished writing it and ran in to show it to his mother. She read it and then turned to him angrily: "You should be outside playing with the rest of the boys in the street," she said. "If you were a real boy, that's where you'd be." The boy looked as if he would faint.

SMYTH: Could you backtrack just a bit. There's something I didn't get.

ANDREWS: You don't have to. The machine will.

SMYTH: Just to get it straight myself, for the conversation.

ANDREWS: So you can ask the right questions.

SMYTH: Exactly.

ANDREWS: He had written a little story about Jane, you see.

SMYTH: No, I understand that part. I meant the mother's anger. Why was she angry? What was she angry at?

ANDREWS: I really don't know. Maybe *she* didn't.

SMYTH: But what would you guess?

ANDREWS: I couldn't begin to.

SMYTH: *(Pressing him)* Was she worried that he might not be—well—what do they call it—a "regular fellow"?

ANDREWS: Maybe.

SMYTH: You think that did worry her.

ANDREWS: Maybe. Otherwise why would she have said it?

SMYTH: Said what?

ANDREWS: About playing in the street more.

SMYTH: She wanted him to play in the street more. With the rest of the boys.

ANDREWS: No, it seems to me that's exactly what worried her. He was out in the street so much with *that* kind of boy.

SMYTH: What kind?

ANDREWS: The ones he would play with.

SMYTH: I'm afraid you've lost me.

ANDREWS: Oh, well.

(Pause)

SMYTH: You think then—just to clear this up—that his mother disapproved of the crowd of boys he was hanging out with. On the streets.

ANDREWS: I really couldn't say. It was so long ago.

SMYTH: I know how hard it is to recall these things. It must be forty years ago, isn't it? At least.

ANDREWS: I should think. Something like that. You probably know better than I.

SMYTH: Sometimes I think I know him very well. Then it turns out there are whole episodes I've never even heard of. This story about Jane, for example.

ANDREWS: Remember, I didn't want to tell it. I have no confidence in it.

SMYTH: Why don't we try it again. If you don't mind. Tell it to me again.

ANDREWS: *(Sighs)* It's like this. He was not the sort of boy—mind you, this is only as I remember him—who was much for the usual horseplay and sports. Now and then he'd enjoy it. In fact he was a good athlete. Quite good, now that I think about it. He used to win cups in summer camp. Best All-Around Midget. That sort of thing. But he liked other things, too. Words, any

81

kind of words. In books, in talk. He liked putting words together.

SMYTH: So he started to write stories.

ANDREWS: Yes. There we are. He wrote that story about Jane. He must have been a tot still. Couldn't have been more than seven.

SMYTH: This is the same story about Jane you just described? The moralistic one?

ANDREWS: *(Surprised)* Were there *two* Jane stories? Huh! I'd always assumed there'd only been the one.

SMYTH: I didn't know of *any.* That is, before today.

ANDREWS: Then why do you refer to two?

SMYTH: The first one you said he wrote when he was about thirteen or fourteen. And now this last one you mentioned you said he wrote when he was about seven.

ANDREWS: I only know of one Jane story.

SMYTH: But you did say earlier he had been thirteen or fourteen.

ANDREWS: Not as I remember. I don't see how I could have.

SMYTH: I could've sworn you said thirteen or four—well, no matter. The machine will have it in any case.

ANDREWS: Perhaps we should rewind and see.

SMYTH: It would be difficult to find the exact spot. I can sort it all out later. It's all there. Anyway, you are now sure he was about seven when he wrote that story.

ANDREWS: Yes, quite sure. I can't swear to it, of course. You know what funny tricks memory can play. But I am reasonably sure he was seven.

SMYTH: Fine. Let's get back then to his mother's reaction. Apparently she didn't like his playing in the streets so much.

ANDREWS: In truth, I think it depended on the boys he was with. Actually, he had several sets of friends. Some the mother liked and some she didn't.

SMYTH: Which did she like?

ANDREWS: *(Thinking)* I wish I could be sure. It seems to me the one she really *didn't* like was the girl across the street.

SMYTH: Not Jane?

ANDREWS: No, no. You've got that wrong. The *story* was about a girl named Jane.

SMYTH: That's what I'd thought.

ANDREWS: Yes, that's right. The *story* was about a girl named Jane.

SMYTH: And the girl across the street?

ANDREWS: Quite something else. She had her hooks into him, you know. Girls aren't very old when they start thinking of marriage.

SMYTH: Yes, but seven—!

ANDREWS: The suburbs. You know how it is. In any case, I wouldn't say seven. No. I couldn't be sure of seven. Not the girl across the street.

SMYTH: She was older then?

ANDREWS: Yes, that was part of the trouble. She was much too old for him. Kept him inside all the time. That's what the mother objected to, you see.

SMYTH: She wanted him out in the street with the boys.

ANDREWS: Right. Playing games. That sort of thing.

SMYTH: Would he and the girl write together?

ANDREWS: They mostly played bridge. Even at lunchtime, during school break. Bridge, bridge, bridge. Became very good at it. A lifelong hobby of his.

SMYTH: Yes. I'd heard that.

ANDREWS: He put himself through college playing bridge.

SMYTH: Really? But he didn't need to do that. He was a wealthy boy.

ANDREWS: He *wanted* to do it. *(Pause)* Bridge is an intricate game. *(Pause)* Do you play?

83

SMYTH: No, not very well. *(Pause)* You and he were roommates in college, weren't you?

ANDREWS: Yes. That is, after the freshman year. *That* may be the most interesting story of all. No memory problem there.

SMYTH: Good.

ANDREWS: But it is painful for me to recall.

SMYTH: I understand.

*(*ANDREWS *is silent)*

SMYTH: *(Trying to coax)* Painful episodes are often important.

ANDREWS: For your book, you mean.

SMYTH: Yes, exactly. *(Pause)* But you know I once dropped this whole project. Gave it up entirely for three months. It was after I talked to a woman in Delaware. The more she talked about the "good old days," the more she drank. By the time it was over I couldn't make any sense of what she was saying. I felt terrible, encouraging her to look back. It was like picking scabs off old wounds.

ANDREWS: Inhuman. Why do you do it?

SMYTH: We have to find out the truth.

ANDREWS: For posterity, I suppose.

SMYTH: We must hold on to past experience. It's all we have to guide us. Without it we'd be like amnesia victims, no moorings at all.

ANDREWS: Each day would be brand-new.

SMYTH: Exactly. Think how disconcerting that would be. Having to start fresh each day.

(Noises from the MACHINE; *the reel has come to an end)*

The reel has ended. *(*SMYTH *goes to the* MACHINE *and starts to turn over the reel)*

ANDREWS: It must have missed that last part. About amnesia.

SMYTH: That doesn't matter. It was just me, gabbing. *(Laughs)* I'm not interested in recording me.

ANDREWS: Those reels aren't very long.

SMYTH: They come in various lengths. I put on a short one. I wasn't sure how long we'd be. (HE *laughs; trying to charm* ANDREWS *into further reminiscence)* But you're a mine of information.

ANDREWS: No one was closer to him, after all.

SMYTH: *(Finishing up with the* MACHINE*)* That does it. I've turned it over to the other side. *(*HE *goes back to his seat)* Now. Just pick up where you were.

ANDREWS: We were talking about bridge, weren't we?

SMYTH: No, we'd finished with that.

ANDREWS: Oh, had we?

SMYTH: I know—we were talking about college. Something you said was very vivid.

ANDREWS: I doubt if it's the sort of thing you want. After all, he's a public figure. This is pretty private stuff. As I say, we were close.

SMYTH: I promise you it will stay private. I want to know everything I can, but I certainly don't intend printing everything.

ANDREWS: Then why know it?

SMYTH: I want to understand why he acted the way he did.

ANDREWS: Just describe his actions, his public career. That's what's important. That's what's affected history.

SMYTH: But it all might have happened differently. I mean, if he'd been a different kind of man, he might have made different decisions, affected history differently.

ANDREWS: Historians shouldn't deal in "ifs," it seems to me. If he'd been different he wouldn't have affected history at all. If he'd been able to screw that girl, he'd never have been a public figure.

SMYTH: *(Stunned)* The . . . girl across the street?

ANDREWS: No, the girl in college. Joan I think her name was. Maybe I'm thinking of Jane again. Joan? Yes, Joan. She came up for the big freshman weekend. Very sexed-up girl. Everybody knew it. They'd been dating off and on. This was supposed to be the big culmination. She'd promised him that if he invited her up for the weekend, she'd have sex with him. He'd told everybody. It was like the wedding night. Everybody knew they were going to do it. There was practically a crowd waiting for them when they came out of the room.

SMYTH: What room?

ANDREWS: I don't know. Funny, everything else is so vivid. Some freshman's room. We had a big party there after the dance. About a dozen couples. Lots of drinking. Something called "purple passion"—gin and grape juice. There was a huge vat of it. An aluminum vat. With large cakes of ice floating in it. We slopped the stuff down. One girl got sick, I remember. Vomited down the stairwell. Quite a sight. Splashed down the stairs.

SMYTH: It wasn't Joan.

ANDREWS: No, no. They were curled up on the floor. Making out. Everybody was. But we had our eyes on them. We were all virgins—except Joan. It was a different generation; you know. He was going to be the first. That night. We could hardly wait. Finally they got up and went into the back room. I think three of us had orgasms on the spot.

SMYTH: Doesn't sound like the kids nowadays.

ANDREWS: Sex was a "big deal" for us. It took a lot of planning and work. Sometimes we had to throw in an engagement ring. The kids today would think we're crazy. For them it's like taking a leak.

SMYTH: They wouldn't believe your freshman prom.

86

ANDREWS: They'd believe it. They just wouldn't care. All those fools in the past. Bury it, forget it. You don't expect them to read your book, do you?

SMYTH: I don't know. I never thought about it. I guess not.

ANDREWS: Why would they? What's it got to tell them?

SMYTH: It could show them how differently people behave.

ANDREWS: So?

SMYTH: It would open up a range of possibilities.

(ANDREWS *laughs*)

ANDREWS: We all know there are insane asylums. But we don't keep visiting them. Who's going to read your book?

SMYTH: Nonfiction sells well. Better than fiction.

ANDREWS: *(Thoughtfully)* I wonder where Joan would fit.

SMYTH: You didn't make her up?!

ANDREWS: I told you how vivid she was. I can see her coming out of that room. Strange expression on her face. Hard to read. Something like his mother's when she saw that story about Jane. His face was less complicated. He was upset. Very upset.

SMYTH: Did he say why?

ANDREWS: Not then. Nobody questioned them. But he said something later to a few of us that they had decided to wait; that Joan was having a period; something like that. (HE *looks at the* MACHINE) Hasn't the tape ended?

SMYTH: *(Getting half out of the chair to look at the* MACHINE*)* No, we still have a ways to go.

ANDREWS: This side seems longer than the other.

SMYTH: It does, doesn't it.

ANDREWS: We must be on pot.

SMYTH: I beg your pardon?

ANDREWS: Pot distorts the sense of time. Haven't you ever smoked?

SMYTH: No. Have you?

ANDREWS: No. Well, what else do you want for the time capsule?

SMYTH: Did he say anything to you later about Joan?

ANDREWS: He said they'd made out on the floor. That he'd come in his handkerchief. She'd understood. She had been very understanding. *(Pause)*

SMYTH: *(Embarrassed; confused)* What is it she had been understanding about?

ANDREWS: About his being afraid. She said it didn't matter that he couldn't get an erection. That often happened the first time. No —wait a minute. I think I've got that confused. That wasn't part of the episode with Joan. It seems to me it was earlier. No; perhaps later. With that call girl, I think it was, in Florida. The taxi driver had taken them to this little house on the outskirts of Palm Beach. Yes, it was a house, not a call girl. All the girls— there must have been five or six—were sitting around a small room rocking slowly in their chairs. Nobody said anything. We sat down. The girls just kept rocking. Finally one of them broke into a laugh. "Come on, boys," she said, "make a choice. We can't spend the whole day." I grabbed the girl nearest me and we went into a back room. She dropped her robe as soon as we got into the room. Then she asked me what I wanted. Everything had a different price. "Round the world" was the big one; I think it cost twenty dollars. I told her I only had seven dollars on me. She didn't believe me, so I let her look in my wallet. She said for seven dollars she could only screw me. We tried for what seemed like hours. And we weren't on pot. Finally she said she'd blow me a little to help me work it up, but that I wasn't to tell the madam or any of my friends or she'd catch hell—for seven bucks she was supposed to give me a straight screw and that was it. The blow job didn't help. She was nice about it. Said not to worry, that married men often came in and couldn't do it either. She squirted some kind of ointment around the opening of my cock. Then she wrapped it in gauze, and put a rubber band around it. She said when my friends saw it they'd think I had screwed her.

(Long pause; SMYTH *is nonplussed;* ANDREWS *sits very calmly)*

I really can't see why you want to know all this.

SMYTH: *(Confused; hesitant)* Well . . . it's fascinating. It . . . uh . . . helps to explain a great deal.

ANDREWS: It does? Like what?

SMYTH: I think it tells me a lot about your—about the—relations with women. I mean, tying that in with writing the story about Jane. And his inability to have intercourse with Joan.

ANDREWS: He had intercourse with Joan. On the floor. I told you that.

SMYTH: Didn't he say they had decided to wait? That Joan was having a period?

ANDREWS: That's what the handkerchief was for.

(Noises from the MACHINE; *the tape has ended)*

SMYTH: Damn! What a time for the tape to end.

ANDREWS: About time. We've been here forever. *(Pause)* Would you do me a favor and backtrack a bit? I'd like to hear that section on the freshman party.

*(*SMYTH *starts to rewind the* MACHINE *)*

SMYTH: Of course. I'd be glad to.

ANDREWS: I want to be sure I got it straight. *(Pause)* She was a very moralistic girl, that Jane. Mary Jane.

*(*SMYTH *stops the* MACHINE, *then starts it forward again)*

MACHINE: "She kept pouring water over his little body . . ."

SMYTH: *(Startled;* HE *stops* the MACHINE*)* I thought that section was on the other side. That was all much earlier.

(ANDREWS sits quietly. SMYTH again rewinds the MACHINE for a few seconds, then starts it forward)

MACHINE: ". . . something to a few of us that they had decided to wait; that Joan was having a period . . ."

(Slight pause; then a FEMALE VOICE on the tape)

FEMALE VOICE: "We can't spend the whole day."

(ANDREWS looks up startled; SMYTH stops the MACHINE)

ANDREWS: Who was that?

SMYTH: *(Laughs)* Sorry. That sometimes happens. I reuse the tapes after the typist makes a transcript. Sometimes they don't erase fully. But you *had* said they decided to wait. You see it is as I remembered it: they did not have intercourse. I thought that was what you'd said.

ANDREWS: They did have intercourse, as I've already told you. But not to climax. The handkerchief. I was quite distinct about that.

SMYTH: *(Nervously)* Tapes don't lie.

ANDREWS: Neither do I.

SMYTH: *(Placating)* Why don't we just try it from scratch? I can put on a new reel. Or we can record right over the first version.

ANDREWS: Frankly, this is getting a little tedious. It was, after all, a minor incident. I probably should never have mentioned it. You'll be making too much of it—that he was impotent, or afraid of women, or God knows what.

SMYTH: No, nothing like that.

ANDREWS: Then what will you say?

SMYTH: Well, to the extent that I understand it—

ANDREWS: —don't be modest. It's unbecoming in an historian. Makes people doubt your word.

SMYTH: Well, it seems to me—

ANDREWS: —bad start. *(Peremptory)* Who was Jane?

SMYTH: Jane was a fictional character about whom he once wrote. When he was a child.

ANDREWS: Good. Turn on the tape recorder.

(SMYTH *hesitantly complies*)

Now come sit down.

(SMYTH *returns to his chair*)

Who was the real-life character?

SMYTH: Joan?

ANDREWS: You're sure you don't want to say his mother?

SMYTH: *(Hesitantly)* Quite sure.

ANDREWS: You don't sound sure.

SMYTH: *(More firmly)* I'm quite sure. Joan was very real to him. You made her sound very real.

ANDREWS: What made her so real?

SMYTH: Her kindness.

ANDREWS: Is the machine recording?

SMYTH: Yes.

ANDREWS: You're quite sure.

SMYTH: Yes.

ANDREWS: In what way was she kind?

SMYTH: She read to him. Moralistic little tales. Useful, though, when a child is growing up. And they would play games. Card games, like bridge. They were very close throughout childhood. Very close.

ANDREWS: You have the feel of it. That girl was important to him. How about as they got older?

SMYTH: He went off to college, as boys do.

(ANDREWS chuckles)

ANDREWS: That's a nice phrase: "As boys do." I'd keep that in the book if I were you. Don't worry: the machine's got it.

SMYTH: When it came time for the freshman dance, he didn't know whether to invite her up for it or not.

ANDREWS: I don't remember saying that.

SMYTH: Those weren't your exact words. It was the impression I got. Call it intuition.

ANDREWS: *(Brooding about it)* Yes, yes, I'd say you were right. You've got the essence of it. Truth of mood I suppose you'd call it. Rather than truth of fact. That's very important in good historical writing—to recreate the spirit of the times. Much more important than getting every little fact right. Any fool can check names and dates.

SMYTH: It's the difference between pedantry and poetry.

ANDREWS: Well said.

SMYTH: *(Very pleased)* But the weekend was a disaster. *(A little alarmed at his audacity)* That is, looking at it overall.

ANDREWS: Hmm. Very perceptive.

SMYTH: *(Elated)* They had hoped it would prove to be the consummation of the relationship. But they went to a wild party with friends after the dance. Had too much gin. Besides, there was too much fuss about the whole thing. Almost all their friends knew they were planning to have intercourse.

ANDREWS: Right. That, I think, *is* the key.

SMYTH: It was like performing on a stage. Enough to inhibit anyone. When the time came he was impotent. She was kind about it. Very kind, really. She fondled him; told him not to worry. That made it worse.

(ANDREWS looks up with sharp interest)

ANDREWS: Oh?

SMYTH: It reminded him of the one time he had gone to a whore house. He had been impotent there, too. And the prostitute had been very understanding. She had even put a kind of bandage on his penis, so that his friends would think he had screwed himself bloody.

ANDREWS: *(Delighted)* Excellent!

SMYTH: The memory was very painful. When Joan fondled his penis, it brought the whole episode back. He was groggy anyway, from the gin. So he couldn't perform. He told her he'd been having too much sex recently—yes, he frankly confessed that he had been screwing himself bloody.

ANDREWS: Splendid!

SMYTH: She felt sorry for him. And angry. They never saw each other again. He did that to people. He went on to fame and fortune. They disappeared from history.

ANDREWS: You've really extracted the essence. *(Pause)* Play back the very last few lines, would you? You put that so well, I'd like to try to remember it.

(SMYTH goes to the MACHINE, starts to rewind)

Besides, I haven't heard how *your* voice sounds.

SMYTH: *(Stopping the MACHINE)* That should do it. *(SMYTH presses the "Forward" button)*

MACHINE: ". . . again. He did that to people. He went on to fame and fortune. They disappeared from history."

(Another VOICE comes on the MACHINE)

MACHINE: "You've really extracted the essence."

ANDREWS: Good Lord, it doesn't sound a bit like you. You're right: the reproduction is very poor.

(SMYTH stops the MACHINE)

SMYTH: That last bit was *you.*

ANDREWS: Which bit?

SMYTH: "You've really extracted the essence."

ANDREWS: I shouldn't be surprised. Good thing we had the machine here to get it all done.

(HE *rises*) Well then. I think you have all you need.

SMYTH: *(Hesitantly)* I'd hoped you might tell me a little more about what he was like to live with.

ANDREWS: No, that's a complicated story. Not easy to grasp.

SMYTH: Perhaps another time.

ANDREWS: Perhaps. When we're fresh. It *is* an important story. Very important.

SMYTH: Then may I call you again?

ANDREWS: We might have dinner. In two weeks, say.

SMYTH: That would be marvelous.

ANDREWS: Yes, two weeks from tonight should be fine. Come by at seven.

SMYTH: I certainly appreciate it.

ANDREWS: My pleasure.

(Pause, while SMYTH *gathers up the cord, microphone, etc.)*

Interesting business, this looking back. Surprising how much it can stir up after all these years.

SMYTH: *(Sententious)* Well, the only way to free ourselves from the past is to learn it.

ANDREWS: We've got you people to thank for that. (HE *looks at the* RECORDER; *chuckles)* That is, you and the tape recorder. You're going to set all of us free. *(Pause)* In two weeks, then.

SMYTH: Two weeks.

BLACKOUT

THE ELECTRIC MAP:

A Melodrama

PRODUCTION AND PUBLICATION HISTORY:

   The Electric Map was the second half of a double bill (*The Recorder* was the first) of my short plays that opened in January 1970 at the off-Broadway Gate Theater under the collective title *The Memory Bank*. Under that same title, the two plays were published by The Dial Press in 1970.

Backstage at the "Electric Map" of the Battle of Gettysburg. The Map covers the entire upstage area, from floor to ceiling. TED *is above stage, fiddling with a loudspeaker.* JIM *enters stage right.* HE *is carrying a newspaper.* HE *looks around for* TED, *finally spots him on the grid above stage.*

JIM: *(Calling up)* Ted!

(TED *looks up, startled*)

TED: Hey, Jim!

JIM: What the hell are you doing up there?

TED: Checking the wiring. Something's gone wrong with the volume. It keeps jumping up and down. I can't figure it out.

JIM: Will you come down here! There's something I got to talk to you about—now.

TED: Since you're here, Jim, maybe you wouldn't mind—

97

JIM: *(Interrupting)*—I got a few other things on my mind. You need an electrician, go pay for one.

(TED *starts down the ladder*)

TED: We put in a call for one three hours ago. He hasn't shown up. First the volume jumps way up. Then it goes low. Can't figure it out.

(TED *trips on a step of the ladder*)

JIM: *(Sarcastic)* Don't break your neck.

TED: Funny, it's been perfect till today. I guess it's just one of those days.

JIM: *(Bitterly)* Sure as hell is.

(TED *is now on the ground*)

TED: The girl in your office didn't know where to find you.

JIM: *(Agitated)* I haven't been in the office all day.

TED: Well I'm glad she got the message through to you. I was afraid she wouldn't be able to reach you.

JIM: *What* message?

TED: *(Startled)* To come over here.

JIM: *(Slowly, as if to be sure HE understands)* You left a message with my office for me to come over here? I see. *You* sent for *me.*

TED: Well, of course. I mean you're here, aren't you?

JIM: *(Quietly)* Oh, I'm here all right. (HE *puts the newspaper on the table*) Couldn't keep me away.

TED: *(Brightening at what HE thinks is concern for him)* Gee thanks, Jim. It's important or I wouldn't have asked you to come.

JIM: You know, for once I agree with you. It *is* important.

TED: *(Confused)* But you haven't heard what it is yet.

JIM: *(Glancing at the newspaper)* I can read.

TED: *(Alarmed)* Read? What do you mean? Read what? *(HE moves toward the newspaper. JIM blocks access)*

JIM: Your face, your face. I can read it in your face.

TED: *(Relieved)* Oh! *(HE laughs nervously)* Yeah, I guess that's the way it is with brothers. *(HE touches his face)* So it shows in my face, huh?

JIM: You look tense.

TED: *(Trying to slough it off)* Not really. Just a little problem. *(Changing the subject)* How's Ann?

JIM: Fine.

TED: Good. Glad to hear it. And the kids?

JIM: *(Impatient)* Fine. We're all fine.

TED: Good. Glad to hear it. Haven't seen them in a long time.

(Pause. JIM folds his arms over his chest)

JIM: So. *(Pause)*

TED: I miss seeing those kids.

JIM: Look, are you gonna tell me why you asked me here? *(Trace of menace)* Or should I tell you why I came?

TED: *(Nervous laugh)* Isn't that one and the same thing?

JIM: It might be.

TED: *(Looking around; evasive)* I'll bet you don't recognize the old place.

JIM: Of course I don't recognize it. I've never been here before.

TED: What? Sure you have! Mama used to take us here when we were kids.

JIM: Nope, not me. Never been inside the place.

TED: I could of sworn you came along with mama and me. *(Pause)* Well—what do you think of it?

JIM: Reminds me of a morgue.

TED: Wait till you see it when the show starts! It becomes a whole different world. You won't believe it!

JIM: Never have.

TED: Huh?

JIM: Nothing. *(Pause)* How's Warren?

TED: *(Evasive)* Warren's fine. Just fine.

JIM: So we're all fine. Terrific.

TED: Stay and see the show! It's about to start.

JIM: I don't have much time.

TED: *(Cajoling)* Boy! If you were in New York I'll bet you wouldn't go see the Statue of Liberty.

JIM: I might. If it was in the neighborhood. *(Laughs)* I wouldn't give up a piece of ass for it, if that's what you mean.

TED: It's not what I mean.

JIM: Didn't think so.

(Pause)

TED: C'mon! I'll give you the grand tour. *(TED moves up the metal stairway toward the control booth)*

JIM: Hey!—I'm here to talk to you.

TED: *(Halfway up the stairs, pointing)* That's the control booth. That's where I run the show from. *(Gesturing behind the Map)* C'mon, I'll show you the auditorium.

(JIM hesitates)

C'mon, c'mon.

(JIM reluctantly follows TED upstage right. TED pulls back a corner of the curtain so JIM can see into the "auditorium" of the Map. JIM jumps back)

JIM: *(Angrily)* There are people out there!

TED: Why sure there are people out there. That's the auditorium. How many people do you think that auditorium holds?

JIM: No idea.

TED: Well take a guess.

JIM: Three hundred.

TED: *(Pleased)* You're way off. Guess again.

JIM: Who knows. Three-fifty.

TED: On the button! *(Slyly)* That is, seven years ago.

JIM: Huh?

TED: Did you see those two strips of chairs down the side aisles?

(JIM *starts poking around the "private area"* TED *has made for himself beneath the stairway of the Map.* HE *opens* TED'*s footlocker, picks up the magazines lying on a table next to* TED'*s armchair, etc.*)

That was wasted space when I came on the job seven years ago. It was my idea to put those two rows in. And now *(Dramatically)* we seat *four hundred and seventeen* people!

JIM: *(Bored)* No shit.

TED: That's right—four hundred and seventeen people. And filled every performance.

JIM: Don't look filled.

TED: I mean during the tourist season. Summers there's not a seat in the house. Not one.

JIM: Sounds like somebody's making a good buck. Not you, I suppose.

TED: I do important work here. This is a national monument.

JIM: Mmm. Those jobs pay low. Maybe you ought to look around for some other kind of work. Maybe even leave this town. The change might do you good.

TED: *(Indignant)* I would never leave the Map. During the summer we do eight shows a day here. That's three thousand, three hundred, thirty-six people see this show every day.

JIM: The same show, eight times a day?

TED: You don't think we'd change it, do you?!

JIM: *(Quietly amused)* I guess not.

TED: You may not believe this, Jimmy, but when I came here they were doing this show live! Can you imagine?!

JIM: Yeah, if I try.

TED: No, no, you don't understand. The guy who had this job before me would do the show *live.*

JIM: You said that.

TED: He'd just talk into the mike, throwing in this or that, making all kinds of mistakes.

(JIM unscrews one of the bulbs from its socket on the Map, and examines it)

I said, "Oh no! I take this job, it's going to be done *right.* The Battle of Gettysburg happened one way and only one way and that's the way we're going to tell it *every time!"*

JIM: *(Ironic)* Good boy!

TED: *(Missing the irony)* Pretty gutsy, huh?

JIM: You told 'em, all right.

TED: So how do you think we did it?

JIM: Did what?

TED: Got the battle letter-perfect?

JIM: Beats me. Hired a new general?

(THEY laugh, then exchange boyish punches)

TED: *(Still giggling)* No. *(Switching to a serious tone)* I automated the whole show! Every line, every light cue is electronically coordinated!

JIM: No kidding.

TED: Now every show is just like every other one.

JIM: That's terrific. Of course, people only see the show once.

TED: *(Feigned shock; then patronizing)* Jim: you don't seem to understand that this is a national monument.

JIM: Yeah, so you said.

TED: People come here from all over the country. And I mean *all* over. Just last week—now you might not believe this—we had a couple here from Hawaii!

JIM: *(Perfunctory)* Is that right?

TED: Couldn't get over it. Said it was the best thing they'd seen on their whole tour. Better than the Lincoln Memorial at night.

JIM: Oh yeah? I've seen that.

TED: Do you know that man cried?

JIM: What man?

TED: The man from Hawaii. Cried like a baby at the end. Said he wasn't ashamed to admit it. Oh, the end is really something— wait till you see it! During Pickett's Charge, the tears poured down his face, seeing all those young men cut down in their prime.

JIM: It's supposed to be women who cry over that. Maybe statehood's gone to Hawaii's head.

(A backstage phone buzzes and the monitor light next to it blinks on and off)

TED: Whoops!—time to start the show.

JIM: *(Impatient)* Now look, I gotta get back to the office.

TED: All I have to do is start it. It only takes a minute.

JIM: Well make it snappy. I'll wait for you outside.

TED: Oh I can't leave while a show is on! I never leave while a show is on.

JIM: You said it was automatic—

TED:—all kinds of things could happen. A fuse could blow. Anything. That's what I get paid for. Besides, there's that trouble with the volume. (HE *heads for the control booth*) I'll just be a second.

JIM: (*Mumbling to himself*) Jesus Christ!

(TED *is in the control booth.* HE *dims the stage lights, then flicks the tape recorder on. A smooth, husky* VOICE *comes out over the amplifying system*)

VOICE: Good evening, ladies and gentlemen. We welcome you to the Gettysburg National Monument and its famous Electric Map. You are located here,

(*A white bulb on the Map flicks on and off*)

at the center of one of the world's great battlefields, now the site of the nation's eternal light peace memorial.

(*The same white light flickers on and off again*)

We will now replay the Battle of Gettysburg for you on the Electric Map, so that later, when you go out on the battlefield, you will be able to locate your position—and also that of the Enemy. (*Phony chuckle*) Depending, of course, which side you think *is* the Enemy. The battlefield measures six miles North and South

(*Large white bulbs on North/South border of the Map light up*)

and seven miles East and West.

(*Large white bulbs on East/West border of the Map light up*)

On July 1, 1863, General Robert E. Lee, leading the Confederate Army in an invasion of the North, pauses in his march north and west of the town of Gettysburg.

(The red bulbs on the north and west sides of the Map flicker on and off to indicate Lee's position)

General George Meade, commander of the Union forces, takes up a position south of the town of Gettysburg, to defend any possible thrust at Washington, D.C., the federal capital.

(The blue bulbs on the southern side of the Map flicker on and off to indicate Meade's position)

The first engagement of the two opposing armies comes when Heth's division moves forward to make a reconnaissance

(Red bulbs start to flicker to indicate Heth's position)

and finds itself met by Buford's cavalry division.

(Blue bulbs start to flicker to indicate Buford's position)

Buford sends back word to Meade requesting Union reinforcements.

(Other blue bulbs start flickering and move toward the bulbs indicating Buford's division)

The Confederates, too, move in reinforcements.

(Other red bulbs start flickering and move toward the bulbs indicating Heth's position)

The Confederates now begin a two-fold attack on the Union position at Seminary Ridge. One column drives in from the northeast and starts eating up the Union flank. The Federals try to stay in position, but the two-pronged attack soon drives them to the opposite side of the Valley . . .

(TED comes out of the control booth)

TED: *(Shouting over the* VOICE*)* What do you think? Isn't it something?

JIM: *(Shouting back)* Turn the goddamn volume down!

*(*TED *goes over to the monitor and turns it down. Bulbs on the Map continue to flicker and change as the "battle" proceeds in background)*

TED: I had the monitor on so you could hear the show.

JIM: How the hell do you expect us to talk with all that noise?

TED: It's off now. *(Pause)*

JIM: Whose voice is it?

TED: The voice on the tape?

JIM: Yeah. Sounds a little like you.

TED: Oh no. It's a professional actor. At least he was. Somebody said he's an airline pilot now.

JIM: You probably know the whole damned speech by heart.

TED: Sure. If the sound went out, I could pick right up with the microphone. It's never happened, though.

JIM: Mmm. Just as well. Your voice is wrong. I told you that when you were a kid. *(Pause)* Okay: let's get down to business. Warren is *not* fine. I want the facts.

TED: *(Frightened)* Warren?—oh, it's not anything very . . . I mean, well . . . we're in a little trouble.

JIM: So I gather.

TED: It's sort of . . . serious.

JIM: You're not going to drag me into it! You got that?! I got a lot at stake in this town.

TED: You *are* my brother.

JIM: Don't put *that* broken record on. We had the same parents. Period. *(Chuckles)* And I wouldn't swear to that.

TED: I don't think that's funny.

JIM: I don't either.

TED: You could show some respect for mama's memory.

(JIM *laughs*)

JIM: How about papa's memory?

TED: Yes, his too. You could show some respect.

(JIM *gestures toward the Map*)

JIM: You take care of the memories.

TED: If mama was alive you wouldn't say these things.

(JIM *laughs in amazement*)

JIM: Thirty-six years old and still at it with the old lady!

TED: You wouldn't and you know it.

JIM: Wouldn't *what?*

TED: Wouldn't say something like that to mama's face.

JIM: You mean *you* wouldn't. I said plenty to her face, in case you forgot.

TED: *(Resentful)* I remember. I remember very well.

JIM: Glad to hear it.

TED: That's why she told you to leave. You were always making trouble.

JIM: *(Getting angry)* Is that right.

TED: So she told you to clear out.

JIM: Nobody *told* me to leave. I left. Period.

TED: You cried. Hard.

(JIM *is flustered.* HE *tries to make light of it*)

JIM: Are you kiddin' me? I couldn't wait to get out of that place.

TED: Then why'd you keep asking to come back?

(JIM *snorts*)

JIM: Who told you that horseshit?

TED: Nobody told me that horseshit. I was there.

JIM: If I'd ever set one foot in that house again, it would have been too soon.

TED: Well, it's just as well, Jimmy, 'cause you weren't missed.

(JIM *looks as if* HE's *going to leave. The* VOICE *on the amplifier suddenly becomes audible*)

VOICE: To sum up the first day: Union forces had been driven back through—

TED: (*Over the* VOICE) —damn!—there goes the volume control! . . . Don't go, Jim! Please! I didn't mean it. (HE *starts toward the control booth*) Just let me fix the sound. Don't go! Please!

VOICE:—Gettysburg streets and alleys to seek temporary security from the slashing attack, and ended up *right here* where we are located.

(*The white bulb flickers on and off. The stage lights slowly dim*)

During the night, the Confederate lines begin to re-form. Reinforcements arrive from the west.

(*New red bulbs on the Map light up*)

General Longstreet's corps, delayed for two days, reaches camp during the night and takes up a position . . .

(*The volume goes down to inaudible.* TED *comes out of the control booth*)

TED: (*Subdued*) You see what I mean? The sound suddenly jumps. (*Pause*) I'm sorry for what I said. I didn't mean it, Jimmy.

JIM: (*Still angry*) Didn't mean what?!

TED: That we didn't miss you. *(Trying to snow him)* When you left, I cried. I remember that.

JIM: You were grinning from ear to ear.

TED: *Me?!!* Oh no, not me!

JIM: No? Maybe it was her. The two of you get mixed up.

TED: *(With false feeling)* She felt bad, Jimmy. Real bad. She talked about you all the time.

JIM: I'll bet.

TED: She *did.*

(A small amount of activity begins on the Map. Two or three red bulbs flicker and move forward. Two or three blue bulbs then flicker and move forward to meet the advancing red bulbs)

JIM: Look, I don't give a shit. It's thirty years ago. I didn't give a shit then.

(The bulbs on the Map flicker a few times and then go out. Stage lights dim further)

What the hell's the matter with the lights?

TED: It's night.

JIM: What?

TED: It's night on the battlefield.

JIM: It's like a fucking tomb in here.

TED: *(Trying to change the subject; false cheer)* Hey, I got a great idea! *(HE moves toward his footlocker)* How about a little snort, huh?

JIM: I thought you couldn't leave.

TED: Don't have to leave. I keep some here. A little pick-me-up, as mama used to say. Two plastic cups and—dear Old Grand-Dad.

JIM: *(Friendlier)* Old Grand-Dad! Shit, even your bourbon's got whiskers on it.

TED: *(Calling from the locker)* What?

JIM: That's expensive bourbon. *(TED comes back to center stage)*

TED: What the hell—you're my brother, aren't you? *(HE pours the drinks)* It's been months since we got together. This is like a reunion. *(HE hands JIM his drink, then raises his glass)* Here we go. To us—to brothers! As mama used to say, blood's thicker than water.

JIM: Maybe that's why it clots so easy.

TED: *(False appreciation)* Same old character!

JIM: Here's blood in your eye.

(THEY belt the drinks. TED shudders after drinking)

TED: Whew! Nice, huh?

JIM: The old lady got you into *some* good habits.

(TED laughs nervously)

TED: She sure knew how to hold her liquor, didn't she!

JIM: She practiced a lot.

TED: *(Trying to keep it light)* Do you know she never touched a drop during the day? Did you know that?

JIM: I didn't follow her habits too close. The parties were beauts. Those I remember.

TED: *(Defensive)* Mama never had parties. Just a friend in now and then.

JIM: Two people can make a lot of noise. It gets to sound like a party. Anyway, how would you know? You were always sent to Don and Bobbie's for the night.

(TED reacts as if hit. HE goes for the bourbon)

TED: How about another?

JIM: Not for me.

(TED pours himself another drink. JIM, needling)

Good old Don and Bobbie. I wonder whatever happened to Don and Bobbie.

(TED *belts his second drink, then shudders again*)

TED: Oh-h-h! Nice.

JIM: Whaddaya think ever happened to Don and Bobbie, huh?

TED: They were nice men.

JIM: Oh yeah? In what way?

TED: *(Evasive)* Nice. Pleasant. You know. *(Abrupt shift)* Hey!—I'm going to treat myself! I've been a good boy. And this has been sort of a tough day. Yes sir, this has been *sort* of a tough day.

JIM: "Sweet." Isn't that what mama used to call them? "Real sweet men."

TED: I don't like the way you talk about mama.

JIM: I'm talking about Don and Bobbie.

(TED *swallows his third drink*)

JIM: They were real convenient for mama. When "company" came, off went her little Teddy to Don and Bobbie's for the night. She used to say the three of you looked "cute" together. You do remember going to Don and Bobbie's, don't you?

TED: Sort of.

JIM: This town's got alotta bad memories for you. You should get away from Gettysburg. *(Pause; trace of menace)* Soon.

TED: I like Gettysburg. I do important work here.

JIM: *(Sadistically)* If we could find out where Don and Bobbie were, maybe we could send you there. I mean, since they were such nice men, you'd get a kick out of seeing them again, right?

TED: *(Sullen)* I don't even remember Don and Bobbie.

JIM: Now isn't that funny. And you over their place at least once a week.

TED: I was a kid. It's all kind of blurred.

JIM: You weren't a kid. You were twelve. That's why the old man stepped in.

TED: *(Abrupt venom)* *You're* the one who stepped in.

JIM: So you do remember.

TED: *(Shaking his head "no")* Nah. (HE *laughs, a little drunkenly*) I only remember what you make up. Ha! Ha!

JIM: I don't make anything up.

TED: That's what I said—I don't remember anything. Ha! Ha!

JIM: It *was* me who stepped in. *(Pause)* And I'm gonna step in again. But this time I'm not tellin' it to mama. I'm tellin' it to you.

TED: Let's not get back to mama.

JIM: That's right. We're gonna stick to you—and Warren.

TED: Mama was a lovely lady. You never appreciated mama.

JIM: *Forget* mama!

TED: You shouldn't make up stories. Let the dead lie.

JIM: Here's to that! And let's not build 'em tombs either: too many people get locked inside.

(The lights suddenly come up. JIM *looks around, startled)*

Now what?

TED: It's the second day.

JIM: Huh?

TED: It's dawn of the second day. *(Lapsing into monotone)* If the Confederates attack early, they stand a good chance of success. But Longstreet is against an offensive. He argues stubbornly with Lee.

JIM: *(Low)* Okay. Okay . . .

TED: Lee is patient. He hears Longstreet out. It's eleven A.M. before Lee finally orders Longstreet to attack.

JIM: *(Louder)* Cut it out, willya? It's spooky.

TED: By then it's too late. Meade has fortified his position. The Federal—

JIM: *(Interrupting)* —hey—enough! I don't have to hear this shit!

(TED comes out of his trance. Pause)

Christ, once you start, you're hard to stop.

TED: If you stop, you lose track. It's like typing: if you *think* about the keys, you've had it. *(Pause; then a trace of contempt)* I'll bet you don't even know who Longstreet is.

JIM: *(Belligerently)* You bet right. *(Pause)* Now look. I want the facts about last night. What was Warren doing in the bus depot?

TED: *(Evasive)* Warren's a good boy. He's a good boy at heart.

JIM: *What was he doing?*

TED: He's only a boy.

JIM: I'm the one who told you that when you took him in, remember?

TED: The boy needed a home. *(Barbed)* Every boy needs a home.

JIM: Every boy needs a mother *and* a father.

TED: *(Petulantly)* I do what I can for Warren. I don't bother you. I got problems, but I handle them.

(JIM laughs sardonically)

And don't think this job isn't a handful. This is a monument. A national monument. Millions of people come here to—

(HE stops in midsentence in reaction to trumpet blasts over the amplifier and the lights suddenly going up and down—as they might during a cannonading)

It's Little Round Top! Oh wait'll you see this! *(HE starts toward the monitor)* I'll turn the monitor up so you don't miss it.

JIM: Now look, I told you I want—

TED: —I *always* listen to this part. It only takes a second. *(HE turns up the sound volume on the monitor, then sits transfixed, listening)*

VOICE: Meade's chief engineer, Brigadier General Gouveneur K. Warren, is the first to see the strategic importance of Little Round Top. From its height Confederate guns could command all the ground between it and our position here.

(The white bulb flickers on and off again. JIM looks at TED with exasperation, then starts to pace the stage, muttering inaudibly)

Warren rushes reinforcements to Little Round Top. Not a moment too soon. Fifteen minutes later, the Confederates charge.

(Red bulbs move toward Little Round Top)

They are repulsed with great bloodshed, but they re-form and charge again.

(Red bulbs move back to signal Confederate retreat, then, simultaneously with trumpet blasts, move forward again to signal second advance)

The carnage is terrible; it is a high point of the heroic struggle. The Union forces, led by General Dan Sickles, suffer four thousand casualties in two hours. The First Minnesota loses 82 percent of its men within fifteen minutes.

(Some of the bulbs go out)

General Sickles himself is struck by a Confederate shell which leaves his right leg hanging in shreds, the thighbone exposed.

(One blue bulb flickers on and off; then stays on)

But Sickles lives! Indeed he will outlive all other corps commanders, not dying till fifty-one years later, in 1914.

(The lights start to dim. Muffled drum rolls)

And so night falls on the bloody scene.

(TED starts to lower the volume on the monitor)

The field is strewn with corpses, but none has died in vain. They have given their all to defend their principles, each man dying nobly for his . . .

(The volume is now inaudible)

TED: That part always moves me. No matter how many times I hear it.

JIM: What was Warren doing?

TED: *(Still mesmerized)* Doing?! Saving the battle, that's all! The whole *war!* If he hadn't realized that Little Round Top—

JIM: *(Interrupting)—your* Warren.

TED: *(Confused)* My Warren? *(HE giggles)* Oh! *My* Warren. Nothing. He wasn't doing anything.

JIM: *(Exasperated)* That's not what the morning paper says.

TED: *(Horrified)* You mean it's in the—

JIM:—that's exactly what I mean.

TED: What does it say?

JIM: It says that the police are looking for a Warren G. Rucker of ninety-seven Fall Street for resisting arrest last night at the bus depot. *(HE throws the paper at TED)* Have the police been to see you?

TED: Chief Bradford came to the house last night. I told him Warren had left town, that I didn't know where he was. *(Brightening)* But I do know, Jim. He's gone to New York. I know where he is. You can help me get him back. You know everybody in town. You've got influence. You could talk to Chief Bradford.

JIM: Do you know you're goddamn lucky *your* name isn't in the paper. We're all lucky. And I intend to keep it that way.

115

TED: Warren made a mistake, that's all. He's a good boy. You know he is. It's just that he needed money. All kids need money. They have a lot to do. They—

JIM: *(Interrupting)* —let's have it straight. Warren stole some money and was trying to skip town when the police caught him at the bus depot. Right?

TED: *(Indignant)* That's a terrible thing to say! Warren's no thief! You could show a little more respect, you know. You shouldn't talk about Warren that way.

JIM: Then you talk about him. *(Pause)*

TED: *(Nervous)* Well, he . . . he . . . needed money.

JIM: You said that.

TED: Well . . . there aren't many ways a seventeen-year-old can make money.

JIM: He's not seventeen. He was seventeen when he moved in with you three years ago.

TED: Yes, well that's what I meant. Around that age it's hard to make money.

JIM: Lots of twenty-year-olds manage. Why didn't you get him a job here?

TED: He gets bored easy. *(Brightly)* But he likes the Map. He came here one day when he first moved in. Sat through two showings in a row. Said it was "a groove." But he never came back. He did work for a week at the supermarket. But he didn't like punching the register all day. It made him feel like a machine, he said. I couldn't blame him: he was getting fat, sitting all—

JIM: *(Interrupting)* —get to the point.

TED: Yes. Well he . . . he met a tourist last summer. Down at the bus depot. You know how the tourists are—lots of money.

JIM: He's not supposed to show tourists around the battlefield. That's a union job.

TED: Oh no, he didn't do that. He wouldn't do that.

JIM: Well damnit, what *did* he do?!

TED: The tourist was an . . . an older man. He, uh, took a shine to Warren. Rented a car. They took a drive together. But not the battlefield! They didn't drive around the battlefield! When it was over, he told Warren he was grateful for his . . . company . . . and gave him—

JIM: *(Interrupting; exasperated)* —when *what* was over?! Grateful for *what,* for Christ's sake?! Look, for once in your life, can you talk straight?

TED: *(Shouting)* You know what happened! Why should I have to say what happened! You're trying to upset me, that's all.

JIM: *(Menacingly)* Say it. *(Pause)*

TED: Warren was keeping an old gentleman company. Warren's a lively boy. Older people like that. No harm in it.

JIM: *(Finally understands)* So. Little Warren was peddling his ass. *(*TED *doesn't answer)* Once or often?

TED: He . . . got to hanging around the depot. Especially in warm weather.

JIM: In other words: often. Did you know about it?

TED: I came home one day in the middle of the afternoon. I wasn't feeling well. They had to cancel a show. *(Enthusiastically shifting topics)* That never happened to me before. In seven years, I hadn't missed a single show. Imagine: seven years, eight times a day. And not one absence.

JIM: In other words you walked in on Warren and one of his old men.

TED: *(Resentful)* They were just resting. It was part of their drive.

JIM: Sounds like Warren had a nice little concession going—just like all the other merchants in town. Except his souvenirs were unauthorized.

TED: Go away! Just go away! You don't want to help . . .

JIM: I'm going to help all right. *(HE takes money out of his wallet)* I'm going to help all of us. *(Waving the money)* You see this? Take it—take all of it. You buy a one-way ticket out of this town.

TED: If you think I'm going to leave the Map, you're crazy.

JIM: You're the one who's crazy: The police are involved!

TED: *That was not Warren's fault!*

JIM: *(Wearily)* Nothing ever is.

TED: Warren started talking to a man in the depot. Suggested they take a drive. The man turned out to be a detective, from Harrisburg. He tried to grab Warren. Said he was going to turn him in to Chief Bradford. Warren had to get loose. He . . . he hit the detective. Hard. He was bleeding. Warren's a strong boy.

JIM: *(Softly)* Jesus!

TED: I got to get him back, Jim. You could talk to Bradford. He likes you. Tell him the detective tried to pick Warren up. Tell him anything. He'll believe you. He likes you.

(The volume on the amplifier suddenly comes up)

VOICE: Having lost a golden opportunity to destroy the Union line *(TED heads toward the control booth)* the Confederates end their attack for the night.

TED: He likes you. He really likes you. *(HE goes into the control booth)*

VOICE: This brings us to the morning of the third and final day of the battle,

(The lights start to go up)

to the turning point

(Pause)

in the Civil War. Lee decides on a frontal assault. He chooses George Pickett to lead it. Pickett is known chiefly for the ele-

118

gance of his clothes. His dark-brown hair hangs from his shoulders in ringlets, which he keeps carefully perfumed. Fifteen years earlier, in the . . .

(The volume is now inaudible; TED *comes out of the control booth)*

TED: I don't know what's going on. The volume's gone crazy. Up and down. I can't keep it under control. What am I going to do?

JIM: It's all right now. Forget it. There's something I want to say to you.

TED: You've got to help me. You've got to fix it. You know about these things.

JIM: No, I don't. I can't help you. That's what I want to say. I *can't help you.*

TED: *(Getting more upset)* You *have* to help me! You *owe* it to me!

JIM: I owe you *zilch!* You got one choice and only one. Get out of Gettysburg—for good.

(The volume suddenly jumps again; this time it's still louder)

VOICE: At three in the afternoon, Pickett's long gray lines start moving toward the Union troops on the ridge a mile away.

TED: Oh, Christ! What am I going to do?! *(*HE *hurries into the control booth)*

VOICE: The Confederates walk straight into a murderous barrage of Union fire.

(Red and blue lights flicker and then converge on the Map. TED *yells out from the control booth)*

TED: Jim, help me!

JIM: *(Struggling with himself)* It's your goddamn monument, not mine!

VOICE: Some Confederates break ranks and run. One Tennessee sergeant later admits, "For a hundred yards I broke the lightning speed records. But then my conscience got the better of me. I was afraid of being shot in the back and disgracing my family forever."

(JIM *goes into the booth and starts fiddling with the controls*)

Two men from a North Carolina regiment actually reach the ridge. The Union soldiers hold their fire. "Come over to this side of the Lord!" a Union soldier shouts. The two Southerners cross over and surrender, grateful for the mercy shown.

(*A corny hymn, like "Nearer My God to Thee," starts playing softly*)

But for most there is no mercy, only death. Attempts are made to rally the troops for a renewed assault, but . . .

(*The volume suddenly goes off;* JIM *comes out of the booth*)

JIM: There. Best I can tell, there's a short in one of the auditorium speakers. It's okay now, but it'll probably go again. You ought to kill it and pick up with the mike. (HE *hands the mike to* TED)

TED: (*Terrified*) No, it's okay now!

JIM: It's bound to go again.

TED: I don't care. It's near the end. I'll take a chance.

JIM: Have it your way. I got to get back.

TED: Will you speak to Bradford?

JIM: No.

TED: No?! How can you say no?!

JIM: I said it. There's nothing I can do.

TED: You could talk to Bradford. Tell him it's all a mistake. Mistaken identity—yes, that's it, mistaken identity.

JIM: That's what it is all right.

TED: How'll I get Warren back?

JIM: You won't get Warren back. (*Pause*) You'll be lucky if they don't take you in, too.

TED: *(Smothered rage)* You'd like that, wouldn't you?

JIM: I gave you my advice: pack it in. *(Gesturing to encompass the Map)* Close the door on the whole goddamn mess!

TED: *(Getting hysterical)* That's enough, you hear me?! That's enough!

(JIM grabs TED's shoulder)

JIM: If you want to survive, forget Warren and *get out of Gettysburg.* Otherwise you're going to end up in jail yourself.

(TED breaks away)

TED: You'd like to see me in jail, back in the State Boys' Home, wouldn't you? Well I'm not going back, you hear? I'm not going back to jail just to make you happy!

JIM: What the hell you talking about now?

TED: Don't think I don't know why mama sent me to the Home. I know you were behind it. I've always known you were behind it.

(A sudden bleep from the amplifier; the volume comes up loud)

VOICE: No one will ever be able to tally the suffering, the high hopes destroyed, the young men cut down in their prime.

JIM: Will you get in there and stop that noise!

(The amplifier bleeps again; the volume goes down)

TED: I know why I got sent to the Home, taken away from mama!

JIM: If you don't get hold of yourself, they're going to carry you out of here.

TED: You told her what was going on with Don and Bobbie! You told her to send me to the Home, or you'd go to the police. You made mama send me away! You're the one who separated me and mama!

121

JIM: *(Quietly)* No one could ever do that.

TED: You did it! I know you did it! And all because she loved *me!*

(JIM grabs TED and throws him against the railing of the Map. TED crumples)

JIM: Now listen, you! I've about had it with your bullshit. With your fucking Warrens, and your maps, and your mamas! Do you want to know what *really* happened?! You want to hear the *true* story for a change?!

TED: Just get out of here, that's all. Leave me alone. Just leave me alone.

JIM: You are alone. You and your make-believe world.

TED: *(Wailing)* Get out of here!!

JIM: I did tell mama I'd go to the police if she didn't stop shipping you over to Don and Bobbie. And you know what? She said I should go right ahead. She wouldn't mind at all if they took you off to the State Home. You get it? She was glad for the chance to get rid of you. You were a nuisance. You got in the way when she wanted to fuck with the garage mechanic or the delivery man. *She wanted to get rid of you!*

(TED turns to face JIM)

TED: You bastard. You lying bastard. *(TED suddenly lunges at JIM)* I'll kill you! I'll kill you!

(THEY grapple. JIM throws TED to the floor. TED gets up, and weeping goes to JIM and tries to embrace him. JIM knees TED in the groin. TED doubles over in pain on the floor)

JIM: Don't touch me—you freak. *(HE heads for the exit)*

TED: She loved me. She loved me.

JIM: She's all yours. (HE *gestures to the Map*) You can have all of it. All your pretty pictures. None of 'em exist anyway. *Just like you.* (JIM *exits*)

TED: (*Shouting after* JIM) She hated *you!* She hated *you!*

(*The Map goes wild. Loud noises from the amplifier, mixed with words*)

VOICE: On the Union side there is wild rejoicing . . . zzz . . . mmm . . . grinning soldiers everywhere . . . trailing Rebel flags in the dirt . . . zzz . . . mmm . . . "That'll hold the bastards!" "That'll hold 'em . . ." zzz . . . mmm . . .

(*Bulbs flicker all over the Map.* TED *starts to get up off the floor; realizes* HE *must get to the control booth*)

. . . cheers and yells . . . zzzz . . . mmmm . . . zzz . . . victory dance . . . zzz . . . mmm . . . zzz . . . General Hays grabs and kisses a young lieutenant on his staff . . . zzzz . . . mmmm . . . zzzzz . . . "Give me a flag, boy! . . . Give me a flag!" . . . zzz . . . mmm . . . zzz . . . mmm . . . zzz.

(TED *is now in the control booth*)

"We've broke 'em all to hell . . . broke 'em all to hell!" . . . zzz . . . mmm . . .

(TED *shuts off the controls. The sound goes dead. The lights on the Map, and most of the stage lights, go out, leaving* TED *in semidarkness. For a few seconds, there is absolute quiet.* TED *looks upstage through the Map into the "auditorium."* HE *grabs the script of the "show" from above the control booth and tries to find his place in it. Then, trembling,* HE *picks up the microphone*)

TED: (*His voice barely under control*) Ladies and gentlemen . . . this is very unfortunate . . . never in seven years . . . this is the first time in seven years that we have not . . . that our equipment has not functioned. The battle, in any case, is almost over . . . if you will bear with me . . . if you will try to help me . . . I will attempt to finish up . . . to tell you . . . what happened . . .

It was an accident of birth and environment . . . (HE *searches frantically for his place in the script; then, reading from it*) I mean, as the motto on the memorial says . . . nobody could help it . . . "The Accident of Birth and Environment Determined Whether They Would Wear the Blue or Gray." All were good boys. All of them . . . good at heart . . .

And now that it's over, *all finished* . . . Robert E. Lee blames only himself . . . nobody else. As the survivors stagger back across the bloody field, Lee rides out among them and speaks to them. They are crazed with fear until they hear his voice. "His fault," he says over and over again, "his fault." (*Wandering from script*) He comforts them like a good parent, a good mama . . . He gathers them to him. They hug his leg. Their blood streaks his white horse. He does not send them away. She would not send him away . . . She was a good woman, a lovely woman . . . she would not send him away . . . (*Returns to the script*) The battlefield is dark. Lee rides back to his headquarters. It is all over, all over . . . "Too bad; too bad. Oh, too bad!" . . . "We must find the way home," Lee says, "home to Virginia." . . . "Home," he keeps saying, "we must find our way home now . . ." (TED *struggles to control himself*) That, ladies and gentlemen, is the end of our story, the end of the last day of the battle.

(HE *switches on the stage lights. All the bulbs on the Map suddenly light up*)

We hope you have enjoyed your visit to the Electric Map, and that you will have a pleasant day touring the battlefield . . . We close this performance, as is our custom, with lines from the speech Abraham Lincoln made on this same spot . . . four and one-half months after Robert E. Lee led his men home to Virginia . . . lines that even today echo through the free world, giving hope and courage to all mankind.

(TED flicks another switch and "The Battle Hymn of the Republic" starts playing in the background. At the same time the colors of some of the bulbs on the Map change so that they are of equal proportions of red, white, and blue. They all start to flicker simultaneously. The official VOICE comes out over the amplifier)

VOICE: . . . testing whether that nation, or any nation so conceived . . . zzz . . .

(Static interrupts the speech. TED reacts frantically at the realization that even the Lincoln tape is defective. Through the remainder of the speech, as the static and volume grow in intensity, so too does TED's desperate jiggling of the control knobs)

We have come to dedicate a . . . zzz . . . mmm . . . final resting place for those who . . . zzz . . . mmm . . . It is for us, the living rather, to be dedicated . . . zzz . . . mmm . . . to the great task remaining before us—that from these honored dead we take increased devotion . . . zzzzzz . . . mmmmmm . . . zzzzzz . . . here highly resolve . . . zzz . . . mmmm . . . zzzzzz

(As the bleeps, noise, and static drown out the Lincoln speech, the "Battle Hymn" and the red, white, and blue lights reach their climax. TED, near collapse, grabs the microphone)

VOICE: *(Suddenly loud again)* . . . and that government of the people, by the people, for the people, shall not perish from the earth.

TED: *(Shouting hysterically into the mike)* She was a lovely lady!! She hated *him!!*

(As the static and the music peak)

THE CURTAIN FALLS

PAYMENTS

PRODUCTION AND PUBLICATION HISTORY:

Payments, in an earlier version, was performed in work-shop at The New Dramatists in April 1971. The play has not previously been published.

LIST OF CHARACTERS *(In Order of Appearance):*

SAL: Mid-late twenties. The "dynamic young executive."

JEANNE: Early-late twenties. Unjudgmental, tolerant of foibles. Keen insight into people, and the keen wit to express it. Her chief pastime is sex.

BO: About twenty. Pleasant-looking. Southern. Dumb, but likeable.

ALICE: Twenties or thirties. Shrewd, touching. Contrast between her flamboyant style and her attachment to middle-class values. Both "bizarre" and poignant.

NANCY: Mid twenties. The initial impression is of a small-town, pleasant, somewhat-brighter-than-average woman. The second impression, which comes after we see her collusion in her husband BOB's prostitution, is of someone overwhelmingly tough and angry. Both impressions are wrong—or at least incomplete. They represent only two aspects of a many-sided woman whose gutsiness and strength take the form they do because of the limited options available to her. Isolated in lower-middle-class suburbia, confined to friends like the simpering ELLEN, in love with BOB but infuriated by his passivity, NANCY impulsively decides on shock tactics in order to try to free both BOB and herself from what she takes to be their death-in-life. Where BOB capitulates to the world around him, NANCY fights it at every turn; where he is acted-upon, she acts. Her tactics may look ugly, but they spring, paradoxically, from healthy assertion.

ELLEN: Early twenties. Reasonably attractive, but not in any striking way. Timid and traditional. Mouths the clichés of the soap operas: the loyal wife and mother, the importance of togetherness, and so on. Decent, well-meaning. Would never deliberately hurt anyone.

BOB: Early-mid twenties. Handsome in a rugged, all-American way. On the outside, a beautiful animal. But complex to a degree he doesn't himself understand, being neither introspective nor articulate. He yearns for options he hasn't defined, seethes with resentments he can't clarify, longs for someone to "save" him but can envision neither the person nor the process. Not understanding his own turmoil, he denies it, presenting instead a good-guy, easy-going image. He lets the world work him over, is complicitous in the process, refusing to possess his own life. Everything happens to him —and nothing; he remains at the end of the play what he was at the start.

NED: Twenty to thirty. Powerful physical presence. Opinionated, loud. A bully.

RAY: Mid-forties. A second-rate novelist, full of pretensions. Agitated, elegant, verbal, clever. A stereotypic "1950s faggot" in his terrier games of provocation and badinage.

TOM: In his forties. A librarian. Fleshy and unappetizing. Speaks begrudgingly, and then in a pedantic monotone. Concealed and furtive.

LARRY: About twenty. Latin. Self-absorbed, nonverbal. Yet has a decided aura, the result of his single-minded devotion to two things: shoes, and keeping his body in shape.

PAUL: Mid-thirties to mid-forties. Dominated by his sexual appetites, and indulgent of them. Intelligent, socially charming, basically decent and gifted. His attraction to BOB is real, and not merely physical; but his compulsions work to prevent what he most wants.

FRANK: Forty to fifty. Caustic, down-to-earth, brilliant. Prides himself on his "realism"—on his knowledge of how the world "works" (a knowledge usually accurate).

ACT I

SCENE 1

SAL GIOMBO's *living room. The decor is in self-conscious good taste. There is a large, elegant desk at one corner of the room, with two phones on it. A half-dead balloon plant sits to one side.*

SAL *is seated at the desk, going through his files.* HE's *dressed conservatively, in slightly liberated Ivy League style, though his hair and sideburns are long.* HE's *about twenty-five, good-looking, energetic, verbal, shrewd.*

BO, *a blond, Southern boy, about nineteen, stupid but ingratiating, is slouched in an armchair.*

JEANNE, *in her twenties, is lying on the couch.* SHE's *a little too plump, her features too irregular, to be attractive in any standard way, but* SHE's *curvaceous and saucy.* SHE's *sloppily dressed.*

As the curtain rises, JEANNE *is puffing on a joint which* SHE *passes to* BO. *Her foot is resting directly on the couch.*

SAL: The foot, Jeanne, the foot.

(SHE *groans in mock annoyance, and keeps her foot on the couch.* BO *sits up straight in his chair*)

JEANNE: Oh Jesus. (SHE *motions to* BO *to relax*)

SAL: *(Mimicking* JEANNE*)* Oh Mary, Oh Joseph.

JEANNE: *(Holds up her leg so* SAL *can see the sole of her shoe*) Look! My shoe is *clean.* Not a drop of shit on it. *(Giggles)* Which is more than I can say for your couch.

SAL: Juanita hand vacuums that couch once a week. And if you don't shape up, *you* can start doing it.

JEANNE: Cleaning's not my bag.

SAL: The least you could do is water the plants.

JEANNE: You don't water plants, you *pat* them.

BO: Mah mama used to sing to her plants. But they died anyway.

JEANNE: At least they died happy.

SAL: *(Gesturing to ashtray)* And empty those goddamn roaches.

BO: In mah mouth.

SAL: *(To* JEANNE*)* This place is a pig sty since you moved in.

JEANNE: *(To* BO*)* A cleanliness fanatic. Just like my old lady. She empties ashtrays before people use them.

SAL: If you did the cleaning instead of Juanita, I'd save fifteen bucks a week. *(Starts calculating in his head)* Fifteen bucks a week times fifty-two weeks. That's—*(Pause)*—Jesus Christ!—that's $780 a year! I could spend a month in San Juan on that!

JEANNE: You and Juanita, under the palms.

(SAL *makes a playful gesture as if to swat her*)

BO: *(To* SAL*)* You add them sums in your head, man?

SAL: No.

BO: *(Relieved)* Whew. Didn't think so.

SAL: I *multiplied* them.

BO: Huh?

SAL: Fifty times $15 is $750. Then you pick up the other two weeks. Two times $15 is $30. $750 and $30 is $780. Simple. You dig?

BO: You puttin' me on, man. Ah know when you puttin' me on. *(Takes a drag of the joint)*

SAL: Remember: none of that while she's here.

BO: Ah dig. Ah dig.

JEANNE: You don't even know if she's coming.

SAL: *(Looks at his watch, frowns)* Mmm. Ten after three already. *(To* BO*)* How come you're here so early? (BO *sits up straight again)* You know there's nuthin' till five.

BO: Shee-it, man, Monday you sent me out at seven in the A.M.

SAL: That's different. The guy'd been up all night.

BO: Never would have known it!

(BO *slaps his thigh and laughs;* JEANNE *smiles;* SAL *grimaces)*

SAL: *(To* BO, *severely)* You gotta get yourself a routine.

JEANNE: He's got dozens of routines.

BO: *(Smiling)* But no face work. That's where ah draw the line.

(HE *and* JEANNE *laugh again)*

SAL: How come your wife don't need you? Where's she at today?

BO: Naw—she's at Miss Fritzi's. It's a treat, 'cause she made me that pecan pie last night. Ooo-eee! them pies is somethin' else! Finger lickin's the best of it.

JEANNE: So that's why Southerners have sticky fingers.

134

SAL: Who the hell is Miss Fritzi?

BO: The lady what removes hair. *(Laughs)* Alice don't think ah know why she's there, but ah know. She say *(Imitating* ALICE*'s voice)* "just gonna have a few little hairs plucked from under mah arms, honey." *(Laughs)* Shee-it, man, ah know where them hairs is gettin' plucked from. Mah baby's beard is growing back in!

JEANNE: Alice is too old for you.

BO: She ain't either. Ah like older women. They know where it's at.

JEANNE: *(Leaning over and caressing* BO*'s leg)* I know where it's at, too, sweetie. But at least I don't have one there myself.

BO: Don't you touch mah private parts.

JEANNE: Meaning your kneecap, I suppose.

BO: And don't mock mah woman. She's more woman than you are. Mah Alice got a woman's soul—the doctors said so when they done the operation. When they laid her on the table they said—

JEANNE: *(Interrupting)* —what a way to talk.

BO: *(Confused)* Huh?

SAL: We know the operation story.

BO: *(Picking up)* —they said, this is a woman what got caught in a man's body.

JEANNE: Don't we all—when we can.

BO: —and we gonna fix that. And let me tell you, they done it.

JEANNE: *(Southern accent)* "She's all woman now, mah woman."

BO: That's right!

SAL: So how come her beard's growing in again?

BO: 'Cause she's a big woman, that's how.

JEANNE: Oh, la!

BO: It's what the doctors call "residual." Big people got more residual. This friend of Alice—man, all she got is residual. *(Shakes his head)* That's a sad story. Saddest story ah know.

(BO looks around expectantly, but gets no reaction. SAL is looking through his files. JEANNE lies back on the couch with her eyes half closed)

(Hurt) Don't you people care none 'bout Marie?

JEANNE: *(Bored)* Who's Marie?

BO: I jes told you. Marie's Alice's friend. The one with the big residual.

JEANNE: *(Opening her eyes; arch)* It doesn't sound like a sad story.

BO: She had the same operation Alice had. Her name used to be Mort. Got herself changed into this beautiful chick, Marie . . . But no sooner's the operation done, then guess what?

JEANNE: She gives birth to quintuplets.

BO: She falls for a chick named Joan! Can you beat that?! When she was Mort, didn't want nothin' to do with chicks. No sooner she's Marie and she's moonin' over a fox named Joan.

JEANNE: Joan's a dyke, right?

SAL: That's a very sick remark.

JEANNE: Just trying to keep the conversation alive.

BO: Marie don't do nothin' day or night but cry to have her pecker put back on.

JEANNE: Well why don't they, the poor thing?

BO: Can't get it back nohow. When they operate, they cut the pecker into four parts and stuff 'em up to make her a "cootchee." No way to get them parts back together again.

SAL: They can make her a new one. Out of silicone. Lots of dykes have 'em.

BO: *(Offended)* Marie ain't no dyke. Ah told you that.

136

JEANNE: You said *Joan* wasn't a dyke. You never said Marie wasn't.

BO: How could Marie be a dyke when her real name's Mort? You betta lay off that weed, girl.

SAL: *(Pedantic)* The trouble with those silicone cocks is that they never get completely soft.

JEANNE: No kidding?! Can you introduce me?

BO: *(Shaking his head)* Nature's something else. You shouldn't mess with Nature.

JEANNE: Alice managed.

BO: Alice is Southern. Down South we used to lickin' nature. *(Smiles)* Finger lickin'.

JEANNE: Now *that* I believe.

SAL: Alice isn't Southern.

BO: She Southern now. 'Cause now she's mah woman. Mah women is always Southern. You see for yourself when she come by. She lookin' fine. Got new orange hair. Wants to make mine orange, too.

SAL: *(Alarmed)* Alice is coming here?!

BO: Back home we used to stomp this kid with orange hair. Mah folks didn't like it none.

JEANNE: The orange hair.

BO: Dig.

SAL: *(Loud)* Hey!

(BO *jumps*)

BO: Don't do that, man! It hurts mah head.

SAL: Is Alice coming here or isn't she?

BO: She gonna pick me up when she done at Miss Fritzi's. You ain't seen her since the Armory drag last year.

SAL: And I ain't seeing her today! If Nancy Marshall gets one look at your six foot, orange Alice, *(The phone rings)* the whole deal'll be shot. I'm running a business, man *(Picks up the receiver)* not a transsexual tea party. *(Talking into the phone)* Hello . . . *(Laughs)* No, I'm not giving away tea, Carl . . .

JEANNE: *(To* BO*)* The action's starting early. It must be Groundhog Day.

SAL: You in your room at the Y? . . . Good. A dude's due from Jersey about four . . . No, don't call me. It ties up the lines . . . Right. I'll get back to you. *(Hangs up phone. Businesslike)* Listen, you two, I got work to do. Bo, why don't you head Alice off at the beauty parlor? Throw on some clothes, Jeanne. Nancy's due any time.

JEANNE: God, you're cuddly today.

SAL: We can't all lay around doing nuthin'.

JEANNE: That's the thanks I get for the paratrooper last night.

(The downstairs buzzer rings)

SAL: Groovy! It's Nancy. Now remember, you two—cool, very cool. This is a *small-town chick.*

JEANNE: What's she got, for Christ's sake—three breasts?

SAL: No, baby: one husband. One big, gorgeous husband.

JEANNE: Oooh! The plot thickens.

SAL: And he's not for you.

JEANNE: Selfish! *I* share.

SAL: *You're* living rent-free.

(The apartment bell rings. SAL *goes to answer it)*

(To BO) Put that goddamn joint out! *(Sniffs the air)* It smells like a fucking five and dime in here.

JEANNE: *(Mimicking a salesgirl)* Notions! Dream sticks! Come get your orange mama!

138

SAL: Can it! (HE *puts on a big smile, then opens door. His face falls*) Jesus Christ, it's you!

(ALICE *enters.* SHE'*s played by the same actor who later will be* RAY. SHE'*s six feet tall, with orange hair teased up another two or three inches, flamboyantly dressed and made up, exaggeratedly "feminine" in movement*)

ALICE: Herself. Come to mama, Salvadore.

(SHE *gives* SAL *a bear hug.* HE *wriggles loose*)

SAL: Salva*tore*, not Salva*dore*.

ALICE: Tallulah-schmullah. It's all the same in Southern.

JEANNE: Sal's a little unnerved, Alice. We were expecting Rosemary's baby.

ALICE: And how are you, Miss Fresh Mouth?

JEANNE: Don't I rate the Southern accent?

ALICE: Most certainly not. That's for mah sweet sugah. (*Goes over to* BO)

BO: Whaddaya say, baby. (*Kisses her on the cheek*)

ALICE: (*To* BO) Smell the new hormonal cologne?

SAL: How'd you get up here, Alice?

ALICE: (*Still entranced by the kiss*) Ooh! Even on the cheek, it sends me to shiverin'!

SAL: Alice: I asked you how you got up here.

ALICE: Is there more than one way?

JEANNE: "Oh yes!" said the preacher, "there are many ways, and the Lord he loves 'em all!"

SAL: Expensive building. Doorman. What difference does it make?! He never stops *any*body!

ALICE: Why would he stop me? Do I look like a junkie or a nigger?

139

SAL: Well you can't stay! A friend of mine is due any minute.

ALICE: Honey, a friend of yours just arrived.

SAL: No, you don't understand . . . this girl is coming, this girl I used to—

(ALICE *gives* SAL *an indignant look.* SAL *throws up his hands*

ALICE: Whaddaya think *this* is, sweetheart—chopped liver?!

SAL: Mama mia!

ALICE: Ah never seen such manners! Who the fuck you think you are, Sally Mae?

SAL: *(Going up to* ALICE *to console her)* It's a mistake, sweetie, that's all. Mistaken identity.

JEANNE: Don't start with the metaphysics.

(The buzzer rings again)

SAL: Oh no! *(Goes to the door)*

JEANNE: Oh, aren't we going to have a nice reunion!

SAL: Button up!

JEANNE: Well—that's a new one!

(SAL opens the door)

SAL: H-E-L-L-O, Nancy!

NANCY: *(Timidly)* Hi, Sal. *(NANCY enters the room.* SHE'*s an attractive woman in her early twenties.* SHE *has a strong, shrewd side, but at the moment it's subdued. Laughs nervously)* Never thought I'd really make it.

SAL: Great to see you! *(Looks at his watch)* And right on time! I love people who are prompt.

JEANNE: As long as they're pretty, too.

SAL: *(Frowning)* Nancy, this is Jeanne . . . Jeanne—de Maro . . .

JEANNE: Ooh—I love that!

SAL: Jeanne's a cousin of mine from P.A. She's in New York to break into modeling.

JEANNE: Cousin Sal's housing me while I get off—oops!, I mean *on* my feet.

NANCY: Nice meeting you.

JEANNE: *(Disarmed; friendly)* Thanks. Welcome to the big city.

SAL: *(To NANCY)* And this is Bo Shepard. Bo is a freshman at N.Y.U. He's studying to be an airline pilot.

(JEANNE almost breaks up)

ALICE: *(To BO)* The things I don't know!

BO: *(Holding out his hand)* How do, ma'am. Pleasure meetin' you.

NANCY: Thank you. It's nice meeting you.

SAL: And *this* . . . is Alice. She's a showgirl friend of Bo's.

BO: *(Belligerent)* Alice is mah woman.

ALICE: *(Sashaying across the room to greet NANCY)* Sure am pleased to make your acquaintance, Miss Nancy.

NANCY: Thanks.

JEANNE: "*Miss* Nancy!" That's no way to talk to a total stranger.

ALICE: But that's the way I talk to you, Miss Welcome Wagon.

NANCY: *(To ALICE)* That's a lovely dress.

ALICE: *(Pleased) Isn't* it?

NANCY: You can't buy anything like that in New Jersey.

ALICE: Who would try?

NANCY: I live in Jersey.

ALICE: *(Genuine concern)* Poor baby! Oh that's how you know Sal.

SAL: *(Offhanded)* Nance and I are old high school friends. *(To NANCY, expansively)* You just make yourself comfortable, Nance. Everyone else is *about to split.*

ALICE: *(Smiling "sweetly")* I've already done that.

SAL: Bo's on his way to class *(ALICE, still smiling, shakes her head "no," slowly from side to side. SAL is disconcerted)* and Jeanne here is about to shower for an audition uptown.

NANCY: *(To JEANNE, sympathetically)* Modeling must be a hard line of work to break into.

JEANNE: Don't know what I'd do without Cousin Sal here to dry my eyes and help me get back on the horse.

SAL: Jeanne's gonna make it. She's got a special quality.

JEANNE: She's nuts about horses. *(Starts to get up)*

NANCY: Don't rush off on my account. I can only stay a few minutes. A friend's sitting with the baby, and I promised to make the five o'clock bus back.

JEANNE: Oh, you have a baby!

NANCY: A little boy. Two years old.

JEANNE: What a comfort to know another generation's on the way.

ALICE: *(To NANCY)* I thought only spades and thugs lived in Jersey.

NANCY: We live in a small town. North of Trenton.

JEANNE: *(To ALICE)* You used to be fond of spades. I remember you and that very black boy named Buster one night at—

ALICE: *(Indignant)* —ah have *never* had sexual relations with a nigra.

JEANNE: Is that the same as fucking?

(The phone rings. SAL goes to answer it)

NANCY: *(To ALICE)* Sal said you were in show business?

ALICE: *(Surprised):* He did?!

SAL: *(Into phone)* Hello . . . Arthur! How you been?! . . . Is that so? . . . Ah-ha. Great beaches, I hear . . . Hang on a minute, Arthur. *(Puts receiver against his chest; to the OTHERS)* Just go on talking, kids. I won't be a minute. *(Into the phone)* No, he's in L.A. . . . Yeah, the Hollywood bit. *(Laughs)* . . . Well, of course. Don't I always?

ALICE: *(To* NANCY*)* To tell you the truth, I'm not in show business right now, honey. *(Looks affectionately at* BO*)* I'm just home-folks now.

SAL: *(Into the phone, reading from* ARTHUR's *file card)* Let's see . . . Terry you already know . . . How about Jeff? . . . No, the one from Georgia.

NANCY: I guess opposites envy. Home can be a little dull.

JEANNE: *(Looking around)* That depends on your home.

ALICE: *(Lofty)* Show Business is a drag after a while, honey.

JEANNE: *(Directed at* ALICE*)* For some, it's drag from the start.

ALICE: Some of us look good in clothes, and some of us don't.

JEANNE: *(Weary)* Don't start, sweets. You know only black chicks can make me jealous. Like that one at the Armory last year— now there was something gorgeous!

ALICE: *(Angry)* Gorgeous, my ass!

JEANNE: Tsk, tsk! What would Robert E. Lee say?

SAL: *(Into the phone)* Hang on while I see if he's in. *(Starts to dial a number on his second phone, while holding the receiver of the first one against his chest)*

ALICE: *(To* NANCY*)* 'Scuse my language, dear. They do provoke me so. Five years ago at the Armory ball, there wasn't a coon in the lineup. Oh yes, one—that mailman from Secaucus. But her legs were so thick from walkin' the route every day, she never stood a chance in the competition. Then suddenly from nowhere, there were coons in every drag ball on the East Coast.

BO: Don't know their place.

SAL: *(Into second receiver)* Mike, it's Sal . . . You feel like goin' out? . . . *(Turns his back to the* OTHERS *so that his words can no longer be heard)*

JEANNE: *(To* ALICE*)* You're jealous. Those high asses. Those long, thin legs.

ALICE: *(To* NANCY, *ignoring* JEANNE*)* I told my manager straight out: I don't appear in no show with coons. Let 'em get their own show. Besides, Bo don't like for me to work. Isn't that right, sugar?

BO: Woman's place is in the home.

ALICE: Don't you jes love an old-fashioned man?

(SAL has been talking alternately into one phone and then the other. HE now hangs up the second phone. Into first phone)

SAL: Send me mine direct . . . Glad to oblige. Talk to you soon, Arthur. *(Hangs up the phone and looks out at the silent group)* What happened to the small talk?

JEANNE: Small?! We've been having a heart-to-heart on The Race Question. *(Mock Southern accent)* Alice say she won't appear no more with Nigras. But Bo, I think, do not share them views.

BO: Ah do, too.

JEANNE: *(Feigned shock)* 'Land sakes, chile! You mean you ain't goin' t'see that nice black Doctor Williams no more?!

ALICE: That's different. A man can't help what he has to put up with on the job. But we don't socialize with 'em none.

BO: That's right. Bed's one thing. The porch is another.

JEANNE: Don't Doctor Williams ever want to do it on the porch?

ALICE: *(Haughty)* You're bein' common again.

BO: He ain't got no porch. Ain't even got a terrace.

SAL: *(Impatient)* Good, terrific. Now why don't you all skip on to your appointments. Nance has to get back, and we got some things to talk over.

(No one gets up to leave)

ALICE: Ah love reunions. Maybe ah oughta run downstairs and buy a cake.

BO: Yum-my!

JEANNE: Easy, sticky fingers.

ALICE: *(To NANCY)* How long since you two seen each other?

NANCY: About five years. At high school graduation. *(Pause; then pointed)* But we hear about Sal from time to time.

JEANNE: Everybody knows Sal.

ALICE: How'd you meet again?

SAL: *(Trying to shut her off)* Hey, how about it, Alice, huh?

NANCY: We ran into each other on Fifty-ninth Street Monday. I was in the city for a doctor's appointment.

JEANNE: *(To SAL)* That's my corner. Work your own side of the street.

ALICE: *(Lets out a small shriek)* Eee!—I forgot to tell you! Guess who got busted Friday at The Guardsman?

JEANNE: Busby Berkeley.

ALICE: *Doctor* Stanley Rubin!

SAL: No shit?!

ALICE: He was dealin' *right there in the bar*! Selling tooies and Cibas to fifteen-year-old trash.

SAL: Not cool.

NANCY: What's a Ciba?

BO: Cibas is Desert Sahara pills. 'Cause they dry your mouth out. *(NANCY shakes her head in confusion. BO reaches into his pocket and takes out a white pill)* Here go, ma'am. I got a Ciba right here. *(HE offers the pill to NANCY)* It gives you a boss nod.

(NANCY takes the pill and looks at it)

ALICE: *(To BO)* How many times I got to tell you about carryin' them things in the street?

BO: Shee-it, mama. Jes found it.

ALICE: You'll make a widow of me, boy.

NANCY: *(Looking at the pill)* C-I-B-A. But that's the name of the manufacturer. Like Squibb or Rexall.

BO: Ain't never had a Rexall. Is that a up or a down?

JEANNE: It's a trade name.

BO: What is?

JEANNE: Rexall.

BO: Trade? Ah don't dig ya, baby.

JEANNE: Concentrate on your former life.

SAL: Look, why not continue this fascinating discussion somewhere else? Nance and I got a lot to talk about.

ALICE: *Mr.* Rude! You were such a nice boy before you got rich and famous.

SAL: So were you. *(The phone rings)* See what I mean. Once they start I won't get a minute. How about it, huh? *(Into phone)* Hello . . . Who? . . . Wrong number. *(Hangs up)*

JEANNE: That was either the F.B.I. or your mother. Possibly both.

SAL: Will you go uptown, for Chrissake?!

BO: *(To* NANCY*)* Mind if ah have my Ciba back, ma'am?

ALICE: *(To* NANCY*)* You give me that, hear?

BO: Shucks, mama.

ALICE: You are a *bad* boy.

BO: *(Grinning)* Ooo-eee! Guess who's gonna get a spankin'?!

SAL: Check in here around nine, Bo.

ALICE: *(Pouting)* Maybe he will and maybe he won't.

SAL: Suit yourself, honey. It ain't my hair that's growin' in.

ALICE: *(Looks accusingly at* BO*)* What's *that* supposed to mean, exactly?

BO: Beats me, baby.

JEANNE: Never pursue meaning, Alice. It inhibits action.

ALICE: Every hair on this head is mine. Every hair.

JEANNE: You got balls, all right. (ALICE *reacts indignantly*) No, no, you're missing the point. (ALICE *glares,* JEANNE *groans*) I give up!

ALICE: (*Getting up*) I am leavin'. Ah never seen such a lack of etiquette!

SAL: Now, now, Miss Alice. You know we love you. It's just that you caught us at a bad time.

ALICE: (*Pouting*) Grumblin' at me at the door. Making fun of mah hair. That's no way to treat old friends.

SAL: (*Putting his arm around her*) You're right. You're absolutely right. I've been a shit.

ALICE: A cad.

SAL: Okay, a cad. (*Kisses her on the cheek*) Now tell me I'm still your old Sal.

ALICE: I don't know.

SAL: (*Coaxing*) Aw c'mon, Alice. (*Kisses her again*)

ALICE: (*Pulling away, but good-naturedly*) Stop kissin' me. You'll make Bo jealous. Ah have mah home to think of.

SAL: We're still friends?

ALICE: Ah s'pose. But your manners could sure do with improvin'. It's all that Northern trash you hang out with.

JEANNE: (*Butterfly McQueen voice*) If My Gal Sal and Miss Scarlett will 'scuse me, ahs going to change mah lingerie, which is what us Northern trash calls our sweet undies. So bye for now, y'all. See you round the slave quarters. (*Exits into the bedroom*)

SAL: (*Calling after her*) Be sure the shower curtain is *inside* the tub, slob!

ALICE: (*To* SAL) I don't know why you put up with that girl. Common as can be.

SAL: So's her touch—God bless her.

ALICE: *(To BO)* Let's you and me go, sugah. Mah head's about to split.

BO: Where we goin'?

ALICE: Don't you sass me. Here I am still grievin' over poor Mitzi. *(To NANCY)* Mah little Mitzi died last week. Mitzi was Pepi's sister.

SAL: Alice, for God's sake, Nancy doesn't know who Mitzi and Pepi are! You make 'em sound like a vaudeville team.

ALICE: *(To NANCY)* Mitzi and Pepi are mah twin poodles. *(Forlorn)* 'Least they were. Little Mitzi's bladder got stuffed and she died. What do you do with a dead doggie in this city? No way to give her a proper burial. Ah wasn't goin' to let that happen to Mitzi. Ah put her little body in a little suitcase to take it to the country. So there ah am hailin' a cab, with the suitcase restin' on the curb behind me. Ah open the door of the cab, turn around to pick up the suitcase—and, guess what? *(No answer)* It had been swiped.

SAL: Somebody's in for a nasty surprise.

ALICE: Stealin' mah poor baby's body. This city's got no heart.

BO: *(Tugging gently at her sleeve)* C'mon, sugah. Let's go.

ALICE *(to BO, still sniffling)* Remind me to stop at Ann's. She got mah hair protein. *(THEY're at the door; to NANCY)* It was a real pleasure meetin' you, Miss Nancy. Do come visit with Bo and me sometime.

NANCY: Thank you.

SAL: Don't muss that hair. It looks great.

ALICE: Well! I thought you'd never say.

SAL: But *not* on Bo. I've got an investment to protect.

(ALICE looks flabbergasted. BO ducks out of the doorway ahead of her. As SHE follows down the hall, ALICE's voice trails back)

148

ALICE: I'm going to beat your little ass! Soon as you're out of my sight you start blabbin' my private business. Just wait until I . . . *(Her voice is no longer audible)*

(The telephone rings)

SAL: *(Calling after* ALICE *and* BO*)* Don't forget to check in later, Bo. *(Closes the door and moves toward the phone)* Sorry, Nance. Won't be a minute.

NANCY: Don't worry about me. I could use a little time to collect myself.

SAL: *(Into phone)* Hello. *(Pause, then explosively)* What the hell happened to you last night?!! . . . I'll give you "hung up" man! That happened to be one of my regulars! *(Pause; then in a calmer voice)* I'll talk to you later. You got some explaining to do. I don't go for that jive . . . No, I'll call you. About five-thirty—and *be* there. *(Hangs up)* These damn phones. I'll take 'em off the hook or we'll never get a word in. *(SAL presses the "off" button on the phones.* HE *comes out from behind desk)* So—peace and quiet at last! Hey—I forgot to offer you a drink. Some way to start a reunion.

NANCY: Nothing for me, Sal. *(Looks at her watch)* I don't have much time.

SAL: Sorry about all the characters. Just one of those days.

NANCY: You run a wide-open house.

SAL: *(Smiling at what* HE *thinks is* NANCY*'s naïveté)* Yeah, I'm a sociable guy.

NANCY: It pays off, I gather. Despite a large phone bill.

SAL: Most of the calls are local.

NANCY: Does that include New Jersey?

SAL: *(Laughing)* It could. *(Pause)* You surprise me.

NANCY: Oh?

SAL: I remember you as a shy girl. Always hiding under that football hero's arm.

(NANCY *shrugs. A suggestion of bitterness*)

NANCY: The arm isn't as big as it used to be.

SAL: Bob's in shape, isn't he?

NANCY: Relax, Sal. He's still a beauty.

SAL: Hey—easy does it!

NANCY: *(Smiling)* I forgot you like to set the pace.

SAL: Be my guest. I thought I had my work cut out for me.

NANCY: You did your share: "cousin from Pennsylvania"; "freshman at N.Y.U."

SAL: Well, I . . . *(probing)* . . . I thought I'd break the news gently.

NANCY: There's no news to break. You're well known. Even in Ridgeway.

(JEANNE, *dressed to go out, enters from bedroom*)

SAL: *(Pleased)* No kidding? Sal Giombo: Hero of the Leisure Revolution.

JEANNE: You oughta sell franchises—something to go with the fried chicken.

SAL: That was quick.

JEANNE: We're out of toilet paper.

SAL: Get the kind with the floral border.

JEANNE: In *some* matters, utility counts for more than design.

SAL: *Get the floral border*. And make sure it's soft weave.

JEANNE: The world's most tender tush. And he hardly ever uses it.

SAL: *(Good-natured)* Aw-right, you—scram!

NANCY: What's your audition for?

JEANNE: Sleep-in maid. (NANCY *laughs*) Listen! Times are tough!
(JEANNE *is at the door*)

SAL: Goodbye, nut.

JEANNE: Watch him, Nancy.

NANCY: I'll try.

(JEANNE *exits*)

SAL: Jeannie's been to college.

NANCY: What *does* she do around here?

SAL: As I said, she's a model—of how one hand can wash the other. They don't know all my secrets in Ridgeway.

NANCY: They know quite a few.

SAL: Like? *(NANCY hesitates)* C'mon, c'mon . . . The world's changed a lot since we were kids.

NANCY: Small towns haven't.

SAL: Oh yeah? Then how come you're here?

NANCY: I knew—until you asked. *(Evasive)* Money.

SAL: *(Knows SHE's lying)* Always a good reason. But your family's got bread.

NANCY: I'm not allowed to go to them anymore. *(Acid)* Bob's "dignity."

SAL: Very traditional fellow. Like all athletes. Surprised he didn't become a cop, with the rest of the football team.

NANCY: He likes construction.

SAL: Oh, *that's* what he's doing.

NANCY: *Was* doing. He got laid off six weeks ago.

SAL: You sure you can talk him into this?

NANCY: I haven't talked *me* into it yet.

SAL: It's no big deal, Nance. Lots of bread. And for next to nothing —as I told you on the street.

NANCY: I'd like to know more about it.

SAL: Ask anything you want.

NANCY: Well . . . what does "next to nothing" mean?

SAL: Oh, some statue work maybe—you know: a little posing, say. Like a Roman soldier. That type thing.

NANCY: Sex *has* changed since we were kids.

(SAL *laughs*)

SAL: The scenes vary. Like people.

NANCY: That much sounds familiar.

SAL: Clients come in all sizes and shapes. Like the boys. A guy as humpy as Bob can get away with doin' practically nuthin'.

NANCY: That's been the trouble.

SAL: *(Intrigued)* You're a little tough to read.

NANCY: Don't bother. Concentrate on Bob.

SAL: How about a couple clues, huh? I don't want my head handed to me. What line do I take?

NANCY: Go on instinct. That's what I'm doing.

SAL: Well . . . if he's out of a job, obviously I push money.

(NANCY *snorts*)

NANCY: *(Sardonic)* Obviously.

SAL: You know, Nance, *girls* do well in New York. Better than guys.

NANCY: It's important *Bob* does it.

SAL: *(Probing)* Make money . . .

NANCY: *(Vague)* Umm . . . make money.

SAL: Is somethin' wrong with you two in bed?

(NANCY *laughs*)

NANCY: Everywhere but bed. You've got some pretty old-fashioned ideas of your own.

SAL: I don't get it.

NANCY: That makes us about even. I've got a couple glimmers, that's all. And at a certain point you try anything. Even Russian roulette.

SAL: You still love the guy, dontcha?

NANCY: I don't give up easy.

SAL: Yeah—I remember you cheerin' him on from the sidelines.

NANCY: Well now I'm about to quarterback. Bob won't call the play. So—I will.

SAL: What happens if the pass gets intercepted?

NANCY: Then the game's over. *(Suddenly clamming up)* This is silly. I don't even talk to Ellen this way.

SAL: Ellen Kramer?!

NANCY: That's right. We're still best friends.

SAL: The Mouse! My God—whatever happened to her?

NANCY: She married Ned. He works construction with Bob. Only Ned didn't get laid off.

SAL: Well, well, Ellen and Ned. Ridgeway really goes by the book.

NANCY: Don't knock it. They're happy.

SAL: Baby, I don't knock *anything* that works. That's how I got to be rich and famous.

NANCY: How much can Bob make?

SAL: I can send him to three, four Johns—guys—a day if he wants. At thirty a throw.

NANCY: Before or after your cut?

SAL: After.

NANCY: I won't let him come in more than twice a week.

SAL: Whatever you say.

NANCY: At forty a "throw."

SAL: Hey—I can't guarantee that every time! Some Johns only pay thirty.

NANCY: Then you'll have to throw in your commission.

(SAL *lets out a low whistle*)

SAL: Whew! And Jeannie warned *you* to watch *me*!

NANCY: We're both survivors.

SAL: I thought you didn't care about money.

NANCY: I don't. But *you* do. A deal or not?

SAL: A deal.

NANCY: Bob'll call you tomorrow. (SHE *nods toward the phones*) Be sure to take the phones off "hold."

(SAL *laughs*)

SAL: You have my number? I'm not listed.

NANCY: You gave it to me on the street.

SAL: Then I guess we're all set. Good seeing you again, Nance.

(THEY*'re at the door*)

NANCY: It sounded ugly when I tried to make it logical. You made me do that.

SAL: Relax, Nance. Logic is *not* what I deal in.

NANCY: It isn't ugly. It's our last chance. And I'm taking it.

SAL: Dig it. Say hello to all my friends in Ridgeway.

NANCY: Name two.

SAL: Bob and Nancy.

(NANCY *laughs*)

NANCY: I'll tell them both.

SAL: See you, Nance.

NANCY: Frankly, Sal, I hope not. I don't want any details. *(Exits)*

(SAL closes the door, then wanders over to the coffee table, picks up the remains of the joint BO *had been smoking and lights it.* HE *suddenly remembers the phones are off the hook.* HE *goes to the desk, presses the phone button, then leans back in the desk chair and takes a deep drag on the joint. One of the phones rings.* SAL *picks it up. Into phone)*

SAL: Hello . . . Oh, whaddaya say, Mr. Peters . . . Yeah, sorry. The phones have been tied up . . . Sure, I can get hold of Al. Are you at the Plaza, like always? . . . Okay, seven-thirty . . . Yeah, I know: tie and jacket . . . Hang on a second while I try him. *(Picks up the second phone to dial, then has an idea and goes back to the first phone)* Hey, Mr. Peters! How long you gonna be in town this trip? . . . Good! I got somethin' very special comin' in. Probably tomorrow. Home-town boy. All-American athlete. May even be a virgin. *(Laughs)* Yeah, I'll give you a call as soon as I hear. Now hang on . . . *(Picks up the second phone again and starts dialing, as*

THE STAGE BEGINS TO REVOLVE . . .

ACT I

SCENE 2

. . . revealing two separate playing areas.

One, upstage right, is a dimly lit neighborhood bar in Ridgeway. The other, downstage left, is BOB *and* NANCY'*s kitchen.*

SAL *moves from behind his desk into the bar.* HE *becomes* NICK, *the bartender.*

Present in the bar are: BOB, *about twenty-three, ruggedly handsome, non-verbal, suggestions of passivity and evasiveness, unawareness of his own mechanisms;* LOIS *(played by the same actor cast as* BO*), a good-time girl;* NED *(played by the same actor who later will be* DAVE*), hard-nosed, straight, lives by the rules;* DON *(played by the same actor who later will be* LARRY*) a middle-aged shoe salesman;* DOTTY *(played by the same actress cast as* JEANNE*), a middle-aged alcoholic.*

A TV set is on the bar. A jukebox is playing. BOB *and* LOIS *are dancing to a soul number, but separately, without touching. A spot is on* BOB. LOIS *is not as good a dancer as* BOB. SHE *watches his graceful, rhythmic movement admiringly.* HE *is self-absorbed.*

A few moments after SAL *enters the bar,* NANCY *enters her kitchen. Her friend,* ELLEN, *timid, traditional-minded, the wife of* NED, *is sitting at the kitchen table having a cup of coffee.*

NANCY: Hi, sorry I'm late.

(BOB *and* LOIS *stop dancing)*

ELLEN: That's okay. I called Ned and told him to pick me up here.

NANCY: Oh good.

ELLEN: Buy lots of things?

NANCY: *(Momentarily startled)* Huh?

BOB: *(Calling to* NICK*)* Hey Nick, open me another beer.

ELLEN: Shopping. You said you had all those things to buy. You're empty-handed.

NANCY: *(Recovering)* Oh— yeah. Everything was overpriced. We've got too many bills, anyway.

(BOB *goes to the bar)*

BOB: *(To* NICK*)* When do I get a free one?

NICK: When you put on your go-go costume.

157

(BOB *laughs*)

BOB: I got my five-dollar shirt on. Whaddaya want?! *(Goes back to dance floor)*

ELLEN: You should open a charge at Bonwit's. They don't send bills for months. *(Giggles)* Ned won't set foot in the place. He says it's a girl's store. Men are terrible about shopping. They just hate it.

NANCY: *(Impatiently)* Some hate it, some like it. Same as women. Don't make *everything* male/female, huh?

LOIS: You move like a dream.

NICK: Dreams cost money.

(LOIS *and* BOB *start dancing again)*

ELLEN: *(Cowed)* Does Bob like to shop?

NANCY: If it's for Bob, sure.

DON: *(Yelling good-naturedly to* BOB*)* You could use a new pair of shoes, too!

ELLEN: You mean tools and stuff.

(DOTTY *laughs drunkenly)*

NANCY: I mean underwear, and pretty shirts and jewelry. The same things we like.

DOTTY: I thought this was your day off.

ELLEN: Gosh, Ned's not like that.

DON: A good salesman never stops selling.

NANCY: Ned's not like anything. *(Repentant)* Sorry. I guess I'm beat.

DOTTY: I know whatcha mean. Some legs on the kid. You gotta have strong legs to be a good dancer. My old man, Pokey, he had a pair of legs on him that—*(SHE knocks over her drink)*

(ELLEN looks at her watch)

NICK: Take it easy, Dotty. *(HE mops up. Yelling down the bar, while motioning with his head toward BOB dancing)* Hey, Ned! Is that what they teach you boys on construction?

ELLEN: I hope he's not late. Friday night's our movie night.

NANCY: Billy okay?

ELLEN: He cried a little.

NED: Didn't teach *me*.

159

BOB: It's not somethin' you can teach.

NICK: There's modesty for ya.

BOB: *(Boyish)* Naw—I mean, it either comes natural or it don't.

(NANCY starts toward BILLY's bedroom)

ELLEN: I picked him up when he cried. Is that okay?

NANCY: *(Surprised)* What should you do?

ELLEN: *(Hurt)* Some of the books say to let them cry.

NANCY: You and your books! Trust your instincts once in a while. *(Goes into bedroom)*

(NED slams his beer down on the bar)

NED: Bob, you ready?

BOB: *(Sexily)* I'm always ready, man.

NED: I'm headin' off.

(BOB goes toward the bar)

ELLEN: *(Calling after NANCY)* Isn't Bob usually home by now?

BOB: Whatsa hurry? *(Goes to the TV set)* They're gonna rerun the Stanley Cup play-off. *(Turns on the set)*

(NANCY comes back into the room)

160

NANCY: Mmm. Usually. *(Goes to the stove to get some coffee)* Thanks for staying with Billy.

ELLEN: That's what friends are for.

(Pause)

ELLEN: It's almost six-thirty. Ned should be here soon.

NANCY: It'll be good to see a man around the house. Bob hasn't been here in two days.

(NICK reaches up and turns it off)

NICK: That was last night, kiddo.

BOB: Was I here last night?

NICK: Yep. Most of the day, too.

BOB: *(Puzzled)* No shit?

NED: How long since you been home?

BOB: I dunno. Couple days. It's the motor, you know?

DOTTY: Sure, baby, I know.

NED: Butt out.

LOIS: Everybody's a big shot. We need a bigger puddle.

(DOTTY cackles appreciatively)

DOTTY: You tell 'em, sweetie.

ELLEN: Nance, you poor thing!
Why didn't you tell me?

NANCY: He does it all the time.
We call it his wild-blue-
yonder routine. The
disappearing act.

ELLEN: Gosh!

NANCY: Sometimes it's a couple of hours Once, five
days.

ELLEN: Doesn't he call at least?

NANCY: That would kill the
suspense. If he's stranded
maybe. Car in a ditch.
Down to his last dollar.
That kind of thing.

ELLEN: That's terrible

(NANCY *shrugs*)

NANCY: It's him, that's all.

DON: This place is fulla bums.
Dunno what Ridgeway is
comin' to.

NICK: To nothin'. Like all
towns.

NED: *(To BOB)* Ellen's at your
place mindin' Billy.

BOB: *(Disinterested)* Oh yeah?

NED: I'm gonna pick her up
there.

(DOTTY *starts to paw* BOB)

DOTTY: You're awright, kid.

BOB: Thanks. You're not half bad yourself.

ELLEN: You know we'd help if we could, Nance.

NANCY: *(Surprised)* How could you help?

DOTTY: How about a dance with the old girl? My feet dance better than they walk.

BOB: Sure. Why not?

ELLEN: Ned won't let me touch the savings account, or I'd—

NANCY:—oh, money! That's the least of it. Thanks, anyway, Ellen.

(HE goes to the jukebox to put on a record. NED follows him)

NED: I'm going to get Ellen.

BOB: I'm going to get a beer.

ELLEN: We might run into a financial problem of our own soon.

NED: You betta come along.

BOB: Yeah—I'm right behind ya. See ya there in five.

NANCY: Don't tell me they're

going to lay Ned off, too?! My God! He's a one-man crew.

ELLEN: It's Mr. Wellington.

NANCY: The beloved boss man? What about him? Aside from being a louse, that is.

ELLEN: Actually it's her, Mrs. Wellington. She . . . she's got a thing for Ned.

NANCY: For everybody. She keeps a regular stable.

ELLEN: Wellington called Ned into his office yesterday.

NANCY: Uh-oh. A warning, huh?

(NED exits. HE crosses the stage from bar to the kitchen)

BOB: *(Good-humored)* Fuck him if he can't take a joke.

BOB: *(To NICK)* Gimme some High Life.

DOTTY: You *are* high life, sweetheart.

DON: *(To DOTTY)* You're old enough to be his mother.

DOTTY: Why dontcha fight him for my "favors"?

(DON playfully winds up as if to hit her. DOTTY laughs, jumps out of the way, and

ELLEN: *(Timidly)* No . . . not exactly.

(NED *walks in the door.* EL-LEN *jumps up*)

ELLEN: Oh good. I was beginning to worry. *(Kisses him)*

NED: Stopped for a beer. Whaddaya say, Nancy?

NANCY: How are you?

NED: Can't complain. Not with all the tender loving care I get. *(Squeezes* ELLEN*)*

goes over to BOB *at the juke-box*)

LOIS: *(To* DON*)* I'll bet you walk better than you dance.

(BOB *and* DOTTY *start to dance a slow number*)

DON: *(To* LOIS, *good-humored)* You askin' me to cut a rug?

LOIS: God no! These are new shoes!

DON: *(Serious)* Oh yeah? Let's see. (HE *bends down and touches them)* Imitation.

LOIS: Easy! You'll get sweat on 'em!

DOTTY: *(To* BOB*)* You're one good-lookin' boy.

BOB: *("modest")* We're a dime a dozen.

ELLEN: *(Pleased)* Silly.

NANCY: Want some coffee? We're on our eighth.

DOTTY: So here's a quarter. Keep the change.

(The jukebox starts playing Otis Redding's "The Glory of Love." BOB impishly grabs DON's hand and starts leading him onto the dance floor)

NED: Okay, thanks.

ELLEN: We should go, honey.

NED: Yeah, in a minute.

NANCY: I'll make it Instant. *(NANCY goes for the coffee. NED and ELLEN are self-consciously affectionate—for NANCY's benefit)*

BOB: Okay, your turn.

(DON throws his hand off)

DON: You some kind of freak?

(The OTHERS laugh)

BOB: Fuck 'em if he can't take a joke.

ELLEN: *(To NED)* We were just talking about you and Mrs. Wellington.

(NANCY looks up surprised)

DOTTY: *(To BOB)* Give us a solo, baby.

BOB: *(Pleased)* Yeah?

NED: *(Grinning)* Quite a story, huh?

NANCY: I didn't hear much of it.

LOIS: Sure, c'mon. I'm tired of

all this togetherness.

BOB: What the hell . . . (BOB *starts to undulate to the music —slowly, sensuously*)

NED: (*To* ELLEN) How far'd you get?

NANCY: When we paused for the commercial, Wellington had called you into the office and warned you to stay away from his wife.

(NED *laughs*)

NED: Not quite. What he must think of that broad—wow! He wants me to service her.

NANCY: What?!

DOTTY: (*To* BOB) Beautiful, lover!

NICK: You're gonna end up in Hollywood!

DON: Yeah—playin' Frankenstein! (HE *breaks up at his own joke*)

NED: That was the ultimatum. Service her—or look for work elsewhere.

ELLEN: Talk about your evil old world, huh?

NANCY: (*Quietly*) Who knows.

Maybe he loves her. *(Puts the coffee down)*

ELLEN: *Loves* her?!

NANCY: Nothing in it for him.

NED: Except peace and quiet.

NANCY: Maybe. I wouldn't be so sure. Love's funny. *(Gives NED his coffee)* Anyway, it's none of my business.

NED: So whaddaya think I should do?

ELLEN: We want your opinion.

(NANCY chuckles in disbelief)

NANCY: You two are something.

(TWO MEN, RAY and TOM, enter the bar. RAY is stereotypically "effeminate," an agitated, elegant forty-five-year-old, with an accent that wavers between Groton and the Bronx. TOM, about the same age, is phlegmatic, drab, pedantic)

RAY: Excuse us.

NED: *(Proud)* C'mon, c'mon, don't be embarrassed. We got nothin' to hide from good friends.

(BOB slows down his dancing but doesn't stop)

168

NANCY: Too bad.

RAY: We seem to have lost our way. Can you tell us how to get on the Jersey Expressway to New York?

(TOM *starts to ogle* BOB)

NICK: Sure. Just keep on this street till the third traffic light. Turn left and you'll see the sign.

RAY: Oh, what a relief! We thought we were in Denmark!

NICK: You're an hour and a quarter from New York.

(RAY *clears his throat to get* TOM's *attention away from* BOB. THEY *confer for a second*)

ELLEN: *(Smug)* We've learned how important it is to talk everything out.

NANCY: Well look, why not take it on the Johnny Carson Show—that way you can poll millions.

NED: I figure once or twice would do it. She likes variety. Sex is no big deal. We've learned that.

(ELLEN *squirms a little*)

Good jobs are hard to come by.

(NANCY doesn't answer)

NED: So c'mon! Whaddaya think?

NANCY: I told you: it's your business.

ELLEN: You know about these things, Nance.

NANCY: *(Getting angry) What* things?

ELLEN: You've always got an opinion.

NANCY: This time I'm over-qualified. *(SHE turns away)*

NED: You know, Nance, it

RAY: Would you mind if my friend uses the loo?

NICK: The what?

RAY: The Men's Room.

(BOB stops dancing)

BOB: C'mon, I'll show ya. Gotta go myself.

(TOM follows BOB off stage right)

RAY: We drove out to the kennels at Bricktown. Must have taken a wrong turn.

NICK: Happens all the time.

RAY: We were looking for an Afghan puppy.

helps to speak your mind. That's one of the troubles with you and Bob, you don't—

DON: A *who*?

NANCY: *(Angry)* —okay, here's my mind! I think Wellington should take his goddamn job and shove it— up *Mrs.* Wellington. That should make everybody happy.

LOIS: Like the socks. Oh no— that's Argyle.

RAY: You're close, in fact. "Afghan" also means a "knitted woolen coverlet."

NED: Now you're getting hysterical. There's no call for that.

DON: I know them dogs. Foreign dog, ain't it?

ELLEN: No, it's good to get feelings out, honey. Go on, Nance.

NANCY: I gotta get supper ready. *(Turns to the stove)*

RAY: Indeed. They were first bred by the Amir of Pushto. My friend can tell you all about it. He's a mine of unusual information. *(Smiles pleasantly)*

(ELLEN shakes her head pa-

NICK: Seems pretty unusual.

171

tronizingly, then motions to NED *that* THEY *should leave.* NED *signals her to sit down again)*

(ELLEN *and* NED *whisper together)*

NED: Nance, as old friends, I feel I got a responsibility to bring up a certain matter.

NANCY: I thought Friday was your movie night.

NED: We're concerned about you and Bob, Nance. We want to help.

NANCY: Swell. Get Bob a job.

NED: It's okay to sow wild oats. But Bob's no teen-ager no more.

(BOB *comes out of the bathroom)*

RAY: *(To* BOB*)* That was quick.

BOB: *(Grinning)* Story of my life, man. That's why all the chicks complain.

(RAY *giggles)*

RAY: I don't believe *that.*

(TOM *comes out of the bathroom)*

RAY: All ready?

TOM: Uh-huh.

RAY: I guess we're off, then. Thanks, thanks.

NICK: Sure thing.

ELLEN: *(To* NED*)* He hasn't been home in two days.

BOB: *(To* RAY *and* TOM*)* I'm off, too, I'll show you guys the way.

(To the OTHERS*)* Seeya, people. I'm gonna take me down the road apiece. Or maybe a piece down the road.

NANCY: *(Outraged)* I told you that in confidence.

ELLEN: *(Innocently)* Ned and I don't keep secrets.

LOIS: Lookin' for volunteers?

NANCY: Maybe you oughta learn.

BOB: Dunno. *(Gives her a pat on the ass)* Next time the motor starts, I'll buzz your block.

NED: I know Bob hasn't been home. I just left him at Nick's.

DOTTY: If you need quarters to start it up, I got drawers full of 'em.

NANCY: *(Concerned)* Is he okay?

BOB: Stay loose, gorgeous.

NED: He's havin' a ball. Got the whole place lookin' at him, like always.

NANCY: *(Proud)* He's something to look at.

NED: There comes a time when a man's gotta settle down, start buildin' a future . . .

NED: Bob wasn't laid off, Nance. He was fired.

NANCY: *(Concealing her surprise)* Is that supposed to be news?

NED: He told you he was laid off.

NICK: Say hello to the wife.

BOB: Will do.

(HE and RAY and TOM exit)

NICK: *(Calling after them)* Regards to the Amir.

DOTTY: That kid's somethin'.

(BOB points directions to RAY and TOM, then waves goodbye)

DON: How about me?

DOTTY: *(Sardonic)* Yeah, you're somethin', too . . . *(Sadly)* Ah, the legs, the legs . . .

NANCY: How do you know
    what he told me?

                    NICK: Drink up, people. We're
                      in business.

(BOB *walks into kitchen.*   *Lights go out in the bar)*

NANCY: Well, well, Prince Charming.

BOB: Whaddaya say, babe. (To ELLEN and NED) You still here, huh?

NED: Yeah, shootin' the breeze with Nance.

NANCY: Want some coffee, lover?

BOB: Yeah, sure. Good idea.

ELLEN: My, you look tired.

BOB: Who me? Nah. Just gettin' my second wind. (HE *takes off his jacket, goes over to the TV and flicks it on)*

NANCY: Car all right?

BOB: Sure it's all right. Whaddaya mean?

NANCY: Just checking. I like to keep tabs on the family assets.

BOB: Let me worry about 'em.

NANCY: Wish you would. *(The TV set comes on)*

TV VOICE: . . . I'm afraid we've got bad news for you, Mrs. Jones. The cancer has spread to his liver . . .

(Sounds of female sobbing. BOB *flicks the set to another channel. Sounds of a baseball game come on.* BOB *settles into the chair in front of the set)*

BOB: *(To* NANCY*)* Make it a beer instead of coffee.

NANCY: The coffee's ready.

BOB: I rather have a beer.

NANCY: Yes, sir! God's Girl Friday serves again.

BOB: Forget it.

(HE *gets up, goes to the refrigerator and takes out the beer himself*)

TV VOICE: He's been one of the League's steadiest performers at second base over the past seven years. Started as a $90,000 bonus baby way back in sixty-three at age nineteen. One of the few that've worked out.

(BOB *settles down in front of the TV*)

ELLEN: You're gonna get a belly on you with all that beer.

BOB: Can't grow fat on steel, as the wife would say.

NANCY: Used to say.

ELLEN: *(Innocently)* It's good you two haven't lost your sense of humor.

NANCY: We're an easy-going family. We take it as it comes. Right, lover.

BOB: *(Absorbed in the* TV*)* Huh?

NANCY: I said we'd rather sit than fight.

TV VOICE: Two balls and a strike. *(Pause)* Pete Rowan has been big man on attack today for the Tigers. *(Pause; then excitement)* That looked like a screwball! But Rowan got just enough wood on it! It's a ground ball in the hole, a base hit!

NANCY: Will you turn that down!

BOB: Why?

NANCY: Because it's loud.

BOB: Oh.

NED: Who's winning?

BOB: Cubs, one to nothin', last of the sixth.

TV VOICE: We're getting down to the bottom of the order now.

(BOB *turns the set lower*)

176

NED: Had any luck with the job-hunting?

(BOB *gives him a disbelieving, resentful look.* HE *turns back to watching the* TV)

BOB: No sweat.

NED: Did you go see Fred Harmon?

BOB: No.

NED: I hear he's lookin' for somebody.

BOB: He's lousy to his men.

NED: You can't pick and choose these days. (BOB *doesn't answer*) Not with a son to take care of.

BOB: You tryin' to impress somebody?

NANCY: *(To* NED; *angry)* Who gave you a platform?

TV VOICE: We'll give you that one in slow-motion now. Instant replay.

ELLEN: Ned's just trying to be a friend.

TV VOICE: There it goes! Up, up and away! Right over the auxiliary scoreboard!

NANCY: *(To* BOB) Will you *please* turn that down?!

BOB: A lot of noise in here.

ELLEN: Sorry we're not appreciated.

NANCY: I appreciate your staying with Billy.

NED: You got a funny way of showin' it.

TV VOICE: *(In background)* Montreal and Pittsburgh underway. No score at the end of the first. Houston–San Diego night game. After six in Oakland, it's California four, Oakland three . . .

NANCY: That's because I care about some other things more. *(Pause)* Have a good movie.

NED: How about you payin' for it?

NANCY: *(Startled)* What?

NED: Since you got a baby-sitter for nothin', seems to me you could pay for the flick.

NANCY: Well, awright! *(Calling over to* BOB*)* You got four dollars?

NED: Four-forty.

*(*BOB *turns the set down)*

BOB: Whadya say?

NANCY: Do you have any money?

BOB: Yeah. Five bucks.

NANCY: Let me have it. *(*SHE *takes the money from* BOB *and hands it to* NED*)* Keep the change.

NED: Right. We'll get popcorn. From now on, look for another sitter.

*(*ELLEN *looks as if* SHE*'s going to cry.* SHE *and* NED *exit)*

NANCY: *(Calling after them)* Feel free to come by for advice if you can't get it up with Mrs. Wellington! *(Slams the door)*

TV VOICE: So far today Bracken has flied to center and flied to right. The count on him is two balls, one strike. Here's the pitch. It's low and inside. Three balls, one strike.

*(*NANCY *goes over and turns off TV)*

NANCY: Do you *mind?*

BOB: Yeah, I do. *(*HE *leans over to turn TV back on)*

NANCY: *Please,* Bob. *(*HE *hesitates, then removes his hand. Pause)* I'll miss Ellen. Even if she is silly.

BOB: Who needs her.

NANCY: It must be nice not to give a damn about anything.

BOB: *(Quietly)* Yeah, it's great.

NANCY: Oh shit—there's no way to talk to you.

BOB: Try just talkin'.

NANCY: I have. It doesn't get me anywhere.

BOB: Where do you want to get?

NANCY: Sometimes I wonder.

BOB: Mmm.

NANCY: Well, like Ned comes home the same time *every* day. That might be an interesting way to live.

BOB: You don't like routine any more than I do. Look, I told you before we got married what I was, and that's what I been.

NANCY: You told me all you knew. Which is a little different.

BOB: *(Not understanding the implication)* I told you before we got married: when the motor starts, it starts. And when it stops, it stops. I got no control over it.

NANCY: True, you told me that.

BOB: So stop bitching. You knew the deal.

NANCY: Simple, huh?

BOB: Yeah. If you'd let it alone. (HE *gets up and goes over to her, puts his arms around her)*

NANCY: What's "it"?

BOB: Me. Us. It works good most of the time. Right?

NANCY: *(Trying to talk to him)* Bob, can't we just—

BOB: —so let's not hassle, okay. I'm beat. *(Pause)*

NANCY: *(Giving up)* Okay. Go take a nap. I'll wake you for dinner.

(BOB *goes back to the chair)*

BOB: Nah. I'd never get up. I'll wait till later.

NANCY: Did you sleep at all last night?

BOB: No. *(Pause)*

NANCY: What'd you do when the bars closed?

BOB: I went to other bars. Clubs.

NANCY: *(Skeptical)* Private clubs in Ridgeway?

BOB: Newark. I think. Some of the guys took me. I don't remember too well.

NANCY: Like always.

BOB: Yeah. Like always. *(Pause)* When's dinner?

NANCY: I didn't plan on you for dinner. I have to feed Billy first.

BOB: Yeah, I know. When's dinner?

NANCY: Not for at least a couple hours.

> *(Pause)*

BOB: Maybe I will take a nap.

NANCY: You'll never get up if you go to bed now.

BOB: So I won't get up.

NANCY: There's no point my cooking dinner if you're not going to get up for it.

> *(BOB doesn't answer; HE heads for the bedroom)*

Doctor Beyer's nurse called again today. That's the third time. I'm tired of making up excuses.

BOB: Tell her we'll pay when we can pay.

NANCY: She said she'd like to know when that might be.

BOB: Tell her to shove it up her ass.

NANCY: That's a big help.

BOB: I'm going to bed *(Starts for bedroom again)*

NANCY: Maybe *I* should look for work. *(BOB turns around but doesn't say anything)* You're home most of the day anyway. You could keep an eye on Billy.

BOB: That's pretty funny.

NANCY: There are lots of things I could do. Waitresses make good money. Or I could work at the V.A. hospital.

BOB: Yeah, torturing the wounded.

NANCY: Aren't we clever.

BOB: I'm at my best with no sleep. Like I just had this wild idea I was married to a man.

NANCY: You've had wilder. *(Pause)* Women work these days, you know. It's the modern age.

BOB: Yeah, well in the modern age people owe money. My wife doesn't work.

NANCY: Well, I guess that leaves me two choices: find somebody else to pay our bills, or stop being your wife.

BOB: I told you before, babe: any time you want out, just say the word.

NANCY: It's so nice you care.

BOB: You don't work. That's it.

NANCY: So how do we pay our bills.

BOB: Find a fairy godfather.

(HE moves toward the bedroom)

NANCY: Maybe I have. Today, in New York.

BOB: Huh?

NANCY: Remember Sal Giombo, from high school?

BOB: Sure. Smart little Italian kid. Lousy at sports.

NANCY: He lives in New York. He's gotten well known.

BOB: Is he on TV or somethin'?

NANCY: *(Amused)* No.

BOB: What's he got goin' for him?

NANCY: Phones.

BOB: Hey, can you talk English? I'm sorta beat.

(Pause)

NANCY: Remember that experience you told me about in the army?

BOB: I thought we were talkin' about Sal Giombo.

NANCY: When you were out on patrol a couple of weeks and got horny. That guy asked you if—you know, that big guy you always thought—

BOB: *(Interrupting)*—yeah, yeah. What the hell are you drivin' at?

NANCY: Well that's what Sal does.

BOB: What? Give guys blow jobs?!

NANCY: He sets people up. Guys. Guys with lots of bread who are interested in—well, yeah, blow jobs . . .

BOB: No shit?! Didn't know Sal went in for that kind of thing.

NANCY: He goes in for money.

BOB: You got to be crackers to give any guy a blow job who wants one.

NANCY: The *guys* give them.

BOB: Oh—to Sal! *(Shakes his head)* Shit, those little cats are somethin' else! They can come five, six times a day.

NANCY: You still don't get it. Sal *introduces* people. Older men to younger guys. Guys like you . . . straight guys. He says there's a lot of money in it. Forty bucks a throw.

BOB: No shit?! What's in it for Sal?

NANCY: He gets ten bucks from the John.

BOB: The who?

NANCY: A John is what they call a rich guy, an older guy, who pays for sex.

BOB: How come you know all this?

NANCY: Everybody knows what a "John" is. It's in every other movie.

BOB: You must be goin' to the movies without me.

(Pause)

NANCY: I ran into Sal on the street today in New York. When I was in at the doctor's. He looked like a million. *(Pause)* He asked about you.

BOB: Oh yeah?

NANCY: Wanted to know what you were up to.

BOB: You didn't tell him I was outta work, did ya?

NANCY: No, I said you were laid off for a few weeks. You're a big hero of his.

BOB: He always wanted to get in our crowd. Not a bad kid.

NANCY: He said to tell you New York is "up to its ass in money." He said "all you got to do is stoop down and pick it up."

BOB: Stoop down or bend over?

NANCY: I thought I'd give you the message.

BOB: That's some message. Forty bucks a throw.

NANCY: Crazy, huh?

BOB: Hard to believe. At that rate a guy could get rich. *(Starts to pace as his excitement mounts)* Sure beats hell out of buildin' roofs—assumin' I was. A guy could clear a couple hundred a week with no trouble. Tax-free, too!

NANCY: Now, hang on.

BOB: No kiddin', babe, I could get together enough of a nest egg to start my own firm. Or buy a piece of land in Canada . . . turn it into campsites. Way off somewhere. Nobody around for miles—

NANCY: *(Interrupting)*—will you slow down?!

BOB: Huh?

NANCY: I haven't agreed to anything.

BOB: It's no big deal. I can spare a couple loads a week. *(Laughs)* Shit, I might even bottle it. Does that stuff keep?

NANCY: First of all, Sal only fixes people up twice a week. It's . . . the slow season.

BOB: That's okay for starters. How do I contact him? You got his number?

NANCY: Yes.

(HE *goes for her purse*)

BOB: How old are the guys?

NANCY: How the hell do I know? What difference does it make?

BOB: Probably eighty. Young guys don't have bread to throw around . . . Forty bucks a throw—whew! I break my ass all day and take home a lousy thirty-seven-fifty . . .

NANCY: Awright, awright! . . . Don't . . . get carried away . . .

BOB: Uh-oh.

NANCY: What?

BOB: I'll bet it's a union job! That means I'll hafta tickle a few balls to get my papers.

(NANCY *half-playfully throws a dishtowel at him*)

NANCY: Yeah—you may even fall in love!

(BOB *tries prancing around in an awkward parody of a "swish"*)

BOB: *(Lisping)* I'm just *wild* about Harry! . . . (HE *stops, embarrassed. Then flexes his biceps*) Ever seen a faggot who looked like this?

NANCY: Often.

BOB: Don't you know who you married, girl?

NANCY: I know.

BOB: Glad to hear it. (HE *takes the piece of paper out of her pocketbook*) This the number?

NANCY: Umm. It's not listed.

BOB: A white-collar job at last!

NANCY: Twice a week. No more.

BOB: I thought you were sick of me hangin' around the house?

NANCY: I want to be sure there's some left over for me.

(BOB *goes over to her*)

BOB: Remember me? I'm your little old repeater rifle. At least when you're around. (HE *puts his arm around her*)

NANCY: Billy might come in.

BOB: Never too young to learn.

NANCY: Give him until his third birthday, huh?

BOB: He's gonna be a stud. Just like his old man.

NANCY: One's enough in any family.

BOB: Hell, his cock's bigger'n mine already.

NANCY: That's not what makes a stud. It's something inside.

BOB: Why don't you let me demonstrate?

NANCY: What's turned *you* on?

BOB: You.

NANCY: I guess I'll believe it.

(THEY *embrace*)

BOB: Maybe I oughta stay away more often.

(SHE *breaks away*)

NANCY: That's not funny.

(*Pause*)

BOB: I wonder how a guy like Sal got started?

NANCY: He got out of a chair. The rest is easy.

BOB: He always was ambitious.

NANCY: It beats staring at your navel.

BOB: Hey lady, you want to stare at my navel?

NANCY: Two people can't stare at the same one.

BOB: You look at mine and I'll look at yours.

NANCY: Navels aren't my bag.

BOB: For starters. If you stare nice, I'll let you touch it.

NANCY: Gee thanks, sport.

BOB: C'mon.

NANCY: Later. I've waited two days. You can wait two minutes.

BOB: No I can't.

NANCY: Well try.

BOB: If I wait, the price'll go up. *(NANCY gasps)* And you know how short you are of money.

NANCY: *(Amused)* You're too much.

BOB: I'll tell you what! I'll give you a cut rate if you come now. Bargain of a lifetime! Whaddaya say? *(HE kisses her)*

NANCY: *(Laughs)* Let me go check on Billy first. *(SHE heads toward the second bedroom)* Take off the bedspread. I'll be right in. *(SHE stops and turns around)* You are fond of Russian roulette, aren't you?

BOB: *(Misunderstanding)* Baby, I dig everything you do in bed.

(Lights cross-fade as BOB and NANCY exit, revealing SAL's apartment with SAL in the middle of a telephone conversation)

ACT I

SCENE 3

Sitting around the apartment are BO, JEANNE, *and* LARRY, *a muscular twenty-year-old Latin who throughout the scene does isometric exercises, flexing and grimacing whenever* HE *thinks* HE *'s unobserved.*

SAL: *(Into phone)* . . . Yeah . . . All set, Mr. Allen, he's on his way . . . Yeah, strong legs: just what you like . . . Right. Talk to you soon. (HE *hangs up*)

BO: *(Looking up from the* Playboy *magazine* HE *'s been flipping through)* What's "O-ra . . ." *(Struggling to pronounce the word)* "O-ra-gentle-ism" mean?

JEANNE: *(Laughs)* Oragenitalism. You don't have to say it, honey, so long as you can do it.

(As the phone rings, BOB *comes out of the bathroom)*

SAL: *(Into phone)* Hello . . . Hey, Herbie, how's it goin'? . . . Yeah, got a score for you at nineteen Waverly at eight. Name is Art

187

Waldron . . . No, nothin' complicated . . . Right, talk to you
later . . . (HE's about to hang up, when HE remembers something)
Hey, Herbie! . . . Don't talk much. He hates a lot of talk.

(As HE hangs up, BOB sits)

BO: They got some book they trying to sell all about that "Ora" stuff.
(Reading from Playboy) Says here it's a "useful addition to one's
library of plain-spoken literature on all subjects that, until lately,
could hardly be spoken of at all."

JEANNE: You never speak with a full mouth. It's a matter of breed-
ing. (Turning to BOB) Isn't that right?

BOB: (Startled; trying to stay cool) Sure, right.

BO: You mean all that Ora stuff is just sixty-nine? Shee-it, why don't
they say so.

(The phone rings)

JEANNE: Not everybody has your grasp of essentials.

SAL: (Into receiver) Hello . . . Hiyadoin', Dr. Howland? Long time
no hear . . . Hang on just a second, okay? (HE puts his hand over
the receiver) Larry, stop with those goddamn isometrics. I can't
concentrate.

LARRY: (Embarrassed) What isometrics? Whaddaya talkin' about?

SAL: (Into receiver) Yeah, now let's see . . .

(BO raises his hand to volunteer. SAL shakes his head "no")

You like a boy who'll roll over, right? . . .

(BO motions with disgust)

You don't know Pete Derani, do you? . . . Okay, lemme see if
he's in. (Starts to dial a number on the second phone while holding
the receiver of the first against his chest. The rest of the transaction is
inaudible, as the OTHERS talk)

JEANNE: *(To BOB)* False name, of course. It's really Agnew. *Very* big on golf cleets.

BOB: *(Uncertain)* Oh yeah? Sure is a busy place.

JEANNE: Five o'clock rush. We're the new rival to cocktail hour.

SAL: *(Into phone)* Let me know how you like him, Dr. Howland . . . So long. (HE *hangs up*)

(The phone rings again)

BOB: Oh, man!

JEANNE: *(Mimicking SAL)* "Hello . . . Sal's Boutique. Everything *and* accessories . . ."

SAL: *(Into phone)* Hello . . . Yes, I know Frank Dawson . . . Oh—well, I'm glad he gave you my number, Mr. Webber. Any friend of Frank's, as they say . . . Sure, Mr. Webber . . . *(Laughs)* Okay, I'll call you Paul if you call me Sal . . . Right, Paul. Now why don't you tell me a little about your type, and we'll see if we can't fix you up with just the right thing.

JEANNE: *(Mimicking the voice on the phone)* "My idea of perfection, Mr. Sal, is a truck driver who's studying at night to be a forest ranger."

(SAL motions JEANNE to be quiet)

SAL: I see . . . Why sure you can come over and pick for yourself. Only a couple of the fellows are here, though . . . We're at 710 East Sixty-fourth Street . . . Oh—you're right around the corner . . . We'll see you in a few minutes, then . . . 14G . . . Right. (HE *hangs up*) A new John. On his way over.

JEANNE: Wants to pick his own merchandise, huh? Must be a comparative shopper for *Consumer Guide.*

BOB: *(To SAL)* How do you know he's okay?

SAL: What do you mean?

BOB: Maybe he's a cop.

SAL: The only cops we hear from are customers.

BOB: Nobody ever gets busted?

SAL: That's Forty-second Street stuff. The single operators. Anything organized the cops leave alone.

BO: 'T'aint true, neither. Ah knew this nigger madam what got busted.

SAL: You mean Sonny Blue.

BO: You know Sonny Blue?!

SAL: He's a jerk. Asks for trouble. Dealing in stuff. Sending out kids under eighteen. Even the cops got standards.

(The phone rings)

(To LARRY, *who's been making weird facial grimaces)* Larry, will you cut it out, for Chrissakes! It's freaky!

LARRY: *(Mumbling)* I got to do my exercises.

SAL: What the hell are you exercising your *face* for?!

BO: 'Case somebody sits on it, he wants it to look pretty.

SAL: *(Into phone)* Hello . . . Fine, how are you? . . . Hang on a second. *(Puts his hand over receiver)* Bo, it's the Wheaties man.

JEANNE: Ooh—I love him!

BOB: Who's the Wheaties man?

LARRY: *(Disdainful)* One of Bo's steadies.

SAL: *(Impatient)* Hey, c'mon! You want to take it or not, Bo?

BO: Yeah, tell him nine.

SAL: *(Into receiver)* Bo says he'll be there at nine . . . Sure, any time. *(Hangs up)*

LARRY: *(To* BOB*)* Bo feeds him Wheaties out of a silver bowl, while he gives himself a hand job. It's unhealthy.

JEANNE: He could shift to Crunchy Granola.

BO: He's no wors'n Fido.

JEANNE: Now Fido I *don't* like.

BO: *(Competing to shock* BOB*)* Fido's one of *his* regulars. You gotta put a leash on him and walk him around the room. "Bark for mah piss, Fido. C'mon, boy, bark for mah piss." Then you piss in a glass and Fido drinks it.

BOB: You gotta be kidding!

LARRY: Fido's an easy score.

BOB: Easy?!

LARRY: Sure, man: you don't have to come.

BO: Anybody who drinks piss ain't got no class.

JEANNE: More Marxist claptrap.

SAL: Knock it off, you two. *(To* BOB*)* They're givin' you extreme cases. Most of the Johns are ordinary guys.

JEANNE: Jes suckin' and fuckin' like the rest of us.

(The phone rings)

SAL: *(Into receiver)* Hello . . . Hey, Jimmy . . . Nothin' right now, man. I'll let you know . . . Right. *(Hangs up)* On a cold day in hell. Tried to cop the last two commissions.

JEANNE: Rotten kid.

BO: *(To* BOB*)* Larry here's got a bad outlook. Can't handle no one under sixty.

BOB: Huh?

LARRY: The hell you say.

JEANNE: *(Explaining to* BOB*)* Larry likes to fuck his daddy.

LARRY: Bullshit!

JEANNE: Relax, honey. I got nothin' against incest. It helps bridge the generation gap.

SAL: *(Chuckling)* Not with Bill Appleton.

JEANNE: Oh Lord!

BOB: Now what?!

SAL: Bill Appleton was a college boy. Very superior type. But he met a sa*d* end.

JEANNE: He met his father.

LARRY: What the fuck's that mean?

SAL: I sent him to the Carlyle Hotel to meet a Mr. Peter Warner. So he goes to Room 401 of the Carlyle, knocks on the door, and guess who answers?

BO: *(Brightly)* Peter Warner.

SAL: Good. Except Peter Warner wasn't Peter Warner. So . . . father met son.

(BO *lets out a whistle*)

BO: Outasight!

SAL: Never know who's using the alias around here.

JEANNE: Makes it tough on the W-2 forms.

LARRY: So what did they do?

SAL: They said hello.

LARRY: *(Expectantly)* Yeah, and then what?

SAL: Then they said goodbye.

LARRY: Didn't they make the scene?

JEANNE: Larry, sometimes I think you're not well.

BO: It's all that sweatin' you do, man. It's bad for the brain.

LARRY: Go stick your finger up your ass, cracker, and give your Johns a rest.

(JEANNE *puts her hand to her forehead, like an old-fashioned movie heroine*)

JEANNE: Sal, take me away from all this.

192

BO: Take her off! Take her off! Jam! Jam!

JEANNE: Really, Bo!

BO: *(Smiling)* Raw, raw, bloody raw!

JEANNE: Where do you think you are—at a football rally?

BO: Them cheers pop into mah head when girls start actin' like cunts. *(Louder)* Raw, raw, bloody raw!

JEANNE: *(To BOB)* Would you ever guess he was a vegetarian?

BO: When we drive past Sally Lou Higher's house down home, we use the long cheer: "Eat mah anus, Kiss mah cunt, Turn the corner an' ah'll sneak a bunt." Mmm-mm! What a body that chick had!

JEANNE: As good as Bob's?

BOB: *(Smiling)* Leave me out of this!

JEANNE: You are out of it, baby. You're an innocent. That's why you're so attractive.

BOB: I'm no innocent.

JEANNE: Now don't start competing, or *(SHE motions around the room)* you'll end up like them. Rotten to the core.

SAL: Thank you, Ma Barker.

(The phone rings)

SAL: *(Into phone)* Hello . . . He's on his way, Mr. Allen. Can't be more than a few minutes . . . Right. *(HE hangs up)*

JEANNE: *(To BOB)* The moment I laid eyes on your wife I knew you didn't belong in this crowd. I knew right off you—

BOB: *(Interrupting, surprised)*— when did you see my wife?

JEANNE: The day she came up here. Last week, wasn't it, Sal?

SAL: Um-hmm. *(HE tries to signal JEANNE to cool it)*

JEANNE: Tuesday, I think.

BOB: *(To SAL)* She told me she met you on the street.

SAL: She did. I invited her up for a cup of coffee.

JEANNE: No, that was the week *after* you met on the street.

SAL: Good old Jeannie. Memory like an elephant.

JEANNE: *("Innocent")* Have I said something wrong?

BOB: *(To SAL)* Nancy didn't tell me she'd seen you twice.

(The downstairs buzzer rings)

SAL: Ah—the new John. *(Goes to the door)*

JEANNE: If you don't mind, I won't rise when he enters.

SAL: So long as you don't rap either. *(To LARRY, who's started to exercise again)* Larry, *stop twitching!* This guy's too young for you. Deep voice, too. Probably means some far-out scene.

JEANNE: Maybe he's so far-out he'll dig me.

(The buzzer rings on the apartment door)

SAL: Smile, everyone. It's Santa Claus. *(Opens the door)* Paul?

PAUL: *(Offstage)* That's right.

SAL: Well. Come on in.

(PAUL enters. HE's a pleasant-looking, intelligent, conservatively dressed man in his late thirties. HE has a good deal of self-possession and charm)

Meet the gang. *(HE goes around the room pointing to each person; EACH nods or mumbles hello)* This is Bo. Larry. Bob.

PAUL: *(Reaching over to shake BOB's hand)* How do you do?

BOB: Okay. How are ya?

SAL: And, finally, Jeannie.

(JEANNE gets up off the couch. SHE's the only one to have risen)

JEANNE: *("Sweetly")* Did you sign the guest book?

PAUL: *(Confused)* Well, no, I . . .

(JEANNE motions to the seat next to her on the couch)

JEANNE: Come sit here. It's comfy.

PAUL: All right. Thanks.

(Sits on the couch next to JEANNE)

SAL: So Frank Dawson gave you my number. Are you in advertising, too?

PAUL: *(Lying)* Yes . . . that's right . . .

SAL: Lots of our clients are.

JEANNE: It's a word-of-mouth business.

SAL: Haven't heard from Frank in a while.

PAUL: He's been . . . uh . . . traveling. Texas, I think.

LARRY: I had me this John in Dallas. Used to fly me down there once a month. But he had a heart attack—right when we was doin' it. I had to give him mouth-to-mouth restitution.

JEANNE: Father Flanagan would have been so proud.

LARRY: Didn't help him none. He stayed dead.

PAUL: Maybe you didn't breathe hard enough.

LARRY: His breath smelled bad.

BO: *(Brightly)* Ah never been to Texas, but Alice's hairdresser jes come back from Morocco. He said it was one hundred thirty degrees the whole time. Ain't that somethin' else?! One hundred and thirty degrees!

JEANNE: He probably meant rectally. *(To PAUL)* I like your jacket. Hand-tailored in Hong Kong, I'll bet.

BO: That *ape* fur?!

JEANNE: *Hong* Kong, Bo, not King Kong. *(To* PAUL*)* I'm like his mother: no one else can translate the noises. *(To* BOB*)* That jacket'd look great on you.

BOB: *(Embarrassed)* Oh yeah?

JEANNE: Mmm. Conservative cut. Just right for you. Goes with your personality.

PAUL: *(To* BOB*)* Would you like to try it on?

BOB: No thanks.

JEANNE: *(To* BOB*)* Go ahead. You're about the same size.

PAUL: No, Bob's much broader across the back.

BOB: *(To* PAUL, *shyly)* You got a good build on you, man.

PAUL: Thanks, but nothing like yours, I'm afraid.

BO: *(To* PAUL*)* Your build gives you away.

PAUL: *(Self-conscious)* What?

BO: Your sign, man, your sign. Ain't no way but you're a Leo.

PAUL: As a matter of fact, I am.

BO: How about that?! Ah'm a fuckin' genius!

LARRY: Signs got nothin' to do with the body, man. It's to do with personality, a person's feelin's.

BO: *(Feigned disgust)* Shee-it, man. What you think come through the body if it ain't feeling? *(Motions to* PAUL*)* Jes look at that cat. How he carries hisself. Leos is used to gettin' their way. Ain't nobody comes between them and what they want. And they want *plenty.* That's Leo every time.

PAUL: I'd better get myself a new sign.

BO: Leo's best in a chick. Mah Alice is a Leo.

JEANNE: She certainly got her way.

BO: A chick who's Leo got more affection than anybody goin'. *(Grins)* 'Specially for Scorpio. That's mah sign. *(To* PAUL*)* Now if only you was a chick, man, we'd really get it on.

196

PAUL: Frankly, I think astrology is pretty silly.

BOB: It's bullshit. Teeny-bopper stuff.

(The phone rings)

BO: Man, I hope the tides don't hear you, that's all. They'll drag you down to Hades. Put you in a sea dungeon for fifty hundred years.

SAL: *(Into phone)* Hello . . . *(Raises his eyebrows to the ceiling)* Oh, hello . . . Harold.

JEANNE: *(Stage whisper to SAL)* Harold Rosenstock? *(SAL nods "yes"; JEANNE shudders)* Ugh!

BO: Who's he?

JEANNE: You remember—the guy I met at The Gilded Grape a couple months ago. *(BO still looks blank)* The guy who likes oranges.

BO: Oh, shee-it, that creep! After we finished, he asked if ah was wearin' athletic socks or a jock strap. Wanted to buy 'em for twenty dollars. Ah ain't even an athlete.

BOB: I am.

SAL: *(Into phone)* Don't think anybody's free right now, Harold. Hang on a minute. *(Puts receiver against his chest)* Anybody want the score?

(BO and LARRY signal "no")

(Into phone) Nothin' right now, Harold. If anybody comes in I'll give you a call . . . So long. *(Hangs up)* Some Johns *are* a problem.

BOB: What's his scene?

JEANNE: He's queer for oranges. So we call him the Sunkist Orange man. And they *have* to be Sunkist. *(BOB looks mystified)* More juice. *(BOB still doesn't understand)* Squishier when they land. *(Dismissing the subject)* You're not experienced enough.

LARRY: *(To* PAUL*)* Hey, man.

PAUL: Yes?

LARRY: Where'd you get them kickers?

PAUL: Where did I get *what?*

LARRY: Them kickers. Them boots you got on.

PAUL: Oh—these shoes! I bought them in a store called Chipp's.

LARRY: Never heard of it.

PAUL: It's midtown, in the Forties.

LARRY: Anywhere near the Dixie Hotel?

PAUL: Where's that?

LARRY: Midtown, in the Forties.

PAUL: No.

LARRY: You mind if I touch 'em.

PAUL: *(Taken aback)* Well, er, no, no of course not.

> *(*LARRY *kneels in front of* PAUL *and starts to stroke one of his shoes. A kind of peace settles on his face)*

SAL: *(Apprehensive)* Take it easy, Larry, huh?

> *(*LARRY *doesn't answer)*

JEANNE: *(To* PAUL*)* We sometimes lose Larry to the Absolute.

SAL: Hey, Larry! Enough!

LARRY: *(Dazed)* Huh?

SAL: I said, enough. You're embarrassing Mr. Webber.

PAUL: *(Nervously)* No, no, I'm okay. Really. *(To* LARRY*)* Call me Paul.

LARRY: *(Gets up)* Them sure are nice kickers, Paul. *(*HE *goes back to his chair)*

PAUL: Thank you.

(An awkward pause)

JEANNE: *(To PAUL)* Larry poses a lot in kickers.

PAUL: *(To LARRY)* Oh, you model shoes.

LARRY: Sorta.

JEANNE: He stars in a magazine called the *World of Welts.* Just him and his kickers in the altogether.

BO: It's sick, man.

LARRY: Sez who?

BO: Sez me. You'd never get me in one of them magazines. It's for perverts.

LARRY: With a body like yours, you ain't got no worry, man.

BO: Oh yeah? Well ah ain't got a dumbbell for a brain, baby.

(LARRY starts to get out of his chair. SAL jumps up and restrains him)

SAL: Now just take it easy, Larry, you hear me?

JEANNE: Usher! Usher! They're smoking in the Children's Section!

SAL: Take it easy, just take it easy! *(HE coaxes LARRY back into his seat)*

LARRY: *(To BO)* You keep spinnin' me, man, I might have to commence to punch you out.

BO: Ah be on you like stink on shit.

(SAL separates them again)

SAL: If you don't shape up, I'm gonna auction you off at Riis Park.

BO: Aw!—Take it up your nose till midnight.

JEANNE: Ooh, the wrestlers are native tonight! *(Trying to change the subject)* Fond as Larry is of your boots, Paul, they don't quite go with the rest of your outfit.

PAUL: *(Looking at his shoes)* Mmm. Not exactly prep school, eh?

BOB: What school?

PAUL: Prep school. Prep is short for preparatory.

BO: You sayin' reformatory, man?

PAUL: *Preparatory.* It's a school that gets you ready for college.

SAL: What does it do, give you money?

> (PAUL *laughs*)

BOB: Brains help.

PAUL: Not much.

BOB: I guess you been to college, or you wouldn't run it down. People like to make fun of what they got.

JEANNE: Only the nice ones do that.

PAUL: *(Slightly patronizing)* College gives you information. But information's not the same as intelligence.

BOB: *(Impressed)* Sure wish I was dumb like that.

PAUL: There are lots of things you know that college graduates don't.

JEANNE: Name two.

PAUL: *(Fumbling)* Well . . . common-sense things.

SAL: Like how to cop a joint.

PAUL: Exactly.

JEANNE: What's the second?

PAUL: *(Kidding tone)* Can't say in mixed company.

JEANNE: Honey, this company's so mixed they rent out as Waring blenders. What's the second point? If you go to college you won't be able to fuck good, right?

> (PAUL *laughs*)

PAUL: I guess that sums it up.

JEANNE: I've embarrassed Larry.

> (LARRY, *who's been doing isometrics again, looks up startled, as if* HE'*s been caught*)

LARRY: Huh? Whadja say?

JEANNE: I said people who are obsessed miss what's going on around them.

(The phone rings)

BO: What's "obsessed" mean?

JEANNE: It means one bell keeps ringing in your head all the time. Like living in a madam's apartment.

SAL: *(Into receiver)* Hello . . . *(As if talking to a little girl)* Well, hello, Shirley honey! How's my little sweetheart today? . . . "They played a Margaret O'Brien movie on TV last night?" —Aren't they naughty! . . . Now you just hold on a minute, sweetheart. *(SAL puts his hand over receiver)* Hey, Larry, have you been with Shirley Temple yet?

LARRY: Is it a man or a woman?

SAL: A man, of course.

LARRY: How old is he?

SAL: *Way* over forty.

LARRY: What's the scene?

SAL: *(Into receiver)* Hang on, sweetheart. *(To LARRY)* You buy makeup and you go and paint it all over his face. Then you stand back and say, "Ooh! You look just like Shirley Temple." He jumps around yelling, "Ooh, I'm Shirley Temple! Oooh, I'm Shirley Temple." That makes him so excited, he gets off.

LARRY: Who pays for the makeup?

SAL: He does.

LARRY: Okay, it's a deal.

SAL: *(Into receiver)* Shirley, honey, there's a talent scout here from Hollywood who's just *dying* to meet you . . . All right, honey, I'll tell him to come right over . . . Goodbye, sweetheart. *(Hangs up receiver; to LARRY)* You got to get there right away. Shirley says Rona Barrett's coming for tea in an hour. (SAL *starts writing on a desk pad*)

BOB: (*Enjoying it*) Jesus!

PAUL: (*To* BOB) I'm glad I'm not the only one in shock!

BOB: Man, I'm as new as you are!

(SAL *hands* LARRY *the piece of paper* HE*'s been writing on*)

SAL: Here's the address. Get the $6.95 Max Factor kit at the Fifty-fifth Street drugstore.

LARRY: You're sure the guy's over forty.

JEANNE: Who needs Max Factor under forty?

SAL: Believe me, Shirley's all your dreams come true.

JEANNE: Wait'll she sings "The Good Ship Lollipop."

SAL: No more. Her ticker can't take it.

LARRY: (*To* PAUL) Hey, if you ever get tired of them boots, man, you'll let me know, wontcha?

PAUL: Oh, definitely. Sure.

LARRY: I'm willing to pay for 'em.

JEANNE: That already makes you a Leader of the Free World.

SAL: Larry!

LARRY: Catch you all later. (*Exits*)

PAUL: I think I'll have to be going too. (*To* BOB, *casually*) Would you like to come along?

BOB: Uh . . . Sure. Why not . . . (PAUL *gets up*) I'm . . . sort of a beginner.

PAUL: Sounds fine.

SAL: (*To* BOB) Don't plan. Things work out.

BO: (*To nobody in particular*) If you go down on a hole you'll go down on a pole.

SAL: *(To* PAUL*)* You know the deal, right? Forty to Bob and ten to me.

PAUL: Oh? Frank told me thirty.

SAL: Bob's special.

JEANNE: Because he doesn't do anything, it costs more.

BO: *(To* PAUL*)* Mah rate's only twenty, man.

JEANNE: Mah rate's *nothing*. Fat lot of good it does me.

(PAUL, BOB, *and* SAL *are at the door)*

PAUL: *(To* BOB*)* Bob, why don't you go ahead and ring for the elevator. I'll just be a second.

BOB: Okay. So long, people . . .

JEANNE: Have fun on the carousel.

BO: Strikebreaker! Scab!

(BOB *exits)*

PAUL: *(To* BO *and* JEANNE*)* Sorry, this is impolite, but there's something private I have to say to Sal. *(PAUL takes* SAL *aside and the* TWO *start to whisper)*

JEANNE: *(To* BO*)* He wants to know if Bob is Aquarius.

BO: Bob's Gemini. Anybody can see that.

JEANNE: Light a joint, honey. I want to forget Leo and Gemini.

BO: Cain't ever tell what's goin' on with a Gemini. They keep it all inside. But there's a lot of it! I once had this chick, she—

JEANNE: *(Interrupting; impatient)*—come on, baby, light the joint.

SAL: *(To* PAUL*)* Okay. I'll talk to you later, Paul.

PAUL: Fine. *(To* BO *and* JEANNE*)* Goodbye. It was good meeting you.

BO: Stay loose, man.

JEANNE: You be nice to Bob, now. He's practically a virgin.

PAUL: Wish I could say that. See you soon. *(Exits)*

BO: Leos ain't what they seem. Can't trust 'em. They're users.

SAL: *(To* BO*)* You're about to be used.

BO: Huh?

SAL: Paul wants to see you later. That's what the conference was about. At eleven.

BO: Far out.

JEANNE: Well, well. Big appetite, huh?

(PAUL and BOB *move downstage left)*

SAL: That's right, sweetheart. Your blood brother.

PAUL: I only live a block from here.

BOB: Let's stop in a bar.

JEANNE: Oh, those conservative dressers!

PAUL: There's plenty to drink at my place.

SAL: My favorite customers.

BOB: I like bars.

PAUL: Okay. There's one on my corner.

JEANNE: Goody—another entry in the Sexual Olympics. *(To* BO*)* Last year's winner stood in a hammock and fucked a pilot from Icelandic Airlines.

(PAUL and BOB *move further downstage left into a "cocktail lounge," and sit at an empty table. A* FEW OTHER PEOPLE *are in the lounge. A* WAITRESS— *played by the same actress who plays* ELLEN—*comes over to their table)*

BO: Big deal.

JEANNE: While being bitten on the neck by a rabid bat.

(SAL gets to work on his files; JEANNE *and* BO *smoke a joint)*

WAITRESS: What'll it be, boys?

BOB: *("Sexy")* Whaddaya got, baby?

204

WAITRESS: Just about everything.

BOB: So I see.

PAUL: Scotch and water.

WAITRESS: Quick decision. *(To* BOB*)* How about you, handsome?

BOB: *(Looking her up and down)* I'll have all of it.

WAITRESS: Why not a drink for starters?

BOB: Make it the same. No— make it a double.

WAITRESS: Big thirst.

BOB: All the time.

WAITRESS: My favorite customers *(Goes to bar)*

BOB: Groovy chick.

PAUL: She likes you.

SAL: Not a bad day. One new recruit on each side of the ledger.

JEANNE: Marching off into the sunset together.

BOB: *(Boyish)* Yeah. *(*HE *takes out a pack of cigarettes, offers one to* PAUL, *then lights them)*

BOB: Beer's what I usually drink. *(Slaps his belly)* Begins to show in the gut, though.

(Lights dim. THEY *continue to smoke in the semidark)*

PAUL: Doesn't look like you have much to worry about.

BOB: "Can't grow fat on steel," as the wife would say.

(The WAITRESS comes back with the drinks)

WAITRESS: Here we go.

BOB: You're a fast worker.

WAITRESS: Fast crowd. *(Starts to leave)*

BOB: Hey! Don't you want to get paid?

WAITRESS: This is the East Side, sweetie. We trust our customers to the *bitter* end. (SHE *leaves*)

PAUL: You mentioned your wife. Married, huh?

BOB: Yeah. When I was seventeen. Nancy's a year older. *(Grins)* Old enough to be my mother. I got a kid, too. And another on the way. Nancy doesn't think I know.

PAUL: Doesn't she wonder what you're doing in New York?

BOB: Nah . . . She's used to me takin' off. She doesn't ask questions.

PAUL: Sounds like a smart girl. *(Pause)* Does she know Sal?

BOB: *(Evasive)* Not really. I mean, we all went to high school together. *(Raises his glass)* To the wild blue yonder!

(THEY drink)

JEANNE: He reminds me of Marilyn Monroe.

BO: You trippin' out?

JEANNE: I *could* on this shit. Where'd you get it—the A&P?

BOB: Don't they have any dancin' in here?

PAUL: It's just a neighborhood bar.

BOB: We got more action in Ridgeway.

PAUL: What kind of work do you do there?

BOB: Construction. *(Lying)* Used to have my own company—when I was eighteen. Made forty thousand one year.

JEANNE: I'm worried about Bob.

SAL: Huh?

JEANNE: He *likes* Paul.

SAL: You're stoned. Bob's in it for the bread.

JEANNE: So he says.

SAL: And so says his wife. And so says me.

JEANNE: The three wise men.

BO: Jeannie's Pisces, the Prophet.

JEANNE: I'm Leo, smartass.

BOB: Got sick of it, though. I might try athletics full time. I had lots of offers when I was in high school. But I got married—what can I tell ya?

PAUL: You're still young.

BOB: I had this one offer from Indiana. Football scholarship. $10,000 a year, a house for the wife, and a new car every six months.

PAUL: You must be good.

BOB: The Phillies wanted me, too.

PAUL: That's a baseball team, isn't it?

BOB: I played baseball, too. I had all kinds of offers.

PAUL: Why didn't you take any of them?

BOB: *(Evasive)* The wife . . . you know . . . She holds me down . . .

(Phone rings.)

JEANNE: I knew it was too peaceful to last.

SAL: *(Into phone)* Hello . . .

(Spot up downstage left. We see NANCY *at the other end of the phone)*

SAL: *(Casual)* Hey, Nance, how's it goin'?

NANCY: *(Nervously)* Is—everything—okay?

JEANNE: *(To* BO *)* Here we go: Truth *and* Consequences.

SAL: Sure . . .

NANCY: . . . Bob said he'd be back by late afternoon.

SAL: He's goin' great guns.

JEANNE: *(To* SAL*)* Meanie. Just because they wouldn't let you in their high school crowd.

BOB: Couple people have said I should model. Supposed to be good bread in it.

PAUL: So I hear.

BOB: I might go off to the woods. Canada, maybe. Way up. Best time I ever had was when I was twelve and was in the woods for ten weeks with my dog. A guy let me use his land. During the day I built him a campsite. But nobody's ever used it.

PAUL: Why not?

BOB: *(Grinning)* No way to get

209

to it, except to swim around the peninsula. I swam it every day to build the camp. Once some girls stole my clothes.

NANCY: Is he still there?

SAL: No, he left hours ago.

JEANNE: Days ago! Years ago!!

NANCY: Well where *is* he?

SAL: Christ, I dunno, Nance. Probably stopped off in a bar on his way home.

NANCY: Did he leave alone?

SAL: You said you didn't want details. *(To JEANNE, covering receiver)* Now I'm a shrink.

BO: Is that a sign?

JEANNE: Yeah. Of decay.

PAUL: Waitress! *(To BOB)* It's getting late. I think we should go.

(WAITRESS comes to table)

WAITRESS: Leavin' already? I thought you were good for the night.

BOB: *(Smirking)* I am.

WAITRESS: Doesn't look like tonight's it.

(PAUL puts tip on the table. WAITRESS picks it up)

210

NANCY: Did he . . . leave with someone?

SAL: You're makin' a big deal out of nuthin'. Turn on the TV. He'll be home in no time.

NANCY: Uh-huh.

SAL: Relax, relax.

NANCY: If you hear from him, tell him to call me right away.

SAL: Sure, Nance.

(SHE *hangs up the phone and sits there, looking forlorn. The spot stays on her*)

BOB: Business before pleasure.

WAITRESS: You oughta learn to mix the two.

PAUL: He will. Ready?

SAL: Some people don't know their own heads.

JEANNE: I think you mean hearts. No, you don't.

BOB: *(Looking at the* WAITRESS*)* Sure. We all gotta go some time.

BO: Sure glad mah Alice don't pester me like that.

JEANNE: Alice is Southern.

ACT I

SCENE 4

Stage left revolves, revealing PAUL*'s apartment. It's spacious but not overly elaborate. Book shelves are prominent.*

The phone on SAL*'s desk rings. Spot is still on* NANCY.

BO: Hope it's one for me.

SAL: You got the Wheaties man at nine and Paul at eleven.

BOB: . . . some people say Australia's the place to go. Better than Canada. More open space.

BO: Shee-it. What am ah supposed to do till then?

PAUL: Doesn't sound like you're much for city life. Another drink?

JEANNE: We could try the Ouija board.

BO: Shee-it.

JEANNE: Build your vocabulary.

BOB: Sure. Make it a double. I can take it or leave it—the city, I mean.

BO: Ah'm gonna take me to Europe.

JEANNE: You what?!

BO: Ah hear time passes faster there. It's five hours ahead.

(JEANNE shakes her head in disbelief)

(BOB starts looking at the books. HE takes one off the shelf)

BOB: Hey, I know this—*Tom Sawyer!* We read it in high school.

PAUL: That's Mark Twain at his worst. Far too sentimental.

SAL: *(Into receiver)* . . . Just fine.

BOB: Uh-huh. *(Intimidated, HE puts the book back on the shelf)*

213

. . . Why sure, don't I always? . . . Now let's see, you don't know George Wicker, right? . . . Lots of muscles . . . No, natural . . . Well, he only swings in a butch sorta way. But affectionate. And good with his hands . . . Okay. . . . give me a second . . .

(As SAL *starts looking through his files and* JEANNE *and* BO *pass the joint, the lights dim to out in* SAL*'s apartment)*

*(*NANCY *starts dialing. A spot comes up on* NED *answering the phone)*

NED: Hello.

NANCY: Hello, Ned. It's Nancy.

NED: *(Cold)* Yes?

NANCY: I'd . . . I'd like to speak to Ellen.

(Spot comes up on ELLEN, *sitting in a chair next to* NED*)*

Books cost a lot, don't they?

PAUL: I get most of them free. I'm an editor in a publishing house.

BOB: I thought you said—

PAUL: *(Smiling)* —um, advertising. I don't want Sal to know too much.

214

(HE *gives* BOB *his drink.*
THEY *sit*)

NED: Ellen's not home.

(ELLEN *moves as if to get out
of the chair.* NED *motions
her to sit down*)

BOB: Sal's okay.

NANCY: Oh . . . What time do
you expect her in?

PAUL: He's a convenience.

BOB: But you just met him today.

NED: She's not gonna be in.

PAUL: There are other ser-
vices.

(HE *hangs up.* NANCY *holds the
dead receiver. Spot on her goes out*)

BOB: Oh yeah? How many?

PAUL: *(Evasive)* I don't know—three or four, I guess.

BOB: You use 'em *all*?

PAUL: *(Nervous)* Of course not. I just know about them.

BOB: So how come you called Sal?

PAUL: I heard you were going to be there.

BOB: *(Pleased)* No, I mean it. I'm, like, interested in how people get
into the bag.

PAUL: How'd you get into it?

BOB: *(Surprised)* I told ya—I need bread.

PAUL: There are lots of ways to make money.

BOB: For you maybe.

215

(The phone rings. PAUL *gets up to answer it)*

BOB: Just like Sal's.

PAUL: *(Annoyed)* Not quite. *(Into receiver)* Hello . . . *(Embarrassed)* Oh, how are you, Pete? Another furlough, huh? . . . No, not tonight. A friend's here . . . No, I'll be tied up later, too . . . Fine, call me about midday . . . Good, talk to you then. *(*HE *hangs up. To* BOB*)* A friend, in from out of town.

BOB: Uh-huh. So how come you pay for it?

PAUL: *(Still more annoyed)* So how come you ask so many questions?

BOB: *(Surprised)* Me?! Boy, you'd never get the wife to believe that! She says I don't talk enough. I don't express myself too good.

PAUL: You're doing fine.

BOB: I just mean it don't make sense—a guy like you, with smarts, and pretty young, too.

PAUL: As I said, it's convenient. And safer. You never know who you meet on the street, or in a bar. Hoods. Addicts. God knows what.

BOB: You can meet guys like that through Sal, too.

PAUL: Do you mean Bo?

BOB: Who's Bo?

PAUL: That Southern kid at Sal's before.

BOB: Oh him, yeah. I don't know. Just met him myself.

PAUL: *(Worried)* He looked all right.

BOB: I guess you never know. Until you press a wrong button. But guys who get in trouble are usually lookin' for it.

PAUL: Kids on the street are full of wrong buttons. Sal keeps the odds down. He screens people.

BOB: Nobody screened me.

PAUL: Who introduced you to Sal? *(*BOB *looks uneasy)* Oh, I forgot —you know each other from high school.

BOB: Yeah, right.

PAUL: Besides, you can waste a whole night in a bar and still not
. . . *(Realizes* HE*'s revealing more than* HE *intends)* I mean, Sal
saves time. There's never enough of that what with the job and
all. Want another drink?

BOB: Okay. *(*PAUL *goes to the bar)* What does an editor do?

PAUL: He helps authors write their books.

BOB: Why don't you write your own?

PAUL: *(Laughs)* That's what my analyst keeps asking. Maybe I ought
to pay *you* forty bucks an hour.

BOB: You are.

*(*THEY *smile)*

PAUL: I forgot that for a minute.

BOB: Yeah, so did I.

PAUL: *(Looks at his watch)* It's already more than an hour.

BOB: You gotta be some place?

PAUL: As a matter of fact, a friend of mine's due by at eleven.

BOB: You got a lot of friends.

PAUL: That's New York.

BOB: I like talkin' to you. You got a lot to say.

PAUL: I'm enjoying it, too.

(Pause)

BOB: You got a groovy pad here.

PAUL: Thanks. It's 11 percent Des Moines, 89 percent Blooming-
dale's.

BOB: I guess you don't invite just anyone up.

PAUL: Only friends.

BOB: No TV. Don't you get lonesome?

PAUL: Sometimes.

BOB: It would bug me to live alone. I guess that's one thing you can say for marriage. Ever thought about gettin' married?

PAUL: The only people who want to get married these days are priests. (THEY *laugh*) I like to set my own timetable.

BOB: So you can write that book, huh?

PAUL: You *do* sound like my analyst!

BOB: What's the book about?

PAUL: It's a novel.

BOB: Oh yeah? Why don't you write a novel about me? You could call it "Repeater Rifle."

PAUL: *(Turned on)* Sounds good. Maybe we ought to start the first chapter.

BOB: We'd make a million, man.

PAUL: I haven't heard the story yet.

BOB: You know—big man in high school. Football hero. Lots of chicks. My own construction firm. Then—boom! Washed up at twenty-five. A has-been, hustling for bread.

PAUL: You don't look like a has-been.

BOB: *(Pleased)* The wife's got me packed in. She makes me feel like I'm not hittin' on nuthin'.

PAUL: I'm sure you could do anything you want.

BOB: I got alotta plans in my head—you know what I mean? *(Lying)* Took a couple night courses last year. Thought I'd go back to college sometime. Maybe pick up one of those athletic scholarships. Don't have all the weight on me I used to, but I could put it on easy if I start workin' out.

PAUL: I'll tell you what: you go to college and I'll write my novel. What do you say?

BOB: Hey! How about that!

PAUL: Maybe I'll write the novel *about* your going to college.

BOB: For seventy-five bucks a week flat sum, man, I'll tell you my whole story!

PAUL: It's a deal!

(THEY *laugh*)

BOB: No kiddin', man. Maybe you could help me brush up. I'm sorta rusty on the books.

PAUL: *(Gesturing to the shelves)* Your own lending library.

BOB: Sure is somethin'. You got a beautiful life, man. Nobody to answer to. *(Sudden inspiration)* Hey—maybe if I got workin' again, got it together—

PAUL: *(Interrupting)* —I thought you were working.

BOB: *(Trying to cover)* Oh sure. I mean, like full time, my own company again—you know. Right now I'm workin' for somebody else.

PAUL: *(Unconvinced)* Uh-huh.

BOB: *(Picking up the beat again)* . . . so like if I start takin' a course in the city, or whatever—you know? . . . like maybe you'd let me rent a room here from you. I mean you live here alone, right?

PAUL: Currently, yes.

BOB: You ever rent a room to anybody?

PAUL: No, but different friends have stayed here.

BOB: At the same time?

(PAUL *laughs*)

PAUL: They don't usually overlap.

BOB: So whaddaya think, huh? I mean, you got a big pad.

PAUL: *(Incredulous)* Are you serious? What about your family?

BOB: *(Vague)* Oh just a couple nights a week maybe. The nights I go to school, or somethin'.

PAUL: *(With a smile, lightly)* But Bob . . . I mean we hardly know each other.

BOB: *(Suddenly depressed)* Yeah, I guess so. Well, it was just an idea. What the hell.

PAUL: It's difficult to live with somebody. Even part-time.

BOB: Maybe I oughta work for Sal and just forget the rest.

PAUL: I didn't mean it was a *bad* idea. We *might* give your staying here a try.

BOB: *(Brightening)* I'd pay you rent, man.

PAUL: No, don't be silly. It might be nice to have company now and then.

BOB: How about tonight?

PAUL: Tonight?

BOB: You want me to stay over?

PAUL: Well . . . what . . . what about your wife?

BOB: She don't care. I told you: I stay out a lot. She's used to it.

PAUL: It might be hard to explain.

BOB: No sweat, man. Believe me.

PAUL: Well, tonight's not very good. I've got that friend coming by at eleven.

BOB: I could go to Sal's and shoot the shit for a while. Then come back after your friend's gone.

PAUL: It's hard to know when he'll leave. We might be up till all hours gabbing.

BOB: *(Giving up)* Oh. Okay. Whatever you say.

PAUL: Some other night maybe.

BOB: How about tomorrow?

PAUL: I thought people from small towns were shy!

BOB: *(Boyish)* Yeah . . . well, what can I tell ya? . . .

PAUL: Sure . . . tomorrow's fine. Say about ten.

BOB: You want me to stay over tomorrow?

PAUL: Classes haven't begun *yet!*

BOB: *(Disappointed)* Oh yeah, I forgot.

PAUL: Why don't we see how it goes.

BOB: Okay.

PAUL: *(Looks at his watch)* It's getting late.

BOB: Yeah. *(Embarrassed)* I'm pretty new at all this.

PAUL: We'll work it out. Don't worry about it. (HE *starts turning out the lights)*

BOB: Hey, why don't you make me a small one. Sort of a nightcap.

PAUL: If you drink it fast. I don't want that friend walking in on us.

BOB: You're sure it's not a chick, man?

PAUL: *(Laughs)* I'm sure. (HE *starts mixing the drink)*

BOB: You better not two-time me with a chick.

PAUL: Not a chance.

BOB: *(Drunken)* Chicks are a pain in the ass. All they want to do is pin you down. Fuck the chicks. Together we're gonna make a million, right?

PAUL: You liked that waitress.

BOB: Yeah, a nice piece. I think I really turned her on.

PAUL: No doubt about it. Why don't you take the bedspread off. I'll be right in.

BOB: Yeah, these New York chicks are somethin' else.

(Exits into the bedroom. PAUL *turns out the last light and with* BOB*'s drink in his hand, heads toward the bedroom.* HE *stops momentarily, shakes his head in a gesture of bemused delight. The lights go to out)*

END OF ACT I

ACT II

SCENE 1

Lights come up stage left revealing BOB *at a bar.* HE *'s wearing jeans and a tee shirt, and is drinking a beer.*

Lights up in SAL*'s apartment.* SAL*'s on the phone.*

SAL: *(Annoyed)* I *know* it's been three days, Nancy. Your calling every ten minutes helps remind me . . . Listen! I'm not running a Missing Persons Bureau! If I knew where he was, I'd tell ya . . . Hey, cool it, huh?! I got as much right to be pissed as you do.

*(*BOB *finishes his beer, puts his glass down, and picks up two large bags full of groceries)*

He's turned out to be a
real winner . . . *(Lights
dim)* Yeah, yeah . . . *if*
he shows . . . (HE *hangs up.
Lights out)*

BOB: *(To* BARTENDER*)* See ya.

BARTENDER: Nice talkin' to ya. If you're in the neighborhood, drop
in again.

BOB: Looks like I'll be livin' around here.

BARTENDER: Good deal. See ya soon, then.

(Lights go out in bar. Stage left revolves into PAUL*'s apartment.* PAUL
is setting up for a party. The phone rings)

PAUL: *(Into receiver)* Hello . . . Sal, I told you yesterday and I told
you the day before yesterday, I *don't know where he is* . . . Of
course he's not staying here! How could I have seen Dave
yesterday? . . . Yes, if I hear from him, I'll tell him to call you.
Yes, to call his wife, too . . .

(The apartment buzzer rings)

There goes my buzzer! I have to run . . . Right . . . Right
. . . Right . . . I'll talk to you.

(PAUL hangs up and goes to door. BOB enters, carrying the packages)

Ah, good man! I almost gave you up. They're going to be here
any second.

BOB: Stopped off for a beer.

PAUL: As always.

BOB: Right.

PAUL: I thought the wine last night converted you.

BOB: I liked it. But beer's home base, man. Now that lobster—*that*
was somethin' else!

PAUL: The world's full of good things.

BOB: I'm beginnin' to believe it.

(THEY start unpacking the shopping bags)

PAUL: I can finish this. Why don't you go ahead and change?

BOB: Change into what?

PAUL: Something to go with the tie-and-jacket set. *I* like you this way, of course.

BOB: I got nuthin' like that with me.

PAUL: Wear one of my jackets. Hell, if you can use my sheets for three days, why not my clothes?

BOB: Okay. Might as well take a shower while I'm at it. *(Exits into bedroom)*

PAUL: *(Calling after him)* Try one of the Oxford button-downs. They're larger than my other shirts.

(PAUL goes back to unpacking the bags. The apartment buzzer rings. HE goes to the door and opens it. FRANK DAWSON enters. HE's a political columnist, in his forties; tough and bright, aggressive in manner)

Frank, how are you?

FRANK: Freezing! Yesterday spring, today winter. This goddamn city is going to do us all in.

PAUL: You sound like a cabbie.

FRANK: The frost is killing the seeds I planted on the terrace last week.

PAUL: *(Kiddingly)* I wouldn't stand for it!

FRANK: It's probably Nixon's fault.

PAUL: He does do those strange things with his eyes.

FRANK: *(Looking around)* You mean I'm *first!* I always arrive last, so I can dramatically announce that I was putting the column to bed.

PAUL: Only two other people are coming. Ray and Tom.

FRANK: Oh no—those idiots! Have you no consideration?

PAUL: Ray's new novel—*Unwilling Cement*—is just out. As his editor, I'm supposed to congratulate him with drinks every six hours.

FRANK: I keep hoping someday you'll give a *real* party—for all the tricks you've met through all your madams. No—someone might get stomped to death in the crowd.

PAUL: I better get you a drink.

FRANK: Hurry!

PAUL: It's clear you've had a hard day at the typewriter. *(Goes to the bar and starts mixing FRANK's drink)*

FRANK: I've spent seven hours on a column arguing that after New York secedes from the state, Manhattan should secede from New York.

PAUL: The possibilities are endless. Then Forty-second Street can secede from Manhattan.

FRANK: And Sal from Forty-second Street. *(THEY laugh)* So? Where is he? Where's the record-setting Bob? Three whole days—he's got to be a paragon.

PAUL: He's taking a shower.

FRANK: I feel like the father of the bride.

PAUL: Don't say that in front of him. He likes to think of himself as straight.

FRANK: *(Sardonic)* Whereas in fact the two of you are madly in love. Does Sal know Bob's staying here?

PAUL: Not exactly.

FRANK: Does he or doesn't he?

PAUL: Doesn't.

FRANK: Mmm. He wouldn't take kindly to your hogging his new star.

PAUL: Aren't we waspish today. I care about this boy a lot.

FRANK: I believe you. It's been months since you've asked anyone to move in. And God knows you're domestic—though rarely, alas, at home.

PAUL: I haven't asked Bob to move in.

FRANK: Yet. *(Pause)* What about your "habit."

PAUL: *(Stage whisper)* Shush! Keep your voice down. *(Puts* FRANK*'s drink in front of him and then sits)* And find a nicer word than "habit," please.

FRANK: It's the right word. It conveys addiction.

PAUL: What a bent for melodrama! A pity the form's passé.

FRANK: Only in literature, not life. You're a one-man welfare agency for underprivileged boys.

PAUL: And you're a prisoner of the outmoded values of the straight culture. "Promiscuity," *dear heart*, is a function not of hysteria, as the shrinks would have it, but of a healthy insistence on varied sexual experience.

FRANK: How well you've learned the new rhetoric! Pity it can't conceal the fact that you are voracious of people, *not* experience.

PAUL: Christ! Why don't you go home?!

FRANK: It hurts me more than it does you to say these things.

PAUL: Well since you're in such pain, I'd better not tell you about a paratrooper named Dave who Sal sent over yesterday.

FRANK: *Yesterday!* How did you manage that, with Bob here?

PAUL: He "volunteered" to do some errands, while I "pored over a manuscript."

FRANK: You *are* a greedy little bastard!

PAUL: *(Arch)* No—Dave wouldn't interest you: awfully muscular.

FRANK: Wretch!

(THEY *laugh)*

FRANK: *(Mock cajolery)* Of course what I *really* meant before is that your "sexual energy" is a kind of genius.

PAUL: *(Laughing)* That's much better than "greedy little bastard."

FRANK: *("Lyrical")* No sooner do you capture a prize, achieve a goal, than you set a new goal, seek a new prize. Never satisfied, always searching. That fierce obsessive urge to press on! Yes— decidedly a genius!

PAUL: Bravo!

FRANK: Now about that paratrooper—

(The apartment buzzer rings.)

PAUL: *(Arch)* What unlucky timing.

FRANK: I'm going to slay you on the spot.

PAUL: If only you could rejoice in a friend's pleasure.

FRANK: If only you had fewer pleasures.

(PAUL opens the door. RAY and TOM enter)

RAY: Forgive us!—getting a cab on Sunday's *impossible!* We can only stay a minute anyway. We promised Mark Simon we'd— *(Sees FRANK on the couch)* Well! What a nice dividend! Our own Walter Lippmann.

FRANK: *(To RAY)* How are you, Ray? Hello, Tom.

RAY: Wretched! That's all, in honesty, I can say.

FRANK: Honesty above all; including civility. *Hello,* Tom.

TOM: Hello.

PAUL: I think I should warn you that Frank's a little testy today. He's having trouble with his pleasure center.

RAY: I beg your pardon?

FRANK: *(Smiling; pointing to his nose)* My nose. Stuffed nose.

RAY: Oh, Lord! Don't go near Tommy, then.

FRANK: *(Almost to himself)* I promise not.

RAY: The poor baby's already had more than his share.

FRANK: *(To TOM)* Aren't you well, Tom?

TOM: Not very.

RAY: Not very, indeed! A roaring case of the Asian. You should have seen the color of his stools. *Green*, my dear!

FRANK: Maybe it's the new eco-toilet paper—

RAY:—"gangrene!" we thought, "Tommy's got gangrene!"

FRANK: I wouldn't be at all surprised.

RAY: We haven't slept a wink in days. It's been a near catastrophe —with the novel coming out.

FRANK: *("Innocently")* The novel's been a catastrophe? Oh I am sorry, Ray.

RAY: *(Miffed)* It's doing *quite* nicely, thank you.

PAUL: How about some drinks?

RAY: Mmm, yummy. Martini for me.

TOM: Me too.

RAY: *(To* TOM*)* Do you think you should? It could start up the yellow plague again.

TOM: *(Petulant)* I don't care. I want one.

RAY: Very well. Don't expect me to stay up with you all night.

(PAUL *goes to the bar*)

Don't ever write a book, Frank. The publicity people drive you mad. I was so busy last week that when I was masturbating, I didn't have time for a fantasy.

FRANK: I've written a book, Ray.

RAY: *Have* you?! Why does no one tell me these things?

PAUL: *(From the bar)* A collection of Frank's columns came out last year.

RAY: *(To* FRANK*)* Wondrous! You must send me a copy.

FRANK: They're on politics, Ray. Not at all your thing.

RAY: My dear! In times like these who is *not* concerned with politics?! Even *creative* people have the obligation to keep informed.

(PAUL *serves the drinks*)

RAY: Ah, time to sip a little aggression . . . If only the young knew what they were missing, smoking all that foul pot.

FRANK: I always thought of you as part of the avant-garde.

RAY: *(Giggling)* I *was* tempted in California. Everywhere you go out there your Average Lifeguard is handing you a joint to "groove" on. *"Love* to," I kept saying, staring into all those vacant eyes, "*love* to!" But they *would* misinterpret. To preserve sanity, I finally had to flee the state.

FRANK: By vote of the Average Lifeguard Association.

(BOB comes out of the bedroom. HE is dressed very conservatively, in an Oxford button-down, tie, and jacket. PAUL jumps up)

PAUL: Hey—you look great! Chip off the old block.

BOB: *(Pleased)* Looks pretty good, huh?

RAY: *(To TOM and FRANK)* Talk about your firsts! We're actually going to meet one of them!

PAUL: Bob, this is Frank Dawson. Bob Marshall.

FRANK: Hello, Bob. Nice meeting you.

BOB: Thanks.

PAUL: And this is Tom Walters and Ray Richards.

BOB: Hello.

(THEY shake hands)

RAY: I love your outfit. You look like a teen-age stockbroker. Wherever did you find it?

BOB: In Paul's closet.

RAY: *(To PAUL)* The things you have buried, dear boy!

PAUL: That jacket cost $125.

RAY: That's a lot for Gentlemen's Resale. I wonder what it cost the first time.

PAUL: *(To BOB)* How about a drink?

BOB: Yeah. Make it a beer.

RAY: Beer before dinner? How quaint!

BOB: I like beer.

PAUL: Anybody else ready?

TOM: Yes, I think I'll—

RAY: *(Interrupting)* —no, love, we can only stay for the one. We're going to a *straight* party. *(To* BOB*)* I don't suppose you know what I mean.

BOB: I been around.

RAY: Have you? Oh, good. I do hate disguises. Just not part of my nature to dissemble.

BOB: To what?

RAY: Dissemble. To conceal, play the hypocrite.

TOM: Its archaic meaning is "to insult."

RAY: The things you know, Tommy. *(To* BOB*)* Pay him no mind. Now why don't you know "dissemble"? You look like a college boy.

*(*PAUL *gives* BOB *his beer)*

BOB: Not exactly.

RAY: What does that mean?

PAUL: Just what it says.

RAY: Don't get tart. It was a simple question. *(To* BOB*)* I'll bet it's money, isn't it.

PAUL: *(Nervously)* You bet *what's* money?

RAY: The college problem. Nobody has enough money these days. I don't know who can afford to live in this city. The poverty line is now $20,000 a year.

FRANK: For Sunday cabs alone.

RAY: *(To* BOB*)* You do live in the city, don't you?

BOB: I'm from Jersey.

RAY: Where in Jersey?

TOM: *(To nobody in particular)* Do you know how New Jersey got its name? And don't anyone say dairy cattle, or the textile.

FRANK: You took the words out of my mouth.

TOM: Give up?

RAY: *(Annoyed)* Oh, Tommy.

TOM: New Jersey is named after one of the Channel Islands. The state bird is the Eastern Goldfinch.

FRANK: But why is the Channel Island named Jersey?

TOM: *(Startled)* What a curious question.

PAUL: *(To* RAY; *trying to change the subject)* Tell us about the party you're going to.

RAY: *(Turning to* BOB*)* I'd rather hear about Bob and college. You are in college, aren't you?

BOB: *(Awkward)* Well, I—

PAUL: *(Interrupting)*—enough questions, Ray.

RAY: My, you sound severe! Have I made a boo-boo? I was only trying to be friendly.

BOB: Don't worry about it.

PAUL: Will you *please* tell us about the party.

RAY: The party, the party. Oh yes. Well, what is there to tell? Straight parties are like Negroes—they all look alike. *(Giggles)* Ooh, Frank'll beat me for that.

FRANK: Don't get your hopes up.

RAY: *Anyway* . . . Mark Simon is giving it. To celebrate the opening of his one-acters. Though what there is to celebrate, I can't imagine. The chutzpah of some people. *(To* BOB*)* "Chutzpah" is a Jewish word for nervy. You're not Jewish, I suppose.

BOB: No. Are you?

RAY: Me?! What an astonishing idea! I'm a New England Puritan. Direct descendant of Ralph Waldo Emerson.

TOM: Emerson had Jewish blood—that long nose.

FRANK: *(Mimicking RAY)* "The things you know, Tommy." A shame those quiz programs went off the air.

RAY: Those programs were fixed. Tommy isn't.

FRANK: Funny, he *looks* fixed. I leave it up to Bob.

BOB: *(Startled)* Huh?

FRANK: Was Emerson Jewish?

PAUL: *(To FRANK; angry)* You're a big help.

FRANK: *(Flaring)* Don't get protective. You're busy enough.

BOB: I know who Emerson is. He was a friend of *(Mispronouncing "Thoreau")* "Thurrow's." I've read *Walden . . .* twice.

RAY: *"Thurrow"*—ooh, I love it!

TOM: "Thurrow"—as in "furrow"—is in fact how he himself pronounced the name. It says so in *The Annotated Walden.*

PAUL: *(To RAY) Tell us about the party.*

RAY: *(Pleased at the undercurrents)* My everyone's jumpy! *(Supercharm)* Everyone but Bob. He's the soul of composure, *(Waxing lyrical)* the eye of the hurricane, the still center of—

(BOB squirms uncomfortably. PAUL gives RAY an angry look)

("Innocently") Well I *am* a writer!

FRANK: Making fiction out of every fact.

RAY: *(Giggles)* Now where was I? . . . Oh yes! Mark's plays were all about lesbians.

TOM: Two women actually kissed on the lips. Then they wonder why gay people aren't accepted.

RAY: Imagine having to go backstage afterward! All I could think to say was, "Mark: you've set a new standard in the theater."

TOM: We shouldn't have gone backstage.

RAY: We had to.

TOM: We didn't.

RAY: If we hadn't, he would have thought we hated the plays.

TOM: We did.

RAY: That's not the point. With friends loyalty comes before honesty. Don't you agree, Bob?

BOB: Yeah, sure. You gotta be honest.

RAY: *(Giggles)* Lord, a wit, too! *(To* PAUL, *archly)* Aren't you the lucky one. Where *did* you find him? *(*HE *throws up his hands as if to stop* PAUL *from answering)* Don't tell me! I want to guess.

PAUL: Don't.

RAY: You're such a grouch today! You must have Jewish blood, too. Jewish people are impossible on Sunday, the *Christians'* day for talking to God. They hate giving anyone else a turn.

FRANK: *(Sly)* It's Paul's Christian side that works for conversion. *(To* BOB *)* That jacket does look good on you.

BOB: Thanks.

RAY: *(Giggles)* So naughty! I'm getting back to my game: guess if you can, where Paul and Bob first met. Tommy, you get the first guess.

TOM: At a party.

RAY: Isn't he sweet? Never a nasty thought in his head. *(To* TOM *)* No, love. Without even consulting the principals, I can tell you that is not the answer. Frank, your turn.

FRANK: Frank says it's none of your business.

RAY: Of course it isn't. If it was, the game wouldn't be any fun.

PAUL: It's not fun. Cut it out, Ray.

RAY: You met in a Turkish bath. *(*PAUL *laughs with relief)* I guessed it, didn't I?

PAUL: Not quite.

RAY: *(Looking at* BOB *)* One could hardly not notice the wedding ring. And married men always go to the Turkish baths. Either that or tearooms—depending on how eager they are to be arrested. Don't you find that's true, Bob?

BOB: That what's true?

RAY: That married men go to Turkish baths or tearooms.

BOB: What the hell is a tearoom?

RAY: You've never heard of a tearoom?! How extraordinary! I could have sworn we first met you in a tearoom. No matter. He who has a good memory has a failed heart, I always say. *(To* BOB*)* In any case, dear boy, a tearoom is a public rest room. They're quite the rage in certain circles. A sociologist has even written a book about them.

FRANK: What?!

RAY: See—you don't know everything. Tommy and I were reading aloud from it last night. He brought it home from the library. *(To* BOB*)* Tommy is *chief* librarian at the Mechanics' Institute. Anyway, scientific language is *very* erotic. Much talk about "insertor" and "insertee." *(Giggles)* The book should be banned.

FRANK: How in God's name did the author gather data?

RAY: He served as a "watchqueen." (BOB *squirms uncomfortably.* RAY *turns to him)* That's the one who coughs when a police car stops nearby. Very diligent man. Watched hundreds of hours of fellatio.

FRANK: Why?

RAY: Because it was there.

*(*RAY, TOM, *and* FRANK *laugh.* PAUL *squirms at* BOB*'s discomfort)*

TOM: He's also discovered that sexual encounters in public rest rooms involve very little conversation. Of the few words he heard, like "not so hard" and "thanks," all were whispered and none in full voice.

RAY: Now I call that a real contribution. Isn't social science wonderful?

(This time PAUL *laughs too, but begrudgingly)*

TOM: He's also found no indication that men who frequent tearooms "seek homosexual contact as such."

RAY: No indeed! They go there only because the naughty vice squads have "narrowed the behavioral options of the lower classes."

FRANK: What?!

RAY: Translation: vice squads have closed the two-bit bordellos, thereby doing away with the sort of fast, impersonal service every male requires. (THEY *laugh*) Here's a crusade for you, Frank!—in the name of mental health, the government should install "milking machines" in every public comfort station! Insert a quarter and your dilly-do and—whush!—instant tension-reduction. Would do wonders for the nation's irritability. You ought to write a column.

(ALL *except* BOB *laugh loudly.* BOB *gets up abruptly*)

BOB: (*To* PAUL) Hey, man: I gotta go.

PAUL: Go?! Don't be silly! Ray and Tom are leaving any minute. (*To* RAY) Aren't you, Ray?

RAY: (*As if to himself*) Pick up the cue, unwanted guests. (*To* PAUL) Indeed we must. By now Mark will have turned up the volume on Bette Midler, so we'll be saved having to discuss his plays. (*Pointed*) Besides, Mark always has divine food.

TOM: Pignolia nuts, perugina lemon, and pontefract cakes.

BOB: I gotta go.

RAY: Young man, your life seems ruled by impulse. You're sure you're not off to the Turkish baths?

BOB: (*Angry*) Yeah, I'm sure.

RAY: Oh my, a note of hostility. And it's been such a pleasant afternoon. Come, Tommy. It's off to warmer climes.

(THEY*'re at the door*)

RAY: Goodbye, goodbye. Many thanks for the drinks. *(Over his shoulder to* BOB*)* Lovely to have met you, dear boy. I do hope your schedule takes on some form. Mustn't leave everything to chance, you know. Ta!

*(*TOM *and* RAY *leave)*

FRANK: I have to go, too. Column-writing time. *(At the door; to* PAUL*)* I'll talk to you tomorrow. Next time, let's have a *quiet* drink. Just we two. *(Remembering* BOB*)* Or we three. Goodbye, Bob. Nice meeting you.

BOB: Goodbye.

PAUL: *(Calling after* FRANK*)* Talk to you tomorrow. *(Closes the door, comes back into room)* Sorry about that. Hope they didn't bother you too much.

BOB: Kinda freaky, dontcha think?

PAUL: Ray's a little strange.

BOB: They all are.

PAUL: Not Frank. Ordinarily.

BOB: Okay. Listen, I gotta go, man.

PAUL: You keep saying that! Go where?

BOB: I don't know. Out. Jersey, maybe.

PAUL: I don't get it.

BOB: I got a wife and kid, remember? She's gonna be pissed off.

PAUL: You're awfully protective of her suddenly.

BOB: I like my wife.

PAUL: You'd never know it. You disappear for three days and don't even call her.

BOB: She understands.

PAUL: You don't treat someone that way if you care about them.

BOB: *(Angry)* You're sure of that, huh?

PAUL: It's none of my business, I suppose.

236

BOB: That's right.

PAUL: *(Trying to hold him)* I've enjoyed the last few days, Bob. I like having you here.

BOB: Uh-huh . . .

PAUL: You can stay, you know. There's . . . plenty of room.

BOB: I'll think about it, okay?

PAUL: I was the one who was supposed to be thinking about it.

BOB: I guess we both betta. *(Heads toward the door)*

PAUL: I'll find out about classes.

BOB: *(Unenthusiastic)* Okay.

PAUL: Ray and Tom aren't really friends of mine. We publish Ray's novels.

BOB: Weird bunch of guys. *(THEY're at the door. BOB opens it)* Oh wow!—I still got your clothes on!

PAUL: Don't worry about it. You can bring them back when you come in next time.

BOB: *(Uncertain)* They'll look funny in Ridgeway. Nobody'll recognize me.

PAUL: You don't look *that* different.

BOB: I guess not. Felt that way for a while. *(Pause)* Well . . . I'll give you a call.

PAUL: When?

BOB: Soon.

(PAUL moves toward BOB as if to embrace him. BOB goes out the door. PAUL crosses to the couch and sits forlornly. HE then gets up, goes to the phone and starts dialing, as the lights go to out)

ACT II

SCENE 2

Lights come up on BOB *and* NANCY's *kitchen.*

Evening of the same day. BOB *enters the front door. Hearing his key,* NANCY *crosses the room and busies herself with the dishes.*

BOB: I'm back.

NANCY: So I see.

BOB: Without turning around?

NANCY: I remember your voice. Even after three days. (BOB *takes off his coat and heads toward the bedroom*) Where are you going?

BOB: To bed. I got a big head.

NANCY: *(Sudden explosion)* I thought you were dead, for Chrissake! *(Near tears)* Jesus, couldn't you have called?

BOB: Hey! What's the big deal? You know I go till I stop.

NANCY: This was a little different.

BOB: What's different? . . . it's the motor, babe, like always.

NANCY: *Please*, Bob! Please . . . can't we . . . *talk* for once?

BOB: Tomorrow. I'm beat. Look: I'm back.

NANCY: I want to *talk*. We can't . . . bury it. Not if it's going to mean anything for us.

BOB: What's "it"? I became a breadwinner again—like you wanted. (HE *puts some money down on the kitchen table*) Next time maybe you oughta win it with *your* body. It's easy work, like you said. I'm going to bed.

(NANCY *picks up the jacket* BOB *left on the chair*)

NANCY: Your taste has changed. Or didn't you choose it?

BOB: Some chick gave it to me. Them people in New York got more money than they know what to do with.

NANCY: I called Sal. He said he didn't know where you were. He said you'd left with—

BOB: (*Interrupting*)—what's the big idea callin' Sal?! I don't like people knowin' my business. And I don't like you checkin' up on me!

NANCY: You said you'd be gone three hours. Where *were* you?

BOB: New York. Where you sent me.

NANCY: But Sal said he hadn't—

BOB: (*Interrupting*)—the scene at Sal's strung me out. I didn't dig it. I went to some bars.

NANCY: What didn't you dig?

BOB: The whole scene.

NANCY: You mean the Johns?

BOB: You heard me: everything. Bunch of weird cats, faggots. Good thing Jeannie was around for a change of pace.

NANCY: Was she as good as the guy you left Sal's with?

239

(For a second it looks as if BOB *will hit her. Then* HE *turns toward the bedroom)*

NANCY: Bob, I'm sorry! You make me say these things! You won't *talk* to me!

BOB: Whaddaya wanna say? Say it.

NANCY: I . . . I'm glad you're back . . .

BOB: *(Sarcastic)* Terrific. I may even stay. But I've had some good competitive offers. *(*HE *again turns toward the bedroom)*

NANCY: Glad you found a job you like.

BOB: Oh definitely! This one chick I met can't do enough for me, she—

NANCY: —oh it's chicks now.

BOB: One chick after the other. Three days of it. Even the old repeater rifle finally drew a blank.

NANCY: *(Quietly)* Okay. I guess we can't talk.

BOB: *(Exploding)* What's this big thing you got with *talk?* Talk, talk, talk! You some kinda fuckin' parrot? Polly wanna cracker? Polly wanna cracker?

NANCY: No, Polly doesn't want anything.

BOB: Beautiful! Maybe I can get some rest now.

NANCY: All you want. *(Pause)* Bob, I think you should leave. Maybe one of those "chicks" will take you in.

BOB: Nobody "takes me in," sweetheart. And nobody throws me out. I guess you didn't get the message: I'm back for one reason: to pack my bags. Then it's off to that big beautiful New York pad.

NANCY: Umm. They're big on everything in New York. Especially variety.

BOB: Is that right.

NANCY: Sal sends some of his "clients" a different boy every day.

BOB: You seem to know the whole routine. When did Sal fill you in—on your *second* visit?

NANCY: I told you I went to Sal's.

BOB: You *told* me you met him on the street.

NANCY: Then we went to his apartment.

BOB: That's not how Jeannie remembers it.

NANCY: Since when do you believe Jeannie?

BOB: Since I stopped believing you. You been tellin' me one lie after the other—

NANCY: —*I've* been telling lies! You haven't told *yourself* the truth in so long, you wouldn't know how to tell it to anybody else.

BOB: I know one big truth, baby: New York's up to its ass in money and affection. And I'm about to get my share.

NANCY: *(Bitter)* Affection?! All you want is someone to enjoy you enjoying yourself in the mirror. That ball game's over. It's time for *me* to crinkle my nose real cute at the crowd, shake my fanny —and disappear.

BOB: If you ever shake it in New York, look us up. We'll buy ya a soda pop.

NANCY: You and who else?

BOB: The chick I'm movin' in with. The one who can't do enough for me. The one who buys me all these pretty jackets. The one who's gonna send me to college. The one who—

NANCY: —how big is this chick's cock?

(Pause; BOB fights to control himself)

BOB: About the same size as yours. *(Pause. HE goes to the door)*

NANCY: What . . . what about your—things . . . ?

BOB: I'll buy new ones. I told you: she's rich.

NANCY: You can . . . stay till morning.

BOB: Now's as good a time as any.

NANCY: Suit yourself.

BOB: I'm suiting you. You said you wanted me out.

NANCY: I said I wouldn't put up with any more shit.

BOB: Same thing.

> *(As* BOB *exits, the stage revolves, revealing a dim, noisy bar scene.* BOB *moves into it)*

ACT II

SCENE 3

Most of the characters in the play, in various "disguises," are in the bar.

As BOB *makes his way to the front, several of the* GIRLS *admire him.*

HE *orders a drink.* RAY, *dressed in drag, seats himself on one side of* BOB. BO, *also in drag, sits on the other.* BOB *looks them both over.* HE *shows some interest in* BO.

From another part of the bar, ELLEN *comes boldly up to* BOB, *and starts talking to him.* SHE's *gotten up like a stereotypic dyke—tweedy, severe, no makeup, short hair.*

FRANK DAWSON, *wearing a priest's collar, gets off his bar stool and waves goodbye to* JEANNE, *who's tending bar.*

JEANNE: *(Calling after FRANK)* Have a nice confession, Father!

FRANK *goes out of the bar and crosses the stage toward* PAUL's *apartment.* HE *stops midway and, with his back to the audience, turns his priest's collar into a regular collar with tie.*

BO *and* BOB *start to dance.*

FRANK *enters* PAUL's *apartment. Lights up)*

PAUL: *(Upset)* It must have been because of Ray and Tom.

FRANK: Nobody behaved very well.

PAUL: I don't know why this always happens. Every time I start to care about someone, they disappear.

FRANK: Try it this way: once they disappear, you start to care about them.

PAUL: You'll never understand the attraction of opposites. I keep trying to explain to you that similarities breed friendship; *dis*similarities, love.

FRANK: You grow more theoretical with every year. And they *are* passing. Anyway, there's no getting inside Bob's head. Pathological liars lie so well you can't tell when they're doing it.

(RAY tries to cut in on BO, but BO rebuffs him)

RAY: Greedy little bastard!

PAUL: But *you* can, apparently.

(BO and BOB continue to dance)

FRANK: There is such a thing as trained insight. I have a long background in politics.

(THEY laugh. PAUL gets up to get them another drink)

PAUL: Some of his stories do seem a little far-fetched. Like owning his own construction firm at eighteen.

BO: I love your jacket. You're a regular Joe College, huh?

FRANK: A remarkably mature insight.

PAUL: For me, you mean.

FRANK: Out of little acorns, et cetera. In any case, if he makes up stories, he probably has to. It's called self-defense. You've heard, I trust, of Scylla and Charybdis—otherwise known as you and the wife.

PAUL: Make up your mind! First his stories are "pathological lies," now they're "innocent defenses."

FRANK: The dualistic way you think is irredeemably vulgar. Can't you see the boy's head is crammed with folklore? Most of it, I fear, from the nineteenth century. Poor lad! It must seem to him that you have everything he doesn't.

PAUL: From the soul of cynicism to the soul of compassion.

(FRANK starts to respond)

—yes, I know: your long background in politics.

(BOB shrugs, takes the jacket off and puts it over a bar stool. HE and BO start dancing again. BO unloosens BOB's tie, then slowly begins to unbutton his shirt. As HE does so, BOB gets increasingly passionate. The OTHERS watch the strip. A few of them start tittering among themselves, as if at some private joke)

(BO has BOB's shirt unbuttoned down the front. HE caresses BOB's chest with his hands. BOB tries to feel "her" breasts, but BO coyly slithers away)

LARRY/DON: *(Spanish accent)* Give the kid another—on

(HE *serves the drinks*)

All I know is, I wish he'd come back.

FRANK: He may, he may not. You must learn to be grateful for occasional happiness.

PAUL: He *is* involved with me, even if you don't like the idea.

FRANK: That's clever—turn it into my problem. Of course he likes you. But for what reasons and in what ways?

PAUL: In what ways do *you* like me?

FRANK: Don't be frivolous. I dashed back here in response to your S.O.S., didn't I?

PAUL: You're about to be rewarded. Remember that paratrooper I told you about? He's on his way up here.

FRANK: Incorrigible!

PAUL: I called him after Bob walked out. I can't help it —it steadies my nerves.

FRANK: Then why the hell did you ask *me* back?!

me! Where'd you get them shoes, kid?

(BOB *belts the drink at the bar, then goes after* BO *again*)

(BOB *tries to feel* BO *up.* SHE *holds him tauntingly at arms' length*)

247

PAUL: You both steady my nerves.

FRANK: Two of everything— as always.

BO: Are these what you want, baby?

(BO *strips off his false breasts and tosses them at* BOB. *The bar explodes in laughter.* BOB *is rooted to the spot for a second, then turns and runs.* NED *grabs* BOB's *jacket from the bar stool and goes with it to the door)*

NED: *(Calling after* BOB*)* Hey, Joe College! You forgot something!

(Hilarious, mocking laughter. BLACKOUT*)*

PAUL: Wait'll you see him. Even your puny appetite'll pick up. He's something from the corner of Hadrian's eye. A marvelous body *and* stupid.

FRANK: That's what you said the last time. And the guy turned out to be a seminarian who *(Tone of mock disgust)* taught math to underprivileged children. Needless to say this Adonis has not been invited here to meet me. At best, I'm to get the mortal remains.

PAUL: Why must you put everything in the worst light?

FRANK: Because it's the one in which I find you constantly bathed.

248

(The buzzer rings)

PAUL: Oops! Himself.

FRANK: This better be good.

PAUL: I wish you'd try to remember that you came back here to comfort me.

FRANK: I wish you'd try to remember that you need it.

(PAUL opens the door)

PAUL: Hi, Dave. Good to see you again.

DAVE: Sheet-it, man, you're somethin' else! You ready to go *again?!*

PAUL: Come on in. A friend of mine is here.

(Spot up on BOB *in a phone booth)*

(DAVE enters the apartment. HE's dressed in full paratrooper uniform; muscular, crew cut, slow of speech and movement, vaguely threatening in manner. HE's played by the same actor cast as NED*)*

BOB: *(Into receiver)* Hello, Sal? . . . It's me, Bob . . . *(Controlled fury)* Don't hassle me, man. You got somebody to send me to, or not? . . . I don't care what the scene is—I'll take it . . .

PAUL: I'd like you to meet Frank. This is Dave.

(As BOB *starts to jot down the address, the spot on him goes out)*

(FRANK gets out of his chair. HE's obviously pleased at the sight of DAVE*)*

FRANK: Very glad to meet you, Dave.

DAVE: Likewise.

PAUL: Why don't you make yourself comfortable. I'll get you a beer. It is beer you drink, right?

(DAVE *takes off his coat*)

DAVE: Nah. Nuthin' right now.

PAUL: Nothing at all?

DAVE: I'm a little piped, man.

FRANK: Tough day?

DAVE: You betta believe it. Twisted. Spaced. Hey—you got anything to smoke, man?

PAUL: Sorry. Never touch the stuff.

(DAVE *laughs*)

DAVE: Too old, huh?

PAUL: It doesn't agree with me.

DAVE: It don't do *what* with you?

PAUL: It makes my legs feel rubbery.

DAVE: Man, it makes everything rubbery. That's the point.

PAUL: I used to keep some hidden in the bookshelf for friends. But someone told me my connection was about to be arrested. So I flushed it all down the toilet.

DAVE: *(Horrified)* You what? Ooooh-eee! How much you flush, man?

PAUL: About an ounce.

(DAVE *rolls his eyes in horror*)

DAVE: I betta have that drink.

PAUL: Beer?

DAVE: Why not.

(PAUL *goes to get the beer*)

FRANK: Do you smoke on the base?

(DAVE *laughs*)

DAVE: Nah. That's for Veet.

FRANK: Veet?

DAVE: *(Impatient)* Veetnam, man, Veetnam. Ain't you heard there's been a war?

FRANK: Oh—Vietnam.

DAVE: You got it! Darvon's the big scene on base.

FRANK: Darvon?

DAVE: *(Turning to* PAUL*)* Hey, where'd you find this dude, baby? He sure don't know much.

(PAUL *puts the beer in front of* DAVE)

PAUL: *(Smiling at* FRANK*)* Actually Frank's a very intelligent man, Dave. It's just that he doesn't keep up.

(FRANK *explodes into his drink; some of it spills*)

DAVE: Nervous little fellah, too. *(To* FRANK*)* You oughta take somethin' for steadyin', man. *(Starts reaching into his coat pocket)* I could let you in on a little Darvon, cut rate.

FRANK: What *is* Darvon?

DAVE: It's a painkiller, baby. Most of the base is on it.

PAUL: *(To* FRANK*)* Unless I'm mistaken, you just got a lead for one of your better columns.

DAVE: Sure wish y'all would talk English.

FRANK: What's your outfit?

DAVE: You blind, too, man? *(Pointing to his insignia)* I'm airborne. Just finished basic. It's them six-mile hikes, baby. Uphill. Every day. Didn't have Darvon, I'd flip out. You know how your piss smells after you eat asparagus?

FRANK: Beg pardon?

DAVE: Well, it smells worse after you drop Darvon.

FRANK: Worse than asparagus. Imagine.

PAUL: How do you get the stuff?

DAVE: Sick bay. Orderlies cop it. One dude took five thousand caps. Made himself a nice bundle.

(FREEZE. BLACKOUT. *Cross-fade to a semidark room*)

ACT II

SCENE 4

A mirror covered with bits of gold foil hangs from the ceiling by wire, downstage right. Hanging downstage left is a large poster of "The Sunkist Orange Girl," a smiling bathing beauty sitting on a wooden crate labeled "Sunkist" and holding an orange in each hand. BOB *enters the room, followed by* HAROLD, *a drab, paunchy, middle-aged man, reserved and furtive;* HE*'s played by the same actor cast as* TOM.

HAROLD: See, here it is. Right across the hall from the apartment.

BOB: Uh-huh. *(Looking around apprehensively)* How come there's no furniture?

HAROLD: It's the rumpus room.

BOB: Huh?

HAROLD: The game room. If you have furniture, there's no space to play.

BOB: I like your apartment better.

HAROLD: Things would break. The lamps and all.

BOB: Listen, man, I don't think I can go through with this.

HAROLD: Sure you can! A big, strong college boy like you.

BOB: I'm only in my first year.

HAROLD: But you are on the team.

BOB: What team?

HAROLD: Any team.

BOB: Sure, sure. All the teams.

HAROLD: Name the teams.

BOB: Oh, listen, man—

HAROLD: —name one, just one.

BOB: Football.

HAROLD: You're on the football team. The football team.

BOB: Yeah, I'm a big football star.

HAROLD: You're the star of the college football team. You're the
quarterback. *(HE puts his hand on BOB's bicep)* You've got a
strong arm. A strong pitching arm.

BOB: Yeah, so the wife tells me.

HAROLD: You got to be fast, too. You got to pitch *fast*.

BOB: Look, man, all this other stuff . . . I mean I don't mind if we
play around a little, you know . . . *(HE moves his hand as if
HE's going to put it on HAROLD's crotch)*

HAROLD: *(Almost screaming)* Don't touch me! That's not what you're
paid for!

BOB: *(Guiltily)* Touch what? You're dreamin', man. *(Makes a move
as if to leave)* Let's forget the whole thing, huh? Sal can send
somebody else down to—

HAROLD: —oh no, I like you! I like you a lot. You've got wonderful
arms. I'm going to pay you well. Really well. Five dollars a hit.

254

(Giggles) It isn't easy. I'm a fancy stepper. Now you wait one second. *(Goes behind a screen downstage left)* You're going to *like* it. You'll see. It's fun.

BOB: *(Surly)* How'd you get into this bag?

HAROLD: *(From behind screen)* It was part of my cure.

BOB: Huh?

HAROLD: Aversion therapy.

BOB: Whaddaya talkin' about? *(Starts to pace nervously)*

HAROLD: Oh I'd tried everything: analysis, drug therapy, nude whirlpool baths—everything.

(Throws a filmy negligee over the screen. BOB stops pacing and stares at it)

BOB: You gonna put *that* on?

HAROLD: It's up to you. Some of the boys get more of a kick that way. That's why I bring it along.

BOB: I don't dig it.

HAROLD: What does turn you on?

BOB: Nuthin'.

HAROLD: *(Giggling)* That's the one thing I can't do. *(Gesturing to negligee)* I'll just leave it there. *(HE leaves the negligee on the screen, continues changing clothes)* You see, I had this fetish. I used to assault prams.

BOB: Who?

HAROLD: Perambulators. *(Pause)* You're sure you're a college boy?

BOB: That's right.

HAROLD: Mmm. Anyway, it got serious. Some prams have babies in them. So they decided to try aversion therapy on me.

BOB: Uh-huh. *(Starts pacing more rapidly)*

HAROLD: The doctors stood me on an electric grid, and every time they flashed a picture of a pram, they gave me a shock in my feet. *(Giggles)* But I got to like the shocks. So they switched to apomorphine injections. Those I *didn't* like. They made me throw up. So whenever they flashed a pram on the—

BOB: *(Interrupting)* —listen, man, I don't want to hear this shit.

HAROLD: *You* asked.

BOB: The oranges. I asked about the oranges. I don't want to hear all—

HAROLD: —I'm getting to that. You see, the doctors weren't satisfied at making me vomit at the sight of prams. They wanted me to like girls, too. So they started to show me pictures of her. *(Nods toward the Sunkist poster girl)* They played beautiful music and made me masturbate. But it didn't quite work out the way they planned. *(Emerges from behind the screen, dressed in a bathing suit just like the one worn by the poster girl.* BOB *does a double take)* I got hung up on the wrong things.

BOB: Holy shit!

HAROLD: Now you come over here. *(Drags wooden crate out from the shadows)* This is all for you. *(Opens crate, reaches in, and takes out two oranges. Holds them up for* BOB *to see)* Aren't they *wonderful!*

BOB: They're oranges.

HAROLD: Squishy and ripe. Here. For you. *(Puts the oranges in* BOB*'s hands)*

BOB: They're soft.

HAROLD: More juice that way. *(Moves back toward screen)* Now we're all ready. *(Flicks on stereo hidden behind the screen. "The Indian Love Call" starts playing)* Stay to the left, so you don't block the mirror. I like to watch myself. *(Starts to preen before the mirror. Puts on a big smile—like the poster girl's)*

BOB: Do you . . . uh . . . make any noise?

HAROLD: Sometimes.

BOB: I want you to cheer.

HAROLD: Cheer?

BOB: I want you to cheer me on.

HAROLD: *(Thrilled)* Oh this is going to be a good one!

BOB: *(Nodding toward the negligee)* And put that . . . that thing on.

HAROLD: *Sure! (Slips on the negligee, looks at himself in the mirror, then looks at the poster. Frowns)* It's not like the real thing.

BOB: Wear it.

(HAROLD *grins*)

HAROLD: You sound so mean. *(Taunting)* I'm going to take it off. *(Drops negligee from his shoulders)*

BOB: You better wear it, you cunt.

HAROLD: Such talk! I don't believe you're a college boy at all. So there! *(Dances provocatively in front of mirror. Then cracks a popper and starts to sniff it)*

BOB: Tell me your name.

HAROLD: I don't have a name.

BOB: I want to know your name. *(Brings his arm back to throw)*

HAROLD: La-la. That's my name: la-la! I'm ready! I'm ready!

BOB: I know your name, you cunt. Your name's Nancy.

HAROLD: *(Defiant)* La-La!

BOB: Tell me your name's Nancy!

HAROLD: *La-La!!*

BOB: Cheer me, you motherfucker!

(As HE *throws the orange and* HAROLD *gives a shriek of pleasure,*

BLACKOUT)

ACT II

SCENE 5

Lights back up in PAUL's *apartment.* THEY UNFREEZE *in the middle of conversation.*

DAVE: . . . I met him through Sal. He wants to write a story about me. But I'm worried, man. I got this doubt: maybe the cat's a Communist. Man, I don't want that on my conscience.

FRANK: *(Almost an aside)* Better that than nothing.

DAVE: Say what, man?

PAUL: *(To change the subject)* When do you finish training?

DAVE: Week after next. Got a five-day leave to see my chick in Cincinnati, then it's San Fran and the wild blue yonder.

FRANK: Sounds like you're looking forward to it.

DAVE: Not lookin' for or against. It's a job. Somebody's gotta do it. Do you know them women and kids over there is still comin' right up to our people and tossin' grenades at 'em? They smile real pretty at ya and then—boom! half your head's gone. We gotta get that job *done*. *(Looks at his watch; then to* PAUL*)* Hey, I don't wanna rush the scene, man, but Sal's fixed my next for one, and it's way downtown.

FRANK: *(Getting up)* I guess I'm leaving.

DAVE: Don't split on my account. *(Shrugs)* Shee-it, we can all do it together.

FRANK: That's very generous of you. But Paul's not my type.

PAUL: *Now* you tell me, after all these years.

DAVE: Suit yisself. *(To* PAUL*)* Hey, I gotta use ya head, man.

PAUL: It's the first door to the right.

(DAVE holds out his hand to FRANK: THEY *shake)*

DAVE: Good meetin' ya, man. Do yisself a favor and get into some Darvon. It's heavy stuff.

FRANK: Fine. I'll do that.

DAVE: See ya round.

(DAVE goes offstage to the bathroom. As HE *does,* FRANK *rolls his eyes toward the ceiling while* PAUL *suppresses a giggle)*

FRANK: You've really surpassed yourself this time.

PAUL: Isn't he amazing?

FRANK: That's hardly the word. He's prehistoric.

PAUL: You should see the body.

FRANK: I hope to. But do me one favor: *don't tamper with his ideas.* He'll lose half his charm if you infect him with your liberal jargon.

(As FRANK *is about to open the door, the apartment buzzer rings)*

PAUL: Oh Christ—don't tell me—?!

FRANK: You see how your patience has been rewarded.

PAUL: Sit down. You've got to stay.

FRANK: Why?

PAUL: If it *is* Bob, Dave is with you. He's *your* trick.

FRANK: Now that idea I like.

PAUL: *(Opening the door)* Well! . . . back already . . .

(BOB enters the room)

BOB: Decided not to go to Jersey. *(HE catches sight of FRANK)* —oh, you came back, too, huh?

PAUL: Frank stopped by for a minute with a friend. He's in the paratroopers.

FRANK: *(Pointing over his shoulder)* He's in the bathroom. Been telling us that everyone in his outfit uses Darvon.

BOB: What's Darvon?

FRANK: Some kind of painkiller. Maybe he said brain, not pain.

PAUL: What a way to talk about your new love.

FRANK: That's *why* he's my new love. All you smart people are look-alikes. *(DAVE comes back into the room)* Ah! Here he is. Dave, I'd like you to meet Bob. Bob, I'd like you to meet Dave.

BOB: Hello.

DAVE: Whaddaya say, man. What's happ'nin'? Instead of one leaving, one comes.

BOB: *(To DAVE)* Who was leaving?

(DAVE opens his mouth to answer, but PAUL breaks in)

PAUL: *(To BOB)* Me. I was leaving. *(Attempt at humor)* Thought I'd let the kids have the place to themselves for a half hour—you know.

FRANK: Yes—right! My sister and her husband are in from Long Island. They're using my apartment.

PAUL: *(Desperate for laughs)* Actually, your sister might enjoy Dave.

FRANK: As I've said, I'm not much for threesomes.

DAVE: *(To* FRANK *)* That's why you was leavin', you said you didn't dig threesomes. *(Looking at* BOB *)* You like foursomes better, huh? *(Shrugs)* Okay by me.

BOB: *(To* FRANK *)* So *you* were leaving.

FRANK: Well, no. I . . . er . . . Dave misunderstood. I was going down for some cigarettes, that's all.

DAVE: Man, where is your head *at!!* Oooh-ooh! I never seen such spells.

PAUL: *(To* BOB *)* There's been a misunderstanding.

BOB: Yeah, I guess so.

PAUL: I know what you're thinking, but it's not true.

BOB: It's no big deal. You do what you have to do. I know what that's like.

FRANK: *(Standing up)* At this point I guess I can go.

DAVE: You takin' off again?! Man, you got a strange bag! In and out. In and out.

FRANK: It's from the war, Dave. My nerves.

DAVE: *(Grave)* Figured t'be sumpthin' like that. *(Pause)* We got to get that job *done*. Once'n for all.

FRANK: Why don't you come along with me?

DAVE: Who, me? Hell, that's up to Paul. *(Big grin)* He's my official score.

FRANK: *(To* PAUL *)* Well?

PAUL: *(Ambivalent; stalling)* Dave's a free agent.

DAVE: Don't matter to me where the thirty comes from.

PAUL: *(To* BOB *)* Are you staying?

BOB: I dunno.

(For a second ALL FOUR *are suspended)*

FRANK: Well, *I'm* going home. *Anyone* care to come?

(Pause)

DAVE: *(Looking at his watch)* Guess I'll stay, man. Ain't no time left to shift pads.

(PAUL starts to get up. FRANK waves him back to his chair)

FRANK: Don't bother. I can see myself out.

PAUL: Thanks for coming over.

FRANK: I'd say "you're welcome" but it wouldn't ring true. *(Looking at BOB and DAVE)* If only I could convince you that less is more.

DAVE: Take care of those nerves, man.

FRANK: Take care of that pain, baby. *(Exits)*

PAUL: *(Embarrassed)* Well, who wants a drink?

BOB: Not for me.

DAVE: Can't hack it.

(Pause)

BOB: *(To PAUL)* I'm gonna take a walk.

PAUL: Another one?!

BOB: I can come back later.

PAUL: It would be nice if you'd stay in one mood for five minutes.

DAVE: What time is it, man?

PAUL: Twelve-twenty.

DAVE: I'm supposed to be at West Ninth Street by one. *(Rummaging in his pocket)* Where's that address Sal gimme?

BOB: Oh, Sal sent you here.

DAVE: Yeah! You know Sal?

BOB: Sure.

PAUL: *(Nervously)* You know, it takes nearly half an hour to get downtown, Dave.

DAVE: Hell; one, one-thirty. It don't matter. *(Pointing to BOB)* I like your buddy here. He's together, man. *(To BOB)* How come you know Sal?

262

BOB: He's a friend of my wife's.

DAVE: Oh yeah? I met him through a chick, too! A cunt named Jeannie.

BOB: I know Jeannie.

DAVE: Hey—good piece of ass, huh?

BOB: We never made it.

DAVE: Well do yourself a favor . . . that cunt's an oreo cookie, man —white on the outside, black on the inside! *(To* BOB*)* Hey, this wife of yours, man—she's a good looker?

BOB: That's right.

DAVE: What I'm gettin' at, man—Sal don't deal in chicks, too, does he? I mean, like Jeannie done it for nuthin'.

BOB: What are you trying to say?

DAVE: Don't get uptight, baby! It's like I figured maybe your old lady was out working for ya.

BOB: *(Quiet anger)* She's not.

DAVE: Shit, man, everybody's sellin' somethin'. You gotta use what the good Lord gave ya. *(Grabs his crotch and shakes it)* Me, I'm lucky. He gave me a lot. *(Laughs)* Right, Paul?

PAUL: Mmm.

DAVE: Don't be shy, man! *(Pointing to* BOB*)* He's a buddy, right? *(To* BOB*)* Man, he damn near wore me out yesterday.

BOB: Oh yeah?

DAVE: Yeah, he was number two. Almost didn't make my third.

BOB: You're a big stud, huh?

DAVE: Shee-it, man, I'm down to five times a day. *(Laughs; to* BOB*)* Hey, you ain't a John, are you?

BOB: Maybe. I'll ask my wife.

PAUL: What's that mean?

BOB: Smart lady. Knows lotsa things.

DAVE: Well shee-it, man, in this town you never can tell. Last night Sal sent me to this John, I'm telling you, he wasn't twenty-two years old. Good lookin' kid, too. Big mop of blond hair on'm. Said he modeled in magazines. *(Chuckles)* Sure dug my uniform. Wunt let me take it off. Not even when we was doin' it! I scratched him on the chest with my good conduct medal here. He grooved on that, too. *(Shrugs)* Maybe the kid's a Communist. He laid fifty bucks on me.

BOB: You meet all kinds in New York.

DAVE: Hey, man: how about some music?

PAUL: You feel like it, Bob?

BOB: I don't care.

> *(PAUL gets up and goes to the stereo)*

DAVE: Put on that thing from yesterday. That cool nigger. You know—Otey, Otey somebody.

PAUL: Otis Redding.

DAVE: That's it! Otey Redding. Ain't he somethin' else, man?! Can't beat them niggers for soul. Once had me this chick—she was part Cherokee—wunt let me ball her 'less we had the nigger music goin'. We'd ball all night on it. Till that station went off the air.

BOB: *(Hostility showing)* No shit.

DAVE: *(Catching the tone)* You tryin' to signify something?

BOB: Not a thing.

DAVE: You ain't doubtin' my word, are ya, man?

BOB: I take it as it comes.

> *(Otis Redding's "Let Me Come on Home" starts to play;* PAUL *comes back to his chair)*

DAVE: *(Closes his eyes)* Yah, that's the one. Groovy! I can see me and that little Cherokee now. Um-hmm-m! What a sweet little pussy. *(To PAUL)* Hey, man: You got any pictures?

PAUL: No.

DAVE: That little blond fella last night, he had this film—ooh-eee! The chick in it couldn'ta been more'n fourteen. She took on three dudes at once. They was in and out of every openin' she had. Man, what a groove! Damn near shot ma load before little blondy could get to it. *(Pause; then to* PAUL*)* Hey, man—you know it's hot in here. (HE *gets up and starts to take off his shirt*)

PAUL: *(Nervous)* It's getting late, Dave. It's close to one.

DAVE: Shee-it, man, so what? They love to wait. It make 'em itchy and nervous. Then when I get there, they're extra grateful. *(To* PAUL*)* Now look at you. I was late gettin' here tonight, and you so thrilled you still twitchin' all over. (DAVE *has his shirt off and begins to move slowly to the music)* Ooh, listen to that nigger move it, man! *(Starts to sing the lyrics along with the record)* "Baby, baby, baby, baby, oh let me come on home, oh let me come on home." (HE *grabs* PAUL *as if he's going to dance with him, then veers off laughing, continuing his solo. To* BOB*)* Whatsa matter, man? Don't you dig dancin'?

BOB: Not alone.

DAVE: You want a chick, huh?

BOB: That's right.

DAVE: Well, shee-it, man, you gotta learn to make do. If your chick ain't here, you use what is.

BOB: You askin' me to dance?

*(*DAVE *stops abruptly)*

DAVE: Say that again.

BOB: I don't dance with men.

DAVE: *(Threatening)* Say, you're a pretty funny fellah.

PAUL: Take it easy, Dave. Bob misunderstood you, that's all.

BOB: No, I didn't.

PAUL: *(Emphatically)* Yes, you did.

DAVE: I'd like to hear *him* say that.

BOB: You heard me: I don't dance with men.

PAUL: *(To BOB, angrily)* What the hell are you trying to pull?

DAVE: *(Starting to move toward BOB)* You askin' for it, baby.

BOB: *(Bringing up his hands)* Any time. I'm supposed to tell you, I'm a black belt. You know about karate, right? We pledge to warn people, so they only got themselves to blame if they break up like firewood.

PAUL: You're out of your mind! You're no black belt and you know it! What kind of crazy lie is that?!

BOB: *(Quietly)* You're one to talk about lying.

PAUL: *(Moving between DAVE and BOB)* Lying or no lying, I've had enough of this. *(To both of them)* Now cut it out, you hear. Just cut it out. *(Goes over to DAVE and tries to coax him into a chair)* Come on, Dave, huh? This is getting out of hand. Why don't you put your shirt back on and we'll just forget the whole thing.

DAVE: So he don't know karate, huh? *(Laughs)* How about that? I'll put my shirt on when I get an apology. I ain't movin' till then.

PAUL: *(To BOB)* Bob, it doesn't have to be any big deal. Just say you misunderstood. It's as simple as that.

BOB: *(Almost to himself)* Everybody keeps tellin' me how simple everything is. *(Pause)* I got nothing to apologize for. *(Pause)*

PAUL: *(To BOB)* All right. Then I'll have to ask you to leave.

BOB: *(Quietly)* Oh you want me to leave, huh? You're kickin' me out.

PAUL: I'm not going to have any fighting in here. I'm asking you to leave, that's all. Later on, maybe, when things have—

BOB: *(Interrupting; then mounting fury)* —later on, maybe? Oh, that's beautiful, man. That's really beautiful. Later on, maybe. You mean like after he's shoved his cock up your ass, huh? I'll give you later on, man. I'll give you— *(HE lunges at PAUL and throws*

266

him to the ground. DAVE *jumps in, grabs* BOB *from the back, and starts beating on him.* PAUL, *freed from* BOB's *grip, gets up. There's blood on his forehead)*

PAUL: *(Shouting)* Get him out of here, Dave! Get him out of here! The goddamned fool! *(*DAVE *and* BOB *continue to scuffle, with* DAVE *getting the better of it.* PAUL *begins to cool off.* HE *sees that* BOB *is getting beaten up)* Dave, okay. That's enough, Dave. Stop it! Dave, *stop it! (*PAUL *grabs* DAVE *from the back and manages to drag him off* BOB*)* Cut it out, Dave! That's enough! Help me get him out of here, that's all. Just help me get him out of here . . .

DAVE: *(Still struggling)* Fuckin' little queer! I'll break you in half, you goddamn puke-pot!

*(*BOB *is badly hurt.* HE *struggles to get up. As* HE *does so,* PAUL *and* DAVE *half drag him toward the door. While doing so* DAVE *lands a few more punches)*

PAUL: No more, Dave! That's enough, damn it!

BOB: *(To* PAUL, *mumbling; barely audible)* You liar! You goddamn liar!

DAVE: *(To* BOB*)* Fuckin' fairy face! I'll break your two-inch cock off and shove it in your mouth!

*(*THEY *are at the door)*

PAUL: *(To* DAVE*) Leave him alone!* Don't touch him, you hear me! Don't touch him!

*(*PAUL *opens the door. As* THEY *push* BOB *out,* DAVE *lands one last blow at* BOB's *groin)*

DAVE: There you go, man! Now you got a real coutchee 'stead of a cock. You can get fucked proper!

PAUL: *(Screaming)* You bastard! Let him alone!!!

*(*PAUL *violently pushes* DAVE *away.* DAVE *retreats, laughing.* BOB *is now outside the door.* PAUL *starts to close it)*

BOB: *(Feebly)* You lied to me.

PAUL: I didn't . . . I didn't mean to . . .

(BOB *pushes him away, furiously*)

BOB: You motherfucker. (HE *lurches out*)

PAUL: *You're* the liar. It's your fault, not mine. It's *your* fault. (PAUL *closes the door, then leans against it, breathing heavily*)

DAVE: That punk! I shoulda cold-konked him all over this floor. Wiped up his little ass!

PAUL: *(Still at the door, his back to* DAVE*)* Shut up, Dave, huh? Just shut up for a minute.

DAVE: *(Muttering)* Tryin' to test me! Black belt in karate! *(Snorts)* What a laugh! He's lucky he got outta here alive! (PAUL *moves from door to window.* HE *raises the shade high enough so* HE *can look out*) Whaddaya up to now?

PAUL: *(Quietly)* I'm watching to see he leaves the building. *(Pause; voice choked)* I'm watching to see . . . Dumb kid . . .

DAVE: Dumb ain't the word, man. That cat's tryin' to get some chest. He looked to the wrong man.

PAUL: I don't want to hear anymore . . . Stop it . . . stop it . . .

DAVE: You tryin' to tell me that cat's got a wife?! Oo-ee! Two'll get you three *she* fucks *him!* (DAVE *breaks up at his own joke. Then a considerable pause.* PAUL *remains at the window*) Well, whatta ya say, man? You gonna stand there all night? I'm in business, baby.

(PAUL *doesn't answer*)

Hey!

PAUL: *(Quietly)* What?

DAVE: If we're gonna do the scene, man, let's do it. I gotta be downtown, remember?

PAUL: Yes . . . I remember.

(Pause)

268

DAVE: Well? *Yes* or *no?* I ain't got all night.

(*Pause. The record starts playing Redding's "The Glory of Love"*)

Hey, man, are you hearin' me?

PAUL: I hear you.

DAVE: Make up your mind. (*Pause*)

PAUL: (*Quietly*) Go in the bedroom. I'll be right in.

DAVE: Well make it snappy. (*Laughs; goes over to the stereo and turns the volume up loud*)

> (RECORD: *That's the story of*
> *That's the glory of,*
> *Luh-huh-ove . . .*
>
> *When this whole world*
> *Gets tired of us,*
> *We'll have each other . . .*
> *Yeah, yeah, yeah . . .)*

DAVE: (*To the record*) Sock it in there, baby!

(DAVE *half dances his way toward the bedroom;* HE *starts playing with himself;* PAUL *remains standing at the window*)

You wanna know somethin'? I'm half hard already. Fights do that to me.

(*As* HE *exits to the bedroom, the* RECORD *plays:*
> *Cry a little*
> *Sigh just a little*
> *Let that old wind just blow right by*
> *a little,*
> *That's the story of,*
> *That's the glory of,*
> *Luh-huh-ove . . .)*

(*Lights cross-fade between* PAUL*'s apartment and* SAL*'s*)

ACT II

SCENE 6

3:00 A.M., the same night. JEANNE *is lying on the couch, her eyes closed.* SAL *is completing a phone call.*

SAL: *(Into receiver)* Yeah, I knew you'd like him, Mr. Drew . . . *(Laughs)* Right—a born lifer . . . Glad you enjoyed it . . . Just put it in the mail to me . . . You're welcome. Talk to you soon. *(SAL hangs up receiver, then yawns)* I guess that's it for tonight. *(Looks at his watch)* It's after three. *(Goes to the desk)*

JEANNE: Shall I put the cat out?

SAL: Baby, you can put the whole thing out. *(SAL starts going through some papers on his desk.* JEANNE *looks over at him)*

JEANNE: *(Mock seriousness)* I worry about you, Salva*tore*. All work and no play. A lad your age should be out having fun with the rest of the boys. Bowling or playing darts.

(SAL *laughs*)

SAL: You gotta find a purpose in life. Mine's cost accounting. *(Pause)* Listen, why don't you turn in? I got some paper work to finish up. (JEANNE *opens her eyes wide, puts her hand to her brow*)

JEANNE: *(Soap opera voice)* Oh God, what's happening to our marriage?! Is it my fault all our children turned out to be *female?* I've tried to make it up to you. I've brought boy after boy into this house. But not one has been able to find his way to your heart.

SAL: Quite a few have reached my pocketbook.

JEANNE: Oh, what I'd give to have those early years back again! Just you and me—and "A" Company from Fort Dix—curled up in front of the fire, doing our thing. *(THEY laugh. The apartment buzzer rings)* It's "A" Company! They've come back! They've come back!

SAL: It's Dave, dropping off some bread. *(SAL goes to the door and presses the buzzer)* That's one hard-working boy.

JEANNE: Bad bit of baggage, if you ask me. But I won't tell him so until *after* our nightly calisthenics.

SAL: Forget it, baby. He's been on five calls in thirty-six hours. It's all gone to the paying customers. And *two* of them've been Paul Webber.

JEANNE: *Two?*

SAL: He asked Dave back again tonight. Doesn't think I know.

JEANNE: He's probably embarrassed. I know the feeling.

SAL: Balls! He's trying to chisel. But my boys are loyal.

JEANNE: *(Sarcastic)* Yeah—like Bob.

SAL: Bob's got his values confused.

JEANNE: Meaning he's got more than one?

(SAL *opens the door to the apartment.* NANCY *is standing there*)

SAL: Well for cryin' out—

(NANCY *brushes past him*)

NANCY: That's right, it's me.

JEANNE: Well, well, wife of our hero. What brings you into the big city?

NANCY: The morning air.

(SAL *closes the door and comes back into the room*)

SAL: What the hell's the idea, Nancy? It's three o'clock in the morning.

JEANNE: *(Almost to herself)* Time for a warm bath, Jeannie m'girl. (JEANNE *starts for the bedroom*)

NANCY: *(To* JEANNE*)* Where do you think you're going?

JEANNE: *(Flaring)* Wherever I want to. And without your permission.

NANCY: *(Softer)* I'd like you to stay.

JEANNE: Are you asking or telling?

NANCY: Asking.

JEANNE: Okay. *(Moves back toward the couch)*

SAL: Now look, I told you on the phone twenty times: I don't know where Bob is.

NANCY: I do. What I want now is the address.

JEANNE: What?—Sal give a free address!

NANCY: Could you cut the jokes?

JEANNE: If you give me a reason.

NANCY: Because they aren't funny.

JEANNE: That's good enough.

NANCY: I want the truth, Sal. I'm tired of the run-around.

SAL: *(Getting angry)* Don't hang tough with me. You're outmatched. I told you the truth: Bob left here with a John three nights ago and *that's it!* *(Quieting down)* He's been a real disappointment. There are a few things about him you forgot to tell me—like he doesn't know where he's at two hours out of three.

JEANNE: And the third hour he's trying to get there.

NANCY: *(To JEANNE)* We can't all live off our "cousins"—or anybody else who comes along.

JEANNE: You got it all wrong, sweetheart. I do it for fun, not money. Like Bob.

NANCY: *(Stunned)* Where'd you get a crazy—

JEANNE: *(Kindly)* C'mon, Nance. The only one *not* in on the "secret" is Bob. And he isn't going to be. You tried. It's time to move on.

NANCY: *(Crumbling; attempt at defiance)* I hear you managed to have him yourself a few times.

JEANNE: *(Shaking her head "no")* Uh-uh, I won't bite. Look, Nance: enough. I like your spunk. Do something else with it now. You can't make a man by yanking the balls off a boy.

(Drained, NANCY sits)

NANCY: I figured things couldn't get worse.

JEANNE: You were right. They won't get better, either. A bomb can't detonate unless it hits something solid. *(The apartment buzzer rings)*

JEANNE: Now what—the Mounties?

SAL: Must be Dave.

JEANNE: Just what we need—sweet, loving Dave.

(SAL goes to the door)

JEANNE: *(To NANCY)* Why don't you have a drink, or some coffee?

NANCY: Mmm. Coffee would be good. Thanks, Jeanne.

(JEANNE starts for the kitchen. SAL opens the apartment door. BOB is leaning against it, barely standing, blood on his face and clothes)

SAL: Jesus Christ! Give me a hand, quick!

BOB: *(Half smile; punchy)* Hey, Sal, whaddaya say? It's me, the Sunkist Orange man.

(NANCY sees BOB and jumps up)

NANCY: Oh my God—Bob!

BOB: Well, well, a regular family reunion. Rah-rah, sis-boom-bah, Ridgeway, Ridgeway, rah! rah! rah! *(HE starts to laugh in a crazy way)*

(JEANNE comes out of the kitchen)

JEANNE: Oh no!

BOB: Hey, Jeannie babe!

JEANNE: Bob, what happened?!

BOB: *(Gesturing toward NANCY)* Get her outta here.

SAL: *(To JEANNE)* Help me get him to the couch. *(To NANCY)* Get his jacket off.

BOB: Then *I'll* leave.

JEANNE: You're not going anywhere. Now lie down.

NANCY: He's got blood all over him.

BOB: Yeah—some dude asked me to dance. *(To NANCY)* You'd dig him—a real good talker.

(JEANNE is about to lift BOB's feet on the couch)

SAL: Watch his feet, Jeanne! He's got his shoes on.

JEANNE: For Christ's sake, Sal! I'll re-cover your goddamn couch!

(BOB struggles against lying down)

274

BOB: No, no, leave me alone. I don't want to lie down. *(HE sits upright on the couch, his head in his hands)*

JEANNE: Lean your head back, Bob. Nancy, go get a wet cloth.

(NANCY moves toward the kitchen. SHE suddenly feels faint and leans against a chair. JEANNE sees her and rushes over to hold her up)

JEANNE: *(Kindly)* C'mon, c'mon, we got enough trouble. Just hold on.

(NANCY nods)

(As BOB is about to put his head on the back of the couch, SAL stops him and slips a handkerchief under BOB's head)

SAL: Juanita's gonna have a fit.

(NANCY is now okay. SHE goes to get the cloth)

SAL: *(To BOB)* Now what the hell happened to you?!

BOB: Some Communist scratched me with his Good Conduct Medal. *(HE laughs)* Fuck him if he can't take a joke!

JEANNE: *(To SAL)* Ho-hum, a day in the life.

BOB: *(Barely audible)* Hey, Sal?

SAL: Yeah?

BOB: Is that guy Dave a friend of yours?

SAL: Is *that* what happened?!

BOB: He tried to fuck with me, man. *(Laughs feebly)* Pressed the wrong button. Paul and I were just havin' a friendly argument.

SAL: *(Angry)* So you *were* at Paul's.

BOB: Paul? Paul who? *(Starts laughing)*

JEANNE: *(To SAL)* Don't ever doubt my word again. As Bo said: Pisces, the prophet.

(NANCY comes back with the wet cloth. SHE starts to clean BOB's face with it)

SAL: *(With disgust)* What a mess.

BOB: *(To* NANCY*)* What are you doin' here?

NANCY: I don't know.

BOB: Checkin' up, as always. *(*HE *pushes her away)* Leave me alone. I'm awright.

NANCY: Yeah, you're great, just great.

BOB: Somebody ran over my karate belt. *(Starts to laugh again)*

JEANNE: Take it easy, Bob . . . take it easy.

(BOB *looks at the blood on the cloth)*

BOB: Oh man, I'm out of shape. *(*HE *shakes his head groggily, then starts to lean back on the couch.* HE *catches sight of the handkerchief)* What the hell is that?

JEANNE: It's a doily. Sal's lace-curtain Italian.

(SAL, *annoyed, looks at his watch)*

NANCY: *(To* BOB*)* You want some coffee?

BOB: *(Ignoring her)* You got a beer, Sal?

SAL: You've had enough beer. The party's over. And I mean *over!*

BOB: Fuck him if he can't take a joke.

SAL: It's three-thirty. And we got only two beds.

JEANNE: You can stay with me, Nancy. Bob can sleep on the couch.

BOB: *(To* JEANNE*)* Bullshit. *I'm* sleeping with you. Dave tells me how good you are.

JEANNE: *(Angry)* Is that right. *(*SHE *gets up)* If anybody dies during the night, don't wake me. I got a big audition tomorrow.

BOB: *(Softer)* Hey, Jeannie?

JEANNE: Well?

BOB: I'm sorry, babe. You're a good kid.

JEANNE: Mmm. We're all good kids. That's one way of looking at it. *(To* NANCY*)* But sometimes kids just aren't enough.

NANCY: Goodbye, Jeanne.

*(*JEANNE *exits)*

SAL: Well? What's it going to be? I gotta lock up.

BOB: When you gonna start sellin' chicks, Sal? You know my wife here's a real good-looker.

SAL: That's what she said about you. Once bitten, twice shy.

BOB: While she's workin' off the bills, I could be goin' to college. I'm college material. Bet you didn't know that. *(Laughs again)*

NANCY: I'll go to a hotel.

BOB: A good idea at last.

NANCY: Do you have any money?

BOB: Nope. Couldn't resist that last blonde.

NANCY: You used to be able to get it for free.

BOB: That was before I met you.

NANCY: Maybe now your luck'll pick up again. *(*SHE *gets up)*

SAL: There's a hotel one block east of here. On Sixty-third Street. Real clean.

NANCY: How much is it?

SAL: Eighteen to twenty.

*(*NANCY *looks in her pocketbook)*

NANCY: I need ten dollars.

SAL: I don't lend money. Firm rule of the house.

BOB: You gotta pay your own way around here.

*(*NANCY *goes to the door)*

NANCY: *(To* BOB*)* What'll you do?

BOB: Baby, as you can see, I'm in the big time. And all thanks to you.

NANCY: I think there's enough credit to go round.

(Pause)

BOB: You coulda told me you were pregnant.

NANCY: I figured you wouldn't want to know. Like always.

BOB: Everything gets planned behind my back. It's not good for a man's morale.

NANCY: Not for anybody's. (SHE *opens the door*)

BOB: Nance, I . . . I don't wish you bad.

NANCY: I believe you. *(Near tears)* I hope you'll . . . wish . . . something for yourself . . .

(SHE *exits.* SAL *goes to the door and bolts it*)

SAL: You can stay till morning.

BOB: Got some good scores for me tomorrow?

SAL: I doubt it. You been more trouble than you're worth. You're not exactly Sam Superlay. Well, we'll talk about it.

BOB: You people take everything too serious.

(SAL *turns off the lights. A spot remains on* BOB)

BOB: You know what I might do tomorrow, man? I might go build me a campsite. *(Chuckles)*

SAL: We get up at one. If the phones ring, don't answer. Service'll pick up. That's what they get paid for.

(SAL *exits.* BOB *sits impassively at the edge of the couch. A refrain of "That's the Glory of Love" plays as*

THE CURTAIN FALLS)

ELAGABALUS

PRODUCTION AND PUBLICATION HISTORY:

Elagabalus, in an earlier version, was performed in work-shop at The New Dramatists in November 1973. The play has not previously been published.

LIST OF CHARACTERS *(In Order of Appearance)*

ADRIAN: Twenty-one years old, heir of a wealthy political family. Strikingly beautiful, but has no trace in voice or gesture of what is called "effeminacy." His manner is one of simplicity and guilelessness.

JULIA DONNER: ADRIAN's grandmother; strong, cold.

FAUSTINA: A middle-aged Puerto Rican woman who cleans house for ADRIAN and cares deeply for him.

DANNY: A stable boy, about twenty; rough-hewn, shrewd, treacherous.

SELENA: ADRIAN's mother, in her forties, sensuous, "irresponsible," likable.

DOMINICK: The "chauffeur," mid-thirties to mid-forties, physically strong, emotionally brutal.

DR. ANSCOMBE: The family doctor, fifty to seventy years old; officious, bizarre.

CYNTHIA: A dizzy young model.

SCENE 1

The stage is dark. "Variations on 'America' " by Charles Ives begins playing.

Faint sound of hoofbeats in the distance. Volume gradually builds until it drowns the theater. Sound of steel clashing. Then sudden, total silence.

OFFSTAGE VOICE: *(Powerful, harsh)* Elagabalus! You dance too much! *(Threatening)* The army will not stand for it.

(A huge stereo set lights up on stage. We barely make out the figure of a young man, ADRIAN, *bending over it, adjusting the knobs. The rest of the stage remains in darkness)*

VOICE FROM STEREO (ADRIAN): The Senate will not stand for it.

*(*ADRIAN *leans over and turns up a knob. Applause bursts out)*

The people of Rome will not stand for it!

(Louder applause; then the sound of military drums beating a funeral dirge—Purcell's "Music for the Funeral of Queen Mary." During this, an apartment buzzer rings, each time more insistently)

WOMAN'S VOICE FROM STEREO: *(Mournful, sobbing)* Elagabalus . . . Elagabalus . . .

VOICE FROM STEREO (ADRIAN): The Empire is in decay. The Christians are in the wings.

(Music becomes light and gay)

Elagabalus, the Syrian, ascends the throne in 218 A.D.

(A continuous loud ring on the buzzer. ADRIAN jumps, as from a trance. HE switches the apartment lights on and the stereo off. The apartment decor is ultramodern—stunning and lavish. ADRIAN is dressed in a loose-fitting, white linen shirt—just long enough to suggest a tunic. A large, cone-shaped black onyx ring is on the middle finger of his left hand)

(ADRIAN opens the door of the apartment. JULIA DONNER, an elegantly dressed, aristocratic woman in her mid-sixties, is standing there. Her hair is snow-white, with a faint blue rinse to it)

ADRIAN: *(Pleased)* Augusta Maesa! What a delightful surprise!

(HE bends down on one knee, as if to kiss her hand. SHE brusquely withdraws it and sweeps into the apartment)

JULIA: Stop it! I have no time for nonsense. Your mother sent me.

ADRIAN: Mother?!—come now, Gran'mère! I knew you would visit today. It was in the horoscope. *(SHE gives him a withering once-over)*

JULIA: *(Scornful)* I see you're in "costume."

ADRIAN: Don't be severe, Gran'mère. Linen's an honorable fabric.

(JULIA sits. ADRIAN closes the door)

JULIA: Do you know how long I have been at your door?

ADRIAN: *(Simply)* No.

JULIA: Hours! Days! Trying to rouse you from your . . . your . . . *(Gestures scornfully at the stereo)* . . . victrola! *(ADRIAN whoops with laughter)*

ADRIAN: Divine Gran'mère! Not only do you have the Republican virtues, but the Republican vocabulary.

JULIA: A pity the qualities can't be transmitted through the genes.

(ADRIAN starts to get down again on one knee)

ADRIAN: *("Little boy" quality)* Alas, Augusta, I—

JULIA: *(Interrupting)* I warn you, Adrian. Once more and I shall leave the apartment! *Kindly* rise.

ADRIAN: *(Gets up; sad, voice trailing off)* Ah, kindly . . . I used to be your favorite grandchild, Augusta.

JULIA: You used to allow yourself to be guided. *And do not call me that ridiculous name.*

ADRIAN: *(Smiling)* "Julia" has a sufficient connotation.

JULIA: Julia is my name. *(Sniffy)* To my contemporaries. Must you wear that vulgar ring?

ADRIAN: *(Thoughtful)* Yes.

JULIA: You will disgrace the family. I told your mother you were too young to have your own apartment.

ADRIAN: *(Still serious)* I am very young.

JULIA: At your age I was the head of a family.

ADRIAN: *(Dreamily)* At the temple in Emesa they claim I am still thirteen. Though old enough to rule.

(JULIA rises angrily and starts toward the door)

JULIA: I shall tell your mother to come herself.

(ADRIAN jumps up)

ADRIAN: Emesa is far off, Gran'mère. Syria is hundreds of days by camel. *(JULIA opens the door)* You mustn't leave! I need your advice.

JULIA: *That* is beyond dispute.

(ADRIAN fondles his ring, then holds it up to the light)

ADRIAN: I have been told to marry.

JULIA: *(Nonplussed)* What—?!

ADRIAN: I must experience everything. However unpleasant.

JULIA: More games.

ADRIAN: I am the only male. The continuation of the family takes precedence over everything. Even predilection.

JULIA: Are you serious?

ADRIAN: I am always serious.

JULIA: Your Uncle Paul will be relieved. *(Closes the door)* Does your mother know?

ADRIAN: *(Sad, distracted)* Besides: there's very little time.

JULIA: I asked you a question, Adrian.

ADRIAN: Uncle Paul? How *is* he?

JULIA: *Does your mother know?*

ADRIAN: Mother hates being bothered. Her delivery boys need tending.

JULIA: Don't be rude.

ADRIAN: Mayn't I then be truthful?

JULIA: No you "mayn't." And speak the King's English.

ADRIAN: *(Gleefully)* Indeed I shall try, Gran'mère. For if the King doesn't speak it, who will?

JULIA: *(Makes a gesture of impatience)* Impossible child. Who is the girl's family?

ADRIAN: *(Playful)* Did I say it was a girl?

JULIA: You said you cared about our name.

286

ADRIAN: Quite so. The line must continue. *(Breezy)* But there may have to be several ceremonies. For there are several—disparate —contenders.

JULIA: I am not amused.

ADRIAN: Nor I. *(Dreamy)* The ideal mate would be blind: forever unaware of my blemishes, forever in need of my help. *(Sighs)* Besides, I'm pressed for funds. If my needs could be met by a single companion, I assure you nothing would please me more. *(Looks again at his ring)* But my nature is prodigal.

JULIA: Your bankers agree. You must give up the stables. They sent me to tell you. They seem to think I still have influence with you. I told them they were quite mistaken. Besides, it is your conduct, not your funds, that concerns me. Now that you are of age, your money is your own—and you can waste only your own. But the family name is a joint possession. Besmirch it, and you ruin others besides yourself.

ADRIAN: But what is it I *do*, Gran'mère, that causes so much dismay? I like to ride horses. And dance.

JULIA: You press too hard against the boundaries of form.

ADRIAN: I've never harmed anyone.

JULIA: Precisely. It shows a lack of self-definition. There is talk of insanity.

ADRIAN: *(Lets out a whoop of laughter)* I do know that this is Nueva York, Gran'mère. *Not* Emesa.

JULIA: I am relieved to hear it. I carry an epitaph for you in my head, Adrian. I have hopes you may yet come to deserve it: "He was one of the sweetest men alive. Then he found himself."

ADRIAN: An epitaph, Gran'mère, is what one says at a funeral oration.

JULIA: Or inscribes on a tomb.

ADRIAN: You meant epigram. (JULIA *turns away*) Or epithet. No— epiphany! That's it—epiphany: a feast, a celebration, a manifestation of divinity!

(HE *turns on the stereo: Ives's "Spanish" variation*)

JULIA: I suggest you play your records at lower volume. The sound carries into the hall.

ADRIAN: It's my own composition. *(Melancholy)* Not yet complete. I think I've added too many drums. Do you like it?

JULIA: *Only* the drum. It has simplicity.

ADRIAN: The tune's very old. Properly performed to castanets. That is, for a *spring* dance. Drums are for war. I want to learn the flute. It's Baal's favorite.

JULIA: *(Starts to leave)* I shall tell your mother—and your bankers— that I no longer understand a word you say. Nor care to.

ADRIAN: Why are you so cruel to me?

JULIA: Why do you wear so large and ugly a ring?

(ADRIAN *again holds it up to the light*)

ADRIAN: *(Dreamlike)* It is not a ring.

JULIA: *(Sternly)* Adrian: do not marry.

ADRIAN: *(Smiling)* Augusta: I am of age.

(JULIA *frowns, turns and exits*)

(ADRIAN *locks the door after her, dims the lights and turns on the stereo. HE sits in a double lotus position on the floor, takes off the onyx ring, and places it ceremoniously in front of him.*

Music: reprise of Purcell.

As the military drums beat out their mournful dirge and the WOMAN'S VOICE *sobs, "Elagabalus . . . Elagabalus . . . ,"* ADRIAN *slowly brings his arm and head forward in a reverential bow to the ring*)

ADRIAN: *(Addressing the ring)* Baal . . . beloved Baal . . .

(His forehead remains on the floor as the LIGHTS GO DARK)

SCENE 2

Lights up on ADRIAN*'s apartment, early afternoon. A middle-aged Puerto Rican woman,* FAUSTINA, *is vacuuming. Loud Latin music is playing.* FAUSTINA *shakes to it rhythmically as she vacuums.*

The door to ADRIAN*'s bedroom opens.* HE *appears in a purple silk robe, rubbing his eyes with sleep.*

ADRIAN: *(Childlike, unreproachful)* Faustina, qué pasa?

FAUSTINA: *(Cheerful)* Bueñas dias, Señor Adrian.

ADRIAN: *(Good-natured)* So much noise. How can we sleep? Qué hora es?

FAUSTINA: Tarde! Tarde! Uno y media.

*(*HE *goes over to* FAUSTINA, *puts his arms around her and kisses her.* SHE *flushes with pleasure)*

ADRIAN: *(Warmly)* Como está?

FAUSTINA: Regularo. Y usted?

ADRIAN: Comme ci, comme ça—oops, sorry! I do wish you spoke Aramaic. I'm so bad at Latin, my tutors despair.

FAUSTINA: You have good rest?

ADRIAN: Not really. I dreamt the Parthians attacked the temple at Emesa.

FAUSTINA: No comprendo, Señor Adrian.

ADRIAN: Nobody comprendos. You must stop calling me "Señor." I keep telling you that.

(FAUSTINA *shrugs uncomprehendingly, goes back to vacuuming*)

ADRIAN: Is there fruit or meal-cake?

FAUSTINA: Fruta?

ADRIAN Don't trouble. I'll look. (*Starts toward the kitchen*)

(DANNY *appears in the bedroom door, stark naked.* HE*'s about the same age as* ADRIAN *but otherwise contrasting: dark in complexion, with long black hair; moody, petulant, vaguely threatening, uneducated*)

DANNY: (*Sullen*) What's all the noise? (ADRIAN *gives him a hug and a kiss on the cheek.* DANNY *wriggles free*) C'mon!

(FAUSTINA *giggles and turns her back*)

FAUSTINA: (*Mock embarrassment*) El overcoat! Por favor!

ADRIAN: Nakedness is a mark of civilization, Faustina. Only Persians consider it indecent.

DANNY: (*Bragging*) I am good to look at.

ADRIAN: Shush—be nice! (HE *takes off his robe and puts it over* DANNY. ADRIAN *is left wearing mauve silk shorts.* HE *frowns*) Being half-clothed is true vulgarity.

FAUSTINA: (*Giggling*) Nuevo boyfren.

ADRIAN: Nueva! (THEY *both giggle.* ADRIAN *clears his throat in a formal way)* Allow me para introducir—

(FAUSTINA *lets out a shriek of laughter.* DANNY *sits on a "whoopee" cushion—and jumps up with a yell)*

DANNY: Hey, what kinda nut house is this?

FAUSTINA: No "introducir," Señor Adrian. *"Presentar."* "Introducir" mean to rape!

(SHE *and* ADRIAN *double up again with laughter)*

ADRIAN: Danny, this is Faustina. Faustina, this is Hierocles.

(DANNY *and* FAUSTINA *look confused)*

DANNY: Huh?

ADRIAN: It's a pet name of mine. I'll explain later. Coffee, Faustina?

FAUSTINA: No, no, gracias. Yo vacuno la carpeta.

DANNY: You're gonna vaccinate a notebook?!

(FAUSTINA *reacts with surprise)*

ADRIAN: I didn't know you spoke Spanish, love.

DANNY My father was Ambassador to *Por*to Rico.

FAUSTINA: *(Correcting him) Puer*to Rico.

ADRIAN: *Minister*, not Ambassador.

DANNY: You two tryin' to tell me who I am?

ADRIAN: We'll do our best. But you'll have to cooperate. Now!— we must have cofi. To celebrate Hierocles's arrival. Y cuchifritos. Y BLT con mayonnaise.

DANNY: Make my BLT to "go."

ADRIAN: Bravo, ma cherie! (HE *kisses him)* Du bist wie eine blume. (DANNY *looks confused)* "You are like *one* flower."

(In a burst of high spirits, ADRIAN *dances around.* FAUSTINA *starts to applaud rhythmically, encouraging* ADRIAN *to do a series of strange arabesques)*

DANNY: I want some coffee.

*(*ADRIAN *instantly dances toward the kitchen)*

ADRIAN: Cofi, cofi, cofi! Syrian cofi! *(Exits)*

*(*DANNY *sits.* FAUSTINA, *eyeing him suspiciously, picks up the vacuum)*

FAUSTINA: *(Pointing to vacuum; over articulating)* El va-cun.

DANNY: *(Hissing)* No. La as-pir-a-dora!

*(*FAUSTINA *jumps as if hit)*

FAUSTINA: *(Narrow-eyed)* Como se llama?

DANNY: *(Sly)* Hierocles.

FAUSTINA: Drogaddicto? *(*DANNY *starts whistling)* Policia? *(*DANNY *keeps whistling)* Ladrón?

DANNY: No capish.

FAUSTINA: *(Triumphant)* Hijackquero!

DANNY: *(Whispering)* Secueftrador.

*(*FAUSTINA *is startled.* ADRIAN *comes dancing out of the kitchen, balancing three cups and saucers)*

ADRIAN: Faustina, put *down* el vacun! You're pregnant. It's dangerous. I'll clean later—if I have time.

*(*HE *starts back toward the kitchen for the coffee pot.* FAUSTINA *stops him)*

FAUSTINA: No, niñito! No es proprio! La estufa is para señoras. *(*SHE *exits into the kitchen.* DANNY *calls after her)*

DANNY: No "estufa." *Fogon.*

(FAUSTINA *pokes her head back into the room. Her brow is furrowed*)

FAUSTINA: *(Worried, mumbling)* I don't know . . . I don't know . . . *(Disappears again)*

ADRIAN: *(Still reacting to* FAUSTINA *intercepting him)* Faustina's very traditional. "It isn't proper," she said, "for men to be in the kitchen."

DANNY: I know what she said. She don't even know the right word for "stove." She speaks Spanglish, not Spanish. New York-ese.

ADRIAN: Are you Spanish, darling? I thought you were a stable boy. You aren't from Gaul, are you? No, of course not. You're a Carian. From Nicomedia. You're Hierocles. But let's not get fanatical about historical accuracy.

DANNY: I take care of horses.

(ADRIAN *caresses him*)

ADRIAN: My fierce Turk. How lucky for me you were cleaning the stable when I arrived yesterday.

DANNY: You betta watch that broad. She's low class.

(FAUSTINA *comes bouncing back into the room*)

FAUSTINA: *(Singing)* Aqui el cofi, Aqui el cofi . . .

(ADRIAN *takes up the "song."* HE *grabs* FAUSTINA *around the waist and starts dancing her around*)

ADRIAN: Aqui el cofi, Aqui el cofi . . .

DANNY: I thought she was pregnant.

ADRIAN: Pregnant? Who?

DANNY: *Her!* Ya just said so!

ADRIAN: Oh—that was a fictive pregnancy. To suit last minute's mood. Faustina's too old to bear children. *(Suddenly sad)* And I, alas, am too young. Or the world is. Why do you make me sad, Hierocles? I hate being reminded of experiences I can't have. Come, we'll drink coffee. And make plans.

(The THREE *sit around a small table, center stage.* ADRIAN *pours)*

(To FAUSTINA*)* Lêché, mon vieux?

*(*FAUSTINA *puts her hand to her face in an elegant gesture of refusal)*

FAUSTINA: Ah no—merci mille fois.

*(*ADRIAN *does a momentary double take, then breaks into a big grin)*

ADRIAN: You're both *so* clever. *So* improved. Spoken like my own soul, Faustina. *(As* HE *leans over to embrace her,* HE *burns* DANNY *on the arm with the coffee pot)*

DANNY: Ow!!

ADRIAN: Oh God!

FAUSTINA: *(Genuine)* Oh—pobrecito! *(*DANNY *pulls away gruffly from her touch)* Pobrecit*a!*

ADRIAN: Bring aromatics, jars of unguents, olive oil, hygienic floral perfumes from the East, garlands of—

DANNY: —oh, shut up!

ADRIAN: *(Deflated)* —garlands of, of lampreys, leather scourges, iron spikes . . . *(*HIS *voice trails off.* HE *stares intensely into* DANNY*'s eyes. Rhapsodic)* I love you, you dreary boy.

DANNY: *(Matter-of-fact)* Pour the fuckin' coffee.

*(*ADRIAN *becomes instantly euphoric)*

ADRIAN: Now! What day is it?

FAUSTINA: Wed-nes-day.

ADRIAN: Aii!—Wed-nes-day already, and not a single gala planned for the week!

DANNY: Ya into chicks at all?

ADRIAN: I already told you I love Faustina. And *all* the Vestal Virgins.

DANNY: *(Lewd)* Yeah? Well let's ask a few over for the gala.

FAUSTINA: Fiesta? Fiesta grupa?

ADRIAN: First we must declare an occasion. Without an occasion, there can be no celebration. On some matters I'm firm.

DANNY: *(Sarcastic)* Well, you could make it a wedding ceremony for you and Faustina.

(ADRIAN jumps as if thunderstruck. HE kisses DANNY hard on the lips. DANNY loses his balance and falls over)

ADRIAN: Quiet, please! I have a serious announcement. *(DANNY struggles up from the floor toward his chair)* Hierocles, your attention *please! (Struck at his own line)* Mmm—charming rhyme. *(Savoring)* "Hierocles, your attention please." *(DANNY freezes in position)* This is not a firm proposal, mind. But I'm inclined to offer you *each* a hand in marriage.

(FAUSTINA shrugs uncomprehendingly and starts to drink her coffee. DANNY's mouth falls open)

ADRIAN: The Empire is too large for any one man. *(To FAUSTINA)* You are gifted in tongues. And have a mature vagina. *(To DANNY)* And *you* look splendid in purple. Oh won't grandmother be pleased!

(As we hear reprise of Ives's "Spanish Variations"—

BLACKOUT

SCENE 3

Stage is in darkness.

A porno film—Big Stick—begins running on an oversized screen facing the audience. On screen a teen-age girl with a mop of unruly hair is sucking sensuously on a huge popsicle. She periodically leers at the audience, then sticks her tongue way out, licking the popsicle from bottom to top.

A woman (SELENA), barely visible, reclines on a chaise.

A man (DOMINICK) is standing, his shirt off. He's watching the film, but is alert to sounds elsewhere.

WOMAN'S VOICE (SELENA): *(Bored, irritated)* Hateful! The child's hateful!

MAN'S VOICE (DOMINICK): *(Gruff, thick; lower-class)* Shush—quiet.

WOMAN: *(Indignant)* Don't tell me to be quiet. It's *my* projector.

MAN: Give the kid a chance. That's all.

WOMAN: I'm bored. *(Patting the bed)* Come sit.

DOMINICK: Not now.

SELENA: Why?

DOMINICK: I like to stay on my feet.

SELENA: That's news.

> *(The image on the screen transforms. The popsicle becomes a penis)*

DOMINICK: There ya go! I told ya to give her a chance.

SELENA: Thank God—a male! Where's the rest of him?

DOMINICK: That kid's got alotta talent.

SELENA: They've made the wrong one anonymous. Where *is* he?!

DOMINICK: You're lookin' at 'im.

SELENA: I'm looking at a *penis.*

DOMINICK: *(Suddenly alert)* What the hell is—!!

> *(The lights snap on. JULIA DONNER is standing in the doorway, accompanied by DR. ANSCOMBE, a man of about fifty, conservatively dressed, contained in manner)*
>
> *(DOMINICK grabs a chauffeur's hat, sticks it on his head, and salutes JULIA)*
>
> *(SELENA, clad in a negligee, remains reclining nonchalantly on the chaise)*

DOMINICK: Good evening, Madame.

SELENA: I've asked you repeatedly, Mother, not to barge through a closed door. *(Leans over and casually turns off the film)* For one who prides herself on manners, you can be remarkably rude.

JULIA: *(Acid)* I didn't know your appetite needed artificial stimulation.

SELENA: *Dominick* occasionally falters. *(Acknowledging* ANSCOMBE*)* A very boring film, Dr. Anscombe.

ANSCOMBE: All pornography is boring. Too predictable: oral sex invariably precedes anal sex. Symptomatic of our culture's surrender to Freudian models. Or of the truth of those models.

JULIA: Don't pontificate.

SELENA: Dominick, take that ridiculous hat off.

JULIA: The complete chauffeur.

SELENA: *(Patting the chaise; to* DOMINICK*)* Do sit here. And tell Dr. Anscombe about the film where they do all that sniffing of the toes. His experience seems limited.

JULIA: Dr. Anscombe has just returned from Washington.

*(*DOMINICK *puts his shirt on)*

DOMINICK: *(To* JULIA*)* If you don't need me, Madame, I'll look after the car. The front tire needs changing.

SELENA: *(Sexily)* The whole chassis needs lubricating. A lot of good it does me.

JULIA: No need, Dominick.

ANSCOMBE: *(Protesting)* I do think it would be better, Julia, if—

JULIA: *(Interrupting)* —I said no need.

DOMINICK: As you wish, Madame.

SELENA: *I* wish to see the film.

ANSCOMBE: Selena, I'm here at the request of your mother, to discuss Adrian.

SELENA: *(Laughing, to* ANSCOMBE*)* Dominick's far more interesting.

*(*ANSCOMBE *turns to* JULIA*)*

ANSCOMBE: Perhaps another time. When the libido is less stimulated.

SELENA: There's no such time.

JULIA: Like mother, like son.

SELENA: Do leave Adrian alone. The child's harmless. Though not, bless him, boring. Except for his taste in men.

JULIA: *(Looking at* DOMINICK*)* I would have said your tastes quite coincide. Indeed I rely on it. *(Directly at* SELENA*)* Adrian intends to marry.

*(*SELENA *bursts out laughing)*

SELENA: Perhaps he is mad.

JULIA: A *man*.

SELENA: Oh. That's better. Are you sure?

JULIA: He's proposed to one of the stable boys.

SELENA: Charming!

JULIA: *And* to his Puerto Rican maid, Faustina. He called to tell me the happy news this morning. He's planning a gala in celebration. A run-round-the-city.

SELENA: The boy must be out of party ideas. Hire him a cruise director.

JULIA: *(Stern)* Selena: the news has reached Washington.

ANSCOMBE: I was at the Secretary's for dinner last night. He took me aside and asked for confirmation of the story.

SELENA: So confirm it. That will be taken as certain proof in Washington that the story is false. *(To* JULIA*)* I thought Adrian told *you* only this morning?

JULIA: He did.

SELENA: *(More subdued)* I see. Brother Paul, as always, heard it first. Probably *before* Adrian proposed.

ANSCOMBE: This will put your brother's chances in grave jeopardy.

SELENA: My brother is too powerful already.

JULIA: *(Barely controlled fury)* Be *serious!* This is the closest we have ever been to—

SELENA: —"we?"

JULIA: Your brother. Adrian's delusions will be used against Paul. "Emesa" and "Elagabalus" are bad enough, but—

SELENA: —Adrian is not delusional. It's a calculated conceit. The boy wants more than one life. So should we all.

ANSCOMBE: We call that schizophrenia. Delusional schizophrenia.

SELENA: I don't care what you call it. I'm telling you what it *is.* Dominick, *do* take that shirt off. *(Smiles lovingly at him; then to* JULIA *and* ANSCOMBE*)* Isn't he wonderful? Positively Praetorian.

JULIA: You're as foolish as your son.

SELENA: A comment one could never make about you—or *your* son. *(Flicks the film back on)* You'll have to excuse us now. We have more foolishness planned.

JULIA: I expect you to talk to Adrian.

SELENA: Whatever about?

JULIA: Paul is determined.

SELENA: . . . later, later . . . I must see how the film comes out. The suspense is killing me. *(Giggles)*

(As the lights dim, ANSCOMBE *picks up on the giggle, soon drowning out* SELENA*)*

(Stage becomes dark, except for the screen. The porno film begins rolling again, from where it left off. CLOSEUP *of teen-age girl sucking on penis.* ZOOM *to penis.* FREEZE.*)*

(Spot comes up on DR. ANSCOMBE. HE *speaks in a monotone, as if in a trance)*

ANSCOMBE: It's one of the largest . . . one of the largest in my whole collection . . . perhaps the very largest . . . Except for the black one . . . Luke . . . *(Chuckles)* I told Luke the operation would be Einfeldt Procedure Number Two . . . a curettage . . . to scrape the infected tissue from the cavity walls . . . simple and painless . . . and *absolutely necessary* . . . Einfeldt Procedure Number Two . . . Could I help it the tissue turned out to be malignant and that more—extreme—measures were called for? . . . During the trial I quoted President Lincoln's eloquent words: "One must never destroy a life to save a limb, but one must sometimes sever a limb to save a life." . . . There wasn't a dry eye in the courtroom . . . Luke's wife told me later how relieved she was . . . The man had been a sex fiend . . . Wouldn't leave her alone . . . I keep it on my desk in a ceramic jug . . . thick, oblong, immense . . . like calcified stone . . . like onyx . . .

BLACKOUT

(The sound of applause is heard faintly in the darkness. It gradually builds in volume. Lights come up slowly on ADRIAN'*s apartment. Over the taped applause,* HE *is recording into a microphone)*

ADRIAN: *(Into microphone)* . . . thank you . . . thank you . . . I knew you would like the flamingos . . . Beautiful birds, are they not? Far too beautiful to kill . . . Baal must have his sacrifice, I know . . . Baal *will* have his sacrifice . . . But . . . But . . .

*(*ADRIAN *hesitates, then stops.* HE *turns the tape to "Replay," then sits on the couch to listen)*

REPLAY VOICE: . . . flamingos . . . Beautiful birds, are they not? Far too beautiful to kill . . . Baal must have his sacrifice, I know . . . Baal *will* have his sacrifice . . . But . . . But . . .

*(*ADRIAN *jumps up scowling, and turns off the machine.* HE *paces in distress)*

ADRIAN: Danny! . . . Danny! . . .

(DANNY comes out of the bedroom. HE wears a wig of ochre hair, topped by a diadem of plastic daisies and lotuses. Tendrils of false curls fall over his shoulders. His eyes are painted black. HE's smiling broadly. As HE appears in the doorway, HE opens his palms to the ceiling, strikes a pose, and stands stock still, like a statue. ADRIAN, pacing the floor, doesn't immediately see him)

Danny! . . . Dan- —*(Turns around, sees DANNY and lets out a shriek)* Santa Maria Maggiore!! *(DANNY smiles complacently)* Is *that* what they sent from Bergdorf's?! It's absolutely wrong!

(DANNY's face falls)

DANNY: Aw shit, man! How many of these fuckin' things do I have to—

ADRIAN: It's *archaic Greek.* A good seven hundred years off the period! I *told* Bergdorf's that Mastrokakis was the wrong man. *(Motions impatiently to DANNY)* Take it off, take it off!

(DANNY removes the wig)

Chauvinist pig. Thinks all history is Greek history. *(Picks up the wig gingerly, then drops it as if burnt)* Plastic lotuses—ugh! *(Looks at DANNY)* And why the black paint, may I ask?

DANNY: That was my idea.

ADRIAN: It's authentic for the period. How did you know?

DANNY: It just come to me.

ADRIAN: Faustina thinks you're a psychic. At the *least.*

DANNY: Things come to me.

ADRIAN: You *said* that. *(DANNY turns away to go into the bedroom. ADRIAN jumps up and throws his arms around him)* I'm sorry, love! Don't pout. I know I'm being mean. But everything's going rotten. Only three weeks to the party. And I can't even decide on what the sacrifice is going to be. Listen to this.

(HE turns on the tape deck)

REPLAY VOICE: . . . flamingos . . . Beautiful birds, are they not? Far too . . .

DANNY: What's flamingos?

ADRIAN: Beautiful birds!

REPLAY VOICE: . . . Baal must have his sacrifice, I know . . . Baal *will* have his sacrifice . . . But . . . But . . .

(ADRIAN *turns off the tape*)

ADRIAN: By interrupting, you missed the key section.

DANNY: You gonna have birds at the party?

ADRIAN: Yes. But I'd only sacrifice paper ones. Baal would understand. Baal is the sun, bringing life. But birds aren't enough. I'm stumped for a climax. It isn't every day I get married. Twice.

DANNY: Nuthin's ever enough.

ADRIAN: Quite right. But there are moments of temporary satiation.

DANNY: Huh?

ADRIAN: I need a climax.

DANNY: Ask Faustina. I'm beat.

ADRIAN: Maybe the Hare Krishna people would play their tambourines.

DANNY: It ain't authentic to the period.

ADRIAN: True. Don't forget to depilate your legs.

DANNY: Huh?

ADRIAN: Never mind—it's a detail. (*The apartment buzzer rings*) Faustina. I sent her to be fitted for purple buskins. They probably measured her ears.

DANNY: Hey—this won't make *me* married to Faustina, will it?

ADRIAN: Another detail. (HE *opens the apartment door:* SELENA *is standing there*) Mum! What an amazing moment! I haven't seen you since boarding school!

SELENA: I never leave the house. Kiss me. We're all we have in the world.

ADRIAN: Our line goes back to the Divine Severus.

SELENA: Well it may not go forward. I've come on serious business. *(Spotting* DANNY*)* Who's that?

ADRIAN: One of my brides. Danny.

SELENA: Oh dear, it is true. Hello, Danny. Congratulations. You've found a wonderful boy. *(To* ADRIAN*)* Rather cute. Is he good with his Johnson?

ADRIAN: He worked in the stables.

SELENA: That's not a direct answer. Now look, honey, I've only got a minute.

ADRIAN: You've come at just the right moment. I need help with the party. Danny, be sweet and get Mum some cofi. *(DANNY reluctantly gets off the couch)*

SELENA: *(To* DANNY*)* I love your slouch. Did you get it in the saddle?

DANNY: Mmm. Fighting the Parthians under Macrinus.

SELENA: Indoctrinated already.

DANNY: Won't Gran'mère be pleased. *(Exits)*

ADRIAN: He and Faustina don't get along.

SELENA: Is Faustina the "other one"?

ADRIAN: I may have to get an Arabian divorce after the party's over. You know— *(He snaps his fingers)* "I hereby declare us divorced."

SELENA: That's a Hebraic divorce. I saw it once in a sixteen millimeter.

ADRIAN: The Near East isn't what it used to be. They'll never be able to live together. And I can't stand bickering.

SELENA: Mulattoes are very intolerant.

ADRIAN: Faustina is not mulatto. She's Puerto Rican. That's darker.

SELENA: You have a wonderful color sense, dear. Why aren't your walls pumpkin? Never mind. Julia says that Faustina's too old to bear children. And you distinctly told her that was your motive in getting married.

ADRIAN: That was my *serious* motive. Always the least important.

SELENA: Julia's in a rage. *And* your uncle.

ADRIAN: Uncle who?

SELENA: Now, Adrian, stop it. You know perfectly well *who*. My only brother. Your only uncle. *Julia's* only son.

ADRIAN: I've forgotten his name. What's ever become of him?

SELENA: *(Amused)* Paul. He practically won the war single-handed. He's a hero. Much talked of in the Senate.

ADRIAN: *(Excited)* Do you mean the war's over—the Parthians beaten, the temple free?! We'll get a full set of silk streamers! No—an entire dress uniform: jeweled choker, pointed cap, braided belt!

SELENA: You *can* be trying. *(DANNY reappears with the coffee)*

ADRIAN: Danny: great news! The temple in Syria has been liberated.

DANNY: No shit.

ADRIAN: Baal is free to join us! A whole new cycle begins! I feel inspired already! Mum—take off your clothes!

SELENA: What do you think this is—Egypt?!

ADRIAN: I want you to practice the ballet sequence with Danny. Cynthia can't get here till later.

SELENA: Cynthia, the mulatto?

ADRIAN: Stick to one topic, Mum. Since Faustina's one of the brides, I can't put her in the ballet sequence. So I've hired Cynthia.

(The key turns in the apartment door. FAUSTINA appears in a black Robin Hood hat with long, green feathers, curling down under her chin.

ADRIAN *groans and buries his head in his hands.* SHE *leaves the door ajar)*

ADRIAN: Aooh—they've done it again. Archaic Greece, now Hollywood Renaissance.

SELENA: Is it Errol Flynn?

FAUSTINA: *(Grinning)* Bonita, no?

ADRIAN: No.

DANNY: It matches my eye paint.

SELENA: I've been meaning to ask you about that.

FAUSTINA: *(Presenting herself)* Señora Robin Hood!

ADRIAN: *Señorita.* And it'll stay that way, if the two of you don't learn your parts better.

SELENA: I gather you are Faustina.

FAUSTINA: Si, señora.

SELENA: Señor*ita.* I am Adrian's mother.

FAUSTINA: *(Overcome)* No-o-o-o! *(Clasping her hands in exclamation)* Madre de Dios!

ADRIAN: *(Blushing)* That's going too far. I haven't even been crowned. Take off your hat.

SELENA: Put on your shirt. Ooh I'm sorry—that's from the other reel.

*(*DOMINICK *appears in the door of the apartment.* HE *wears his chauffeur's uniform)*

DOMINICK: Ready yet?

SELENA: Come in, Dominick, and close the door.

ADRIAN: *(Staring at* DOMINICK*)* Faustina, you left the entrada open.

FAUSTINA: *(Gesturing toward* DOMINICK: *stage whisper)* No es portero. No es el super.

SELENA: *(To* DOMINICK*)* I'll be a few more minutes.

*(*DOMINICK *enters and closes the door behind him)*

DOMINICK: I'm parked in front of a church.

(Music, very low: Ligeti's "Volumina")

ADRIAN: *(Awestruck)* How did you know?

DOMINICK: Huh?

ADRIAN: How did you know it was a church?

DOMINICK: The stained-glass window.

ADRIAN: It must be an omen. Hard upon the peace. The new cycle begins.

*(*FAUSTINA *moves away in fear from* DOMINICK*. Music off)*

SELENA: Adrian, this is Dominick, the new chauffeur.

ADRIAN: *(Ignoring her)* Welcome. Welcome, honorable priest. Welcome from your long journey. We must celebrate your arrival. *(Continues to stare at* DOMINICK*)* Faustina: silver plates. The dolphin steak. Stuffed eggs with oyster sauce. Baked giraffe, crested with skystone mushrooms.

FAUSTINA: *(Puzzled)* Fruta? Queso? Ice cream?

DANNY: *(Enthused)* Ice cream?—yeah! You got any Haagen-dazs? The boysenberry sherbet's outasight.

ADRIAN: *(His eyes still fixed on* DOMINICK*)* Danny, wash your eyes. It now approaches sacrilege.

DANNY: *(Resentful)* Who is this dude? What's goin' on?

*(*FAUSTINA *tries to get* ADRIAN *aside)*

FAUSTINA: *(Whispering)* Tiber. Tiberún!

ADRIAN: Shush! Calma! You must do as I say, Faustina. Promise me you'll do as I say.

FAUSTINA: Ai, ai, no me gusta . . .

ADRIAN: Promise?

FAUSTINA: *(Reluctant)* Si, Señor Adrian, si . . .

SELENA: Adrian, don't be tiresome. Remember I rarely leave the house. The event is due some consideration.

ADRIAN: The event is enshrined.

FAUSTINA: Qué lastima! Lastimoso! *(SHE exits toward the kitchen, her voice mournful, reminiscent of the sounds from the stereo in the first scene)* Elagabalus . . . Elagabalus . . .

DANNY: *(Calling after FAUSTINA)* If it's not boysenberry, forget it. *(Exits into bedroom)*

(ADRIAN's eyes remain fixed on DOMINICK. HE motions him to the largest chair, pulls up a cushion and sits cross-legged at DOMINICK's feet)

ADRIAN: Did you come by way of Tyre or northward from the Aegean? What news from the capital? Is the colonnade intact, the columns still four abreast? Mother says the war is over, the temple liberated. I shall be recalled in honor to Emesa, drive my chariot to the temple door, be made immortal at Baal's altar.

DOMINICK: *(To SELENA)* The car's gonna get towed.

ADRIAN: No one else knows it as a church.

SELENA: *(To ADRIAN)* Are those two making it? I swear I don't know what's to become of this city.

DOMINICK: It *was* a church. It's a library now.

ADRIAN: So are they all.

SELENA: Would you mind answering your mother.

(ADRIAN finally averts his eyes from DOMINICK)

ADRIAN: *(To SELENA)* Nothing's to become of this city, mother. You're too political.

DOMINICK: The car's gonna get towed.

(SELENA *rises*)

SELENA: *(Bored)* Conversations never change. Give me a silent film any day.

(FAUSTINA *appears from the kitchen carrying a tray at the same moment that* DANNY *appears at the door of the bedroom wearing his ochre wig. At the sight of him,* FAUSTINA *screams and drops the tray; the tone is terror, not humor.* ADRIAN *rises quickly)*

ADRIAN: *(To* DANNY*)* Try to be more considerate.

DANNY: Just tryin' to help the festivities along.

FAUSTINA: No me gusta. No me gusta.

ADRIAN: *(To* FAUSTINA*)* Don't be afraid . . . don't be afraid . . .

(DOMINICK *rises slowly from his chair)*

FAUSTINA: No es portero. No es el super.

ADRIAN: *(To* DOMINICK*)* Faustina's frightened of you.

DANNY: Of *me!* It was my wig made her jump.

ADRIAN: Don't be competitive. It will give you wrinkles. *(To* DOMINICK, *apprehensively)* You are from Emesa, aren't you?

(Low reprise of Ligeti music. SELENA *sprawls in a casual position on the couch.* SHE *picks up a magazine and starts thumbing through it)*

DOMINICK: I'm from uptown. The car's gonna get towed.

(The sound of the drums intensifies. ADRIAN *goes to the stereo and in an effort to stop the sound, turns knobs off and on. But the sound continues to mount in intensity, with words interspersed)*

VOICE FROM STEREO: . . . Maggiore! . . . beautiful birds . . . No-o-o . . . *will* have his sacrifice . . . *will* . . .

ADRIAN: . . . I don't understand . . . If you're not from Emesa, how could you have known it was a church . . .

DOMINICK: What's the big deal? Ain't ya ever seen stained glass? Rome's fulla stained glass . . . I once drove this rich family around Rome. Every third house was a church . . . Pretty spot. To visit, I mean.

(The lights dim, except for a spot on SELENA, *who starts to chuckle over her magazine)*

SELENA:—it's called "Spanglish"—can you believe it? Hey, is anybody listening to me?!

(As the lights go out, ADRIAN*'s voice, barely audible, melancholy)*

ADRIAN: Rome . . . Rome . . .

*(*BLACKOUT, *except for spot on* SELENA*)*

SELENA: When a Puerto Rican in New York says "vacunar la carpeta," she means "to vacuum the carpet." A real Spaniard wouldn't understand her. To him, "vacunar la carpeta" means "to vaccinate a looseleaf notebook"! *(*SELENA *laughs uproariously)*

(Spot goes out. Ligeti music continues in the dark, diminishes, then fades)

SCENE 4

Lights slowly come back up on ADRIAN*'s apartment. It's daytime.* HE*'s alone with* DR. ANSCOMBE.

ANSCOMBE: Yes, I'm surprised. I thought you wanted to talk about yourself, not your mother.

ADRIAN: I want to do both. And still more beyond that.

ANSCOMBE: As always.

ADRIAN: Quite. I worry about Mother. She's merely frivolous; her pleasures derive wholly from *traditional* ritual. She's not a good judge of character. *(*ANSCOMBE *smiles)* You find that amusing?

ANSCOMBE: Well, forgive me, Adrian, but there are those—including your mother—who say the same of you.

ADRIAN: I can divine character in an instant. I find it everywhere. That's what upsets people: diversity of taste. Anyone pure of type is attractive. Of course finally there aren't any types. Which is why I find everyone attractive. If pure.

ANSCOMBE: *(Confused)* Innocent.

ADRIAN: Innocently themselves. Which you are not. And Dominick is not.

ANSCOMBE: I can't say I'm following you.

ADRIAN: Of course you are. That's a perfect example of what I mean.

ANSCOMBE: Apparently you want to talk about *me*.

ADRIAN: Only about one of your skills.

ANSCOMBE: I beg your pardon?

ADRIAN: You'll doubtless end in the Senate one day. Remind me to make a public dinner for you. Peas of crystal, yams of gold, lentil soup of liquid rubies. You get to take the dinner home instead of eating it. Well worth a little public ridicule. Perhaps we ought to make up a guest list now. We must have Spurius Maelius—slain by orders of the Senate for distributing wheat to the poor. Yes, and Marcus Manlius, put to death for giving his money to debtors. Perhaps we'll invite a Nubian or two.

ANSCOMBE: Nubian?

ADRIAN: A Nubian, dear doctor, is a black. I dare say you don't know any. Rome was full of blacks. Not all of them slaves. Did you know that in 356 during the Republic a plebeian was made dictator for a year? I wonder why only a year? I'll ask Baal. *(HE rises, goes to the mantel and picks up a piece of black onyx, shaped like a phallus)* Too large to wear on my finger.

ANSCOMBE: I've wasted enough time.

ADRIAN: Why are people constantly rushing from my apartment? It's well decorated.

ANSCOMBE: I'm too busy for games, Adrian.

ADRIAN: Then you've organized your life very badly. I'm glad you came to talk about it.

ANSCOMBE: I came at *your* request to talk about *you*.

ADRIAN: I thought it was at Dominick's request to talk about Uncle Paul. Never mind. Since you're here, we might as well talk about somebody. It can be me, if you like. (HE *leads* ANSCOMBE *back to a chair*) Actually, there *is* a matter I want to discuss with you. A *contemporary* matter. You've been our family physician for a long time, have you not?

ANSCOMBE: That is correct.

ADRIAN: You were the family physician when I was born.

ANSCOMBE: Correct.

ADRIAN: All right, then: Why was I circumcised? A barbaric custom, an ugly mutilation, frowned on by Greeks *and* Romans. It mars my beauty. It weighs heavily on my mind—what with the approaching marriage. (ANSCOMBE *moves to the other side of the room, as if to escape*) Can you manage a reconstruction? Find a foreskin to sew back on? Perhaps Dominick would volunteer. He has a giving nature.

ANSCOMBE: You're a fool, Adrian. A fool. The family won't stand for much more. *(Exits)*

(ADRIAN chuckles. The lights dim)

ADRIAN: I should add that to the tape. "The *family* won't stand for it."

(HE turns on the tape deck)

VOICE FROM STEREO (ADRIAN): The army will not stand for it . . . The Senate will not stand for it . . .

(HE stops the tape, picks up the mike, then turns the tape on again)

ADRIAN *(Into microphone)* The family will not stand for it. (HE *smiles contentedly*)

VOICE FROM STEREO: . . . The people of Rome will not stand for it . . .

(ADRIAN frowns, snaps the tape off)

ADRIAN: *(Puzzled)* The "people"? Did I say that? Mmm. It may be a false note. Danny will know. *(HE sits on the couch, brow furrowed)*

(Lights go to out. In the dark, we hear SELENA's voice)

SELENA: Danny's quite adorable. Though not exactly pure of type. Knows too many words. I'd say *"neo-*Neolithic."

JULIA: That was the sum of your observations?

SELENA: I'm a participant, Mama, not an observer. Besides, Dominick—*pure* Neolithic—interrupted us. And we were having such a good time. I must see more of Adrian. He was *transfixed* with Dominick. That's when it started to get boring.

JULIA: Were you jealous, dear?

SELENA: No. Are you?

(JULIA is momentarily startled, then recovers)

JULIA: Yes—of your brother's future.

SELENA: You know, Mama, you need diversion. You should ask Dominick to take you for rides in the country.

JULIA: Selena—do you care about your son?

SELENA: I adore him.

JULIA: You would miss him, then?

SELENA: I miss him now. One makes choices. Somewhere along the way. That's why I adore Adrian: his refusal to choose.

JULIA: Which leaves the responsibility to others, eh? Well, dear, I know you've done all you could. You look quite peakéd from the effort.

SELENA: I never did find out why Danny was wearing that black eye shadow.

(Lights come up. JULIA *is talking into the telephone.* ANSCOMBE *is seated next to her, reading a paper, drinking tea)*

JULIA: I entirely agree. Selena's an obstacle. *(Chuckles)* She reports Adrian was "transfixed" with Dominick . . . Anscombe? He's here with me now . . . Yes, I'll tell him . . . Yes . . . *(Sound of phone clicking off)* . . . Hello? . . . Hello? Are you still there, Paul? . . . Hello?—Oh, I thought we'd been cut off. Perhaps the line is tapped. You wouldn't do that to your own mother, would you? . . . Mmm, I thought you would . . . Yes, we'll keep you informed. Though it does seem a redundancy . . . Goodbye, dear. *(To* ANSCOMBE*)* How peculiar: the dear boy was quoting Cicero to me. Something about the "concord of the orders," cooperation between the upper classes, business, and the Senate. The connection was bad. *(Pause)* He used to complain so about his Latin teacher at Groton. The strangest things stick in the mind.

ANSCOMBE: Only the strange things.

JULIA: Don't be aphoristic: it's middle class. Paul had a message for you: we're *not* considering Einfeldt Procedure—

ANSCOMBE: *(Shocked)*—Einfel—!

JULIA: *("Gentle" smile)*—Yes, faithful physician. Paul's objections are entirely on pragmatic grounds: Adrian would promptly decide he was Cleopatra and the wedding ceremonies would be shifted to a barge in the Hudson.

*(*DOMINICK *enters)*

DOMINICK: Excuse me, Madame.

JULIA: Come in, Dominick.

DOMINICK: A message from Washington.

JULIA: *(Startled)* From Washington? But I just—

DOMINICK: I was told to deliver it personally.

JULIA: I don't understand. I—

315

ANSCOMBE: *(To* DOMINICK*)* Have you come from Washington?

DOMINICK: No sir.

JULIA: You'd better leave us, Anscombe.

ANSCOMBE: What *is* going on?

JULIA: You'll be informed in time.

ANSCOMBE: *(Hurt)* I thought my trustworthiness had been established.

JULIA: Trust, like all emotions, is evanescent.

ANSCOMBE: I take it I'm being "dismissed."

JULIA: Don't be petulant. You will be kept informed.

ANSCOMBE: *(Pointed)* Exactly whose phone call shall I await?

JULIA: Mine, of course.

DOMINICK: Part of the message *is* for you, sir. It has to do with Selena.

JULIA: *(Surprised)* With Selena? I distinctly told Paul that it was ill advised to involve Selena in any way.

ANSCOMBE: *(To* DOMINICK*)* Your message is from Paul?

JULIA: The message is to me. If any part of it concerns you, you will be notified. *(Dismissing him)* Goodbye, Anscombe.

ANSCOMBE: Most peculiar. *(To* DOMINICK*)* You *are* the chauffeur?

JULIA: Dominick is in *my* employ. *Goodbye, Anscombe.*

> (ANSCOMBE *exits.* DOMINICK *sits in the vacated chair. Ives's "Variations" begins under, very low)*

DOMINICK: Paul thinks it's time you were made aware of certain plans.

BLACKOUT

SCENE 5

ADRIAN's *apartment.*

DANNY *and* CYNTHIA, *both in body stockings, are rehearsing a ballet.* ADRIAN *is preoccupied on the couch.* FAUSTINA *is cleaning.*

ADRIAN: Faustina, have you ever heard of death by sacking?

FAUSTINA: Sacudir?

ADRIAN: Si, si. Shake, jolt. *(Rolling the words)* Mu-erte Sac-u-dir.

FAUSTINA: *(Starts to shake her hips)* El rock and roll, yes? *(Gesturing toward the plants)* Es malo para las plantas.

ADRIAN: Malo for people, too. It was a favorite punishment in Rome.

FAUSTINA: Roma, Roma. *(Starts singing.)* "Arriva derci, Roma."

ADRIAN: Faustina, you're not concentrating. I'm talking of serious matters, however unlikely their eventuation. Danny? Where's Danny? *(HE looks around and sees DANNY dancing with CYNTHIA)* Hierocles—stop it! *(CYNTHIA laughs)*

CYNTHIA: We're playing.

ADRIAN: As the child plays, so shall she reap. *(Frowns)* That's very bad. It must be from Seneca. *(Dismayed)* Whenever I get morbid, I fall instantly into a post-Revolutionary mood. Well it can't be helped. I do feel morbid. Danny, pay attention. Faustina's being frivolous, and I want to discuss the prospects of death by sacking.

DANNY: Just one more *(Mispronouncing)* entree-chat.

(CYNTHIA giggles)

ADRIAN: You'll wear poor Cynthia out before the gala even begins.

CYNTHIA: I'm all right, love. It's a gas.

ADRIAN: Are you sure the tutu's snug, the chamois not chafing?

CYNTHIA: It's a groove—though a bit rough on the old kneecaps.

ADRIAN: Well, put some housemaid on them, and—*(Realizes what HE's said)* See how distracted I am!

CYNTHIA: *(To DANNY)* Have a bit of a chat with him. We can have another turn later. *(DANNY reluctantly goes over)*

DANNY: Okay, what's all this about Sacco?

FAUSTINA: Saco? Saco de noche? *(SHE looks around, spots an overnight bag, and triumphantly waves it)* Vacaciones? A donde, Señor Adrian? A Puerto Rico? A Lisbon? A Madrid?

(CYNTHIA heads to the bedroom to dress)

DANNY: *(To CYNTHIA)* Just throw on a little gauze, babe. We'll have at it again in five.

(CYNTHIA giggles, exits. DANNY looks through the keyhole to the bedroom as CYNTHIA changes clothes)

FAUSTINA: Demasiados boyfren.

ADRIAN: Who is Sacco?

318

DANNY: *Who?* My people's hero—SaccoVanzetti! That's who. You ain't the only one with line-age.

ADRIAN: Lineage.

DANNY: *(Mopey)* Whaddaya wanna know about Sacco?

ADRIAN: How did he die?

DANNY: Murdered by the state.

ADRIAN: Perhaps we *are* on the same subject. Did they put him in a bag?

DANNY: Yeah—a noose.

ADRIAN: An oxhide sack—together with a wild dog, two fighting cocks, four poisonous snakes and—

FAUSTINA: *(Interrupting; beaming)*—and a pear tree!

ADRIAN: *(Sternly)*—and a full-grown ape! Then they sewed up the sack and threw it in the Tiber.

FAUSTINA: Tiber. Tiburón.

DANNY: *(Wrinkling his nose in fright)* Tiburón?—eee!

ADRIAN: Would Mr. and Mrs. Berlitz mind translating for the linguistic poor?

DANNY: A tiburón is a shark.

(FAUSTINA bares her teeth in imitation of a shark)

ADRIAN: Faustina, we've got to get you to a good dentist. You're flashing gold off the ceiling. Perhaps that's why the Treasury's so low. Soon we'll be back to bartering spices. *(To DANNY)* You're right to be afraid of sharks. They're immortal.

FAUSTINA: Immortal!

ADRIAN: Si. El tiburón es immortál.

FAUSTINA: Ostentadora . . . Os-tent . . . —tatious.

DANNY: Whaddaya mean "immortal"? Nuthin' lives forever.

ADRIAN: Except sharks. Wholly regenerative, indestructible. They can regrow any part of their body.

DANNY: *(Skeptical)* An eye?

ADRIAN: You don't need an eye. Lampreys have no eyes. No bones either. I meant any *necessary* part. Like underwear, say.

(CYNTHIA emerges from the bedroom, wearing a chiffon caftan)

CYNTHIA: Is rehearsal over? I have to go uptown and audition for the Turkish Delight commercial.

ADRIAN: Is that tobacco or toffee?

CYNTHIA: *(Puzzled)* I wish I'd thought to ask. Not that my agent ever knows. She always leaves the same message: "Put on the chiffon caftan."

DANNY: It's code: she's gonna sell ya into white slavery.

CYNTHIA: Oh if only she would. All I ever meet are nice people.

ADRIAN: Gran'mère will introduce you to Vedius Pollio.

(CYNTHIA reacts as if to "Clark Gable")

CYNTHIA: Ooh—wonderful!

ADRIAN: He feeds his slaves to lampreys, huge gray lampreys.

DANNY: Lincoln freed the slaves.

CYNTHIA: What's a lamprey?

ADRIAN: If you hadn't had so much schooling, Danny, you'd understand more.

DANNY: *(Misunderstanding; defensive)* All I need's a year equivalency and I get the high school degree.

CYNTHIA: What's a lamprey?

DANNY: I didn't drop out till I was sixteen.

ADRIAN: Too old. The truly original students drop out far earlier. Twelve is the cut-off point. Once puberty sets in, it serves as a gelatin; everything you read or hear gets caught in the sticky mucous and is fixed forever.

CYNTHIA: What's a lamprey?

ADRIAN: Sticky mucous. A big slimy blob of it. With a rasping tongue, covered with teeth on top, like a mace.

DANNY: You talkin' about lampreys or schools?

ADRIAN: It's all one. Pollio feeds in his slaves. The flesh is stripped off.

CYNTHIA: Is it for a commercial?

ADRIAN: It's for sport.

CYNTHIA: I've never done a sports commercial. But I think Frank Gifford is gorgeous. Especially his lisp. It's so twenty-first century.

ADRIAN: *(Sadly)* Now the lampreys have invaded the Great Lakes. It's not their natural habitat. But they can adapt to anything.

CYNTHIA: That lamprey guy sounds spooky. I hope the cops catch him.

DANNY: He is a cop.

ADRIAN: Don't invent, Hierocles. Unless you have a parable to point. Vedius Pollio is a Senator, a friend of Augustus.

(FAUSTINA appears)

FAUSTINA: Vamonos! Vamonos! Vamonos a ir shopin!

CYNTHIA: *(Looking at her watch)* Ooh, it's late. I'm going to miss the audition.

ADRIAN: Here, love, take a cab. *(HE hands her money)* Do me a favor and drop Faustina off at Henri Bendel's. She's due for a fitting on her stola.

DANNY: *(Lewd)* Lots of "folds"—you dig?

(CYNTHIA giggles)

ADRIAN: *(Sternly)* A stola, Cynthia, is a ceremonial tunic.

FAUSTINA: Oh is beautiful, precioso, mi toga! And the color—o-oh! Púrpureo, púrpureo! *(DANNY makes a lewd sucking sound with his mouth)*

DANNY: *(Correcting FAUSTINA)* Pur-púr-eo . . . pur-púr-eo . . .

CYNTHIA: Do I get to wear one, too?

ADRIAN: Certainly not. Are you rubbing on the olive oil at night?

CYNTHIA: Uh-huh.

ADRIAN: Starting tonight, add the floral perfumes. I don't mean to embarrass you, dear, but are you using Binaca after *every* meal?

CYNTHIA: Yes!

ADRIAN: I thought I caught just the whiff of she-goat smell as you and Hierocles trotted by.

DANNY: *(Grinning)* You smelled him-goat. Me Tarzan.

ADRIAN: *He*-goat. *(CYNTHIA and FAUSTINA are at the door)* And study your lines.

CYNTHIA: Gotcha. *(Kisses DANNY)* See you, ducks.

DANNY: See ya, lamprey.

(FAUSTINA embraces ADRIAN)

FAUSTINA: *("Theatrical")* Hasta luego, el amor brujo! *(CYNTHIA and FAUSTINA exit)*

ADRIAN: Hierocles, come cuddle with me. I'm melancholy. My moon must be rising. I hope Baal isn't angry.

DANNY: *(Pinching ADRIAN on the ass)* It ain't his moon.

(THEY lie on the couch together)

ADRIAN: I keep forgetting why we're getting married.

DANNY: So we can have a party.

ADRIAN: I don't feel like a party. It was supposed to be to have a son. Liberum quaerendorum causa—for the sake of getting children. To continue the line of priests. Baal is angry. I know it. *(HE holds up his onyx ring)* Look: no luster in the stone. *(Sighs)* There's been too much levity. Stoic counterweights—that's what we need. More *gravitas*. Perhaps we should experiment with abstinence. Cut our diet to olives and cheese. Dilute all the wine. Then we'll—yes . . . ! *(Mounting enthusiasm)* . . . YES! We'll have a Public Oratory Contest! Get up, Danny! *(HE drags* DANNY *off the couch)*

DANNY: Aw c'mon, man, I'm beat.

ADRIAN: I'll bet you're a marvel at extemporaneous elegies. No— not extemporaneous—I'll set a topic. That has more formality, more *gravitas*. Ready?

DANNY: For what?

ADRIAN: After I announce the topic, you have exactly thirty seconds by the clock—sorry, hourglass—to gather your thoughts before you begin the declamation. Use any style you like, so long as it *is* a style. Shout and bellow. Slap your thigh. Stand aloof and unbending, voluptuously virile. Rise suddenly from a panther crouch—or slowly with senile seniority. Let fire flash from the center of your eye—or tears melt them at the corners. Let long pauses punctuate the—

DANNY: *(Yawning)*—you know: I miss the stables.

ADRIAN: It's that galloping about with Cynthia. No more talking, please. I have to concentrate on a suitable topic. *(HE sits in a double lotus position and closes his eyes)* Alcaeus . . . Menelaus . . . Maelius . . . Silius . . . Sedra . . . Phaedra . . .

DANNY: Hey, is there any soda in the fridge?

ADRIAN: *(Jumping up)* PHAEDRA! Perfect! *(Pointing suddenly to* DANNY*)* Comment on Phaedra's statement in the Heroides: "Jove decreed that virtue is whatever brings us pleasure."

DANNY: Sounds right to me.

ADRIAN: Shush—use your thirty seconds! You might want to start with a drinking song. Or a Pythagorean puzzle. I can't be giving out laurel leaves to simple declarative sentences. *(Staring at his watch)* Read . . . y—GO! *(ADRIAN sits on the floor in the double lotus, staring expectantly at DANNY)*

DANNY: Whaddaya lookin' at me like that for? It's freaky.

ADRIAN: More vivacity! Stick out an arrogant pelvis! Attempt *some* complexity of expression. Iambs, maybe. Or hendecasyllabics.

DANNY: I'm gettin' some soda.

ADRIAN: Only cheese and olives. A few figs perhaps. FIGS! *(Points at DANNY)* "Are Fresh Figs the Preferred Fruit of the Gods?"

DANNY: You're the preferred fruit of the gods.

ADRIAN: *(Disgusted)* Boring boy. It's clear you have no talent for improvisation. I'll *assign* you a role. Nero, perhaps. Yes— Nero. I'll play Agrippina, your mother.

DANNY: Why dontcha save it for the party?

ADRIAN: Pay attention while I outline the plot. Nero became infatuated with a famous courtesan named Poppaea. He wanted to marry her. *(Thoughtful)* Perhaps you should be Poppaea, given your fondness for cosmetics. No—you're no good at fellatio. Anyway—Nero's mother, Agrippina, opposed his marriage to Poppaea. *(Thoughtful)* That seems quite out of character for me. Oh my—the casting's very difficult.

DANNY: So give up.

ADRIAN: Nonsense. You have to learn to play against type. That's how you discover there aren't any types. *(Suddenly inspired)* Danny, I've got it!

DANNY: I hope it ain't contagious.

ADRIAN: You will be *Seneca*.

DANNY: The Iroquois chief?

ADRIAN: Seneca was very treacherous, kept changing sides. He wrote to the Roman Senate on Nero's behalf.

DANNY: I'd rather be Nero.

ADRIAN: Seneca has some wonderful lines: "Man is a thing which is sacred to mankind; but nowadays he is killed in play, for fun." *(Thoughtful)* He doesn't seem to have cared much about womankind.

DANNY: Maybe he was a dyke.

ADRIAN: That makes no sense at all.

DANNY: That's why I thought you'd like it.

ADRIAN: Its *sole* merit is illogic. *(Sighs)* All right, Danny: one last chance. "Who is Lesbia's Lover?"

DANNY: Shee-it. You still talking about dykes?

ADRIAN: *(Sighs)* You disappoint me, Danny. Refusing to give me children shows a suspicious devotion to form. Refusing to be childish borders on the sacrilegious. Baal tolerates everything but dignity. *(Looks at his ring despairingly)* The luster is dimmer still. It's my own fault: oratory's inauthentic to my period. An exercise in conventionality, public ritual. One cannot combat Rome by becoming Rome. Stupid of me . . . stupid . . .

DANNY: You said it. *(Exits into kitchen)*

(ADRIAN remains seated on the floor, his expression melancholy)

ADRIAN: I should be *all* my ancestors—and heirs. *All* who are buried—and who will bury us. Else how to grieve—or find relief from it?

(HE slowly lowers his head between his legs, then remains motionless in a position of meditation. The lights hold at dim)

To be taken always into the sky.
To participate always in the life of the stars.
To be reborn—and reborn again.

(From stage left, in darkness, we hear JULIA*'s voice)*

JULIA: *(Stern)* There is no appeal. You leave at once for the estate at Highlands. Anscombe will accompany you.

SELENA'S VOICE: *(Plaintive)* . . . I don't understand . . .

JULIA: These are decisions of State, my dear. Decided for the General Good. You will be recalled at the appropriate time.

SELENA: I can't bear the country! I'll perish from boredom.

JULIA: In which case, you will not be recalled.

SELENA: Why Anscombe? He's the dreariest man alive . . .

JULIA: One of the doctor's hobbies is closely related to your own.

SELENA: Raising Great Danes.

JULIA: He has a superb film collection. Gathered *pains*takingly over the years.

SELENA: I won't go without Dominick.

JULIA: Darling, don't threaten. You are my only daughter.

SELENA: I must have Dominick with me.

JULIA: *(Ice-cold)* Poor baby. Would that we could satisfy *all* imperatives. Paul asked that I give you one other message. He suggests that after you use the sauna you plunge *directly* into the pond. He's had the bottom resilted with a new weed. Lamprey, it's called. Lamprey. Extraordinary for the skin.

(Spot on ADRIAN *comes up.* HE *is still in a position of meditation)*

ADRIAN: . . . how to grieve, or find relief from it? To fight Rome —and not become Rome?

(Dim spot comes up on SELENA *upstage, behind* ADRIAN. HE *continues to face outward, oblivious of her)*

SELENA: I am sent away, love. The country. They say I will not be bored for long. I believe them. I'm to be under the tutelage of Dr. Anscombe. It's their version of a sense of humor. Cocks to

Newcastle, as it were. *(Music under, low: Ligeti's "Volumina")* What will you do? I wish I had some advice. It never was my strong point. Perhaps that's why you're so alive. Goodbye, dear boy. Never eat the flesh of swine. Oh my—I did have advice, after all!

(Lights out on SELENA, *up on* ADRIAN*)*

ADRIAN: . . . *all* who are buried—and who will bury us. All our ancestors—and heirs.

Baal hears.
Baal helps.
Baal keeps.

(Music out. Lights up)

SCENE 6

Stage right, ADRIAN *comes out of meditation.* HE *draws a deep breath.* DANNY *emerges from the kitchen with a bottle of soda.*

DANNY: Were there alotta lesbians in Rome? I dig watchin' two chicks make it. Especially Oriental chicks. I remember this dyke once picked me up. Wanted me to fuck her lover, this young chick she was keepin'. No—it was the young chick who wanted to be fucked, and the older one agreed: to keep her happy. Man—what a scene! I balled the young one for an hour. Had her moanin' and groanin'. The older one just lay there naked on the bed, watchin'. Once in a while she'd play with her twat. She was waitin' her turn—only she didn't know it. When the young one went to the bathroom to douche, I jumped the old lady. She made like she didn't wanna. But I jammed it in, and you know what she done—? *(HE looks over at* ADRIAN, *who's sat unmoving on the floor)* — Adrian: guess what she done?

ADRIAN: *(Trancelike)* When Claudius ordered Caecina Paetus to kill himself, Caecina's wife, Arria Paeta, plunged a dagger into her own breast and, dying, handed it to her husband. "It does not hurt," she said.

DANNY: Wrong guess. She took my cock out of her cunt—and shoved it up her ass. *(Laughs)* Ain't that somethin'?!

ADRIAN: *(Gently)* Laneium latusculum manusque mollicellas: "Little sides smooth as wool, and soft little hands."

(Dim lights come up stage left. TWO FIGURES are barely visible; the one, FEMALE, is bound naked to the bed, her mouth stuffed with a sock. The other, recognizable as DOMINICK, is dressed in a pleated leather apron and sandals with thonged straps criss-crossed around his calves.)

(THEY simulate various sado-masochistic rituals, in near darkness, almost like a ballet—as ADRIAN and DANNY play out their scene stage right)

ADRIAN: I've come to a decision. The party will take place tonight.

DANNY: Huh—whaddaya talkin' about? Nuthin's ready! We ain't even sent the invitations!

ADRIAN: No one's invited. Except the family.

DANNY: That's some party! No booze, no smoke, no chicks!

ADRIAN: My grandmother will be there. Perhaps they'll let my mother come.

A pantomime of mock protest and muffled sounds from the FEMALE *figure.*

DANNY: Shee-it! Ain't you got no consideration? Cynthia's been trottin' back and forth practicin' in her livin' room for weeks. And what about Faustina—running to Henry Bendel's every three minutes?

ADRIAN: *(Stately)* Go to Faustina. Tell her to bring the stola as is, incomplete. Go then to my mother's house. Gather whoever is there; it hardly matters: they're all one. Except my mother. Who will not be there.

DANNY: *(Frightened)* You don't mean bring Dominick too, do ya?

ADRIAN: Dominick will be here before you return. He'll be the first to arrive. There are certain forms he must understand, certain placements.

DANNY: I ain't doin' my hymnal chant if he's here.

ADRIAN: Hymen*eal.* No need, love. Propitiation is now the theme. Not celebration.

DANNY: Ain't we gonna have a ceremony?

ADRIAN: You may wear the ochre wig. Leave now, Danny. I have a great deal to do. Every detail must be perfect. First I must complete the tape. Then wash my hair with soap from tallow and ashes of elm. Did you know Pyrrhus used twenty elephants in his victory over Rome? I'd hoped we could have elephants at the party. One at least. *(Shrugs)* Oh well— Faustina would have thrown a fit: they're so difficult to clean up after. Why did we never think to have elephants in the stables, instead of horses?

DANNY: They ain't big at Churchill Downs.

ADRIAN: You were born out of time, Danny. You would have adored Carthage.

The "chicks" had Oriental features. Semites, akin to the ancient Jews.

DANNY: Jewish broads talk too much. Stubborn, too.

ADRIAN: Women in Carthage were admitted to high posts in the priesthood— in the worship of Baal. *(Derisive)* Rome spread the lie that they sacrificed live babies.

DANNY: Why does Dominick hafta come? He's a chauffeur.

ADRIAN: Only Rome could invent such a story. Rome demanded three hundred children from Carthage as hostages—and then burnt the city to the ground anyway.

(DOMINICK drops tallow from a burning candle on the WOMAN's buttocks)

ADRIAN: We should hire a scribe for tonight, Danny. Otherwise, our history, too, will be written by Rome. Another chapter in Carthaginian treachery. More babies burnt for Baal.

DANNY: I ain't wearin' the wig tonight.

ADRIAN: Suit yourself. Propitiation, in any case, hinges on the unpredictable. I have one other commission for you.

DANNY: Is Cynthia comin' or not?

ADRIAN: I want you to buy a truck of snowballs, put a gold coin inside each one, then rush down Forty-second Street distributing them to the prostitutes. Say to each one, as you deposit the snowball in his or her hand: "From Adrian. A protest against Nature."

DANNY: Where do ya expect me to find snow in April?

(ADRIAN *laughs*)

ADRIAN: Perhaps you *do* have a sweet soul. I was so afraid you'd ask where to find gold coins. Hurry now. Faustina first. Tell Gran'mère that out of consideration for Uncle Paul, I am willing to discuss canceling the wedding. That will bring her.

DANNY: Is he comin' too?

ADRIAN: Uncle Paul? *(Laughs)* Mon chère—il n'existe pas. He's too important to exist. Es persona de influencia. *(Spanish accent)* Beegweeg. Comprehende?

DANNY: I'm telling you in plain English: I'm in the dumps.

ADRIAN: You and Baal both. Keep a stiff upper lip, your shirt on, and the ball rolling. Demain il fera jour.

(Kisses him. DANNY *exits.* ADRIAN *goes to tape machine and begins to set up for a recording session. Lights dim)*

(Lights up stage left. DOMINICK *removes the sock from the* WOMAN*'s mouth.* SHE *turns toward the audience for the first time. It is* JULIA*)*

JULIA: Can you love a prostitute?

DOMINICK: I can love a she-goat.

JULIA: *(Dreamy)* Next time I want a dim cubicle. Obscene pictures above the door. Everywhere the impression of filth and dis-

ease. Only certain plea-
sures are permitted to
each age. Wisdom consists
in identifying and enjoy-
ing them. The imbecile
Christians are always in
the wings, eager to disdain
all things terrestrial.

DOMINICK: I'm sweatin' like a
stuck pig.

JULIA: Next time you will first
kneel at my feet: we must
establish where the power
is, in order to enjoy its re-
versal. After you've knelt,
I'll hand you the birch
branch, an oxhide strap, a
cane. You will insist I
learn the grammar.

DOMINICK: I'm gonna take a
shower.

JULIA: A father has the right to
kill an adulterous daugh-
ter—and her accomplice.
However, I pardon you.
Go to Adrian now. Soon
you will have your own es-
tates, kegs of salt fish from
the Black Sea, an ivory
harness for every horse,
bellies with no ears. Go to
Adrian.

BLACKOUT

(Lights up stage right. ADRIAN has gone into the bedroom. The tape deck is playing)

VOICE FROM STEREO (ADRIAN): . . . the family will not stand for it . . . *(Sound of military drums)* . . . Nero, infatuated with Poppaea, agreed to the matricide. Poison would not work: Agrippina's habitual use of antidotes defeated it. Nero arranged a shipwreck; Agrippina swam to safety. His men pursued her to her country estate. They seized her. She bared her body; "Plunge your swords into my womb," she said. It took many blows to kill her. Viewing the mangled corpse, Nero remarked, "I did not know I had so beautiful a mother."

(Apartment buzzer rings insistently. ADRIAN emerges from the bedroom. HE is dressed in a flame-colored tunic, belted with a jeweled silk sash. His arms are bare, his fingers and toenails painted red to match the tunic. HE turns off the tape, then opens the apartment door. DOMINICK enters)

ADRIAN: You have every virtue—even punctuality. This very second, I finished painting the henna on my toes.

DOMINICK: You're a sight awright.

(ADRIAN closes the door behind him)

ADRIAN: Technically, we should not speak directly to each other. It is uncommon even to meet before the rituals begin. Salute me, Dominick. You're in the presence of Baal's bride. *(DOMINICK perfunctorily tips his chauffeur's cap)* No, no. A wider sweep. A more encompassing gesture. But in no sense imply servility. *(DOMINICK complies with an elaborate bow)* Excellent.

(HE goes up to DOMINICK and kisses him solemnly on both cheeks)

DOMINICK: Your grandmother told me to come ahead. She's waitin' for Anscombe. He's been delayed in the country.

ADRIAN: *(Alarmed)* Oh no!

336

DOMINICK: Whatsa matter?

(ADRIAN *goes up to* DOMINICK *and brushes something off his cheek*)

ADRIAN: I'm *so* sorry! I seem to have gotten a speck of dough on your cheek. My nocturnal mask is made of dough and asses' milk. Perhaps I'd better wash my face again. Do sit down. I'll only be a moment.

DOMINICK: Make it snappy, huh? They'll be here any minute.

ADRIAN: Oh I hope not. I must get to know you better. And to have news from the Capital.

DOMINICK: Huh?

ADRIAN: Here in the provinces we're so cut off. (HE *turns the tape deck on*) Do some homework while you wait. Gran'mère's already heard this part.

(ADRIAN *exits to the bedroom. The tape deck begins playing*)

VOICE FROM STEREO (ADRIAN): . . . Poppaea was a wanton woman, whose life consisted entirely of cosmetics and fellatio . . . In 65 A.D. Poppaea suddenly died, in advanced— (ADRIAN *hurries out of the bedroom*) —pregnancy, allegedly from having been kicked in the stomach by Nero . . .

(ADRIAN *turns the tape off*)

ADRIAN: Oops, I forgot to rewind. Not even Faustina and Danny have heard that part yet. (HE *rewinds the machine*)

DOMINICK: Where are those two?

ADRIAN: You miss them, don't you. They are sweet. Faustina's the purer soul. But Danny has a darling sense of humor. And of course is better hung.

DOMINICK: Are they in the bedroom?

ADRIAN: Life in the Capital must be very strange. (DOMINICK *stands up*) Do you need the bathroom? *(Laughs)* Next thing, you'll be

337

suggesting a "golden shower." I didn't know you were part French.

DOMINICK: I don't understand a word you're—

(ADRIAN stops the tape)

ADRIAN: —ah—here we are. This is the part I wanted you to hear. *(Turns the tape on)* Now I won't be a minute. *(Looks directly at* DOMINICK*; seriously)* My dear Dominick: be calm. We're traveling the same road. Each must proceed in his own way. *(Exits)*

(DOMINICK paces in agitation)

VOICE FROM STEREO (ADRIAN): . . . thank you . . . thank you . . . Baal must have his sacrifice, I know . . . Baal *will* have his sacrifice . . . But . . . But . . .

(As if the needle is stuck on a record, the VOICE *keeps repeating)*

VOICE FROM STEREO: . . . but . . . but . . . but . . . but . . . but . . . but . . .

DOMINICK: *(Yelling)* Hey! *You!* Hey! . . .

(ADRIAN hurries out of the bedroom. A false beard is hanging, half pasted on, from his face)

ADRIAN: Now what, Dominick? Can't you see I'm preparing for—

DOMINICK: —your machine's broken. *(Seeing the beard)* What the hell is that on your—

ADRIAN: —oh, you mean all the "but's."

VOICE FROM STEREO: . . . but . . . but . . . but . . . but . . . but . . .

ADRIAN: Isn't it lovely? Happened quite by chance. In the section on flamingos. I was stumped for the next line. "But . . . but . . ." was all I could sputter out . . . *(*HE *turns up the volume on the tape)*

338

VOICE FROM STEREO: *(Loud)* . . . but . . . but . . . but . . . but
. . . but . . .

(ADRIAN *turns it down*)

ADRIAN: *(Smiling)* Then I realized I'd achieved an exact duplication
of the flamingo's mating call. Inadvertence is often its own
reward. (HE *turns the tape up again*)

VOICE FROM STEREO: . . . but . . . but . . . but . . . but . . .

DOMINICK: *(Yelling)* Cut it out, damn it! It's drivin' me crazy!

(ADRIAN *turns the machine off*)

ADRIAN: *("Placating")* Aren't you fond of birds? Oh my, we're into
such different things . . . Never mind: opposites, at last, always
meet. You'll adore the later sections . . . Do sit back down. I
want to hear about the Capitol. Surely we have common ground
there. Has the Senate agreed to restore the cavalry? Frankly, I
think it's a great mistake. What's past is past. (HE *continues to
fiddle with the beard, trying to paste it on his face*) One should never
look back—except in honest emulation. Which of course pre-
sumes an honest emulator.

(DOMINICK *scowls*)

Therein—and I can see from your expression that you're way
ahead of me—lies the problem. Any fruitful union is predicated
on two *pre*existing parts. Lincoln understood that. But then
Lincoln understood everything. Which is why he was a manic-
depressive.

DOMINICK: Why the hell are you covering your face with pubic
hair?

(ADRIAN *breaks into a delighted laugh*)

ADRIAN: Ah, you've caught the essence! That's *exactly* what beards
are—*dis*honest emulation. Only a Praetorian could have understood.

DOMINICK: *(Rising menacingly from his chair)* Take it off.

(ADRIAN starts toward the bedroom)

ADRIAN: Oops—I forgot something! I rushed out so fast when I heard you yell, that I forgot to bring in the—

DOMINICK: *(Interrupting)* —take the beard off.

ADRIAN: But all the priestesses of Baal—

DOMINICK: —off! *Now!*

(ADRIAN hesitates a second, then calmly removes the beard)

ADRIAN: There we are. I forgot how special our tastes are in the provinces. And provincialism is always a form of rudeness. You're right to be angry.

DOMINICK: This ain't the provinces. It's New York City.

ADRIAN: I think we'd better check through other details of the procedure. This isn't the kind of thing, after all, that we can do more than once. *(HE twirls around like a fashion model)* Do you approve of the cut? The color? The jewels on the belt? I may have overdone the amethysts. Expert opinion is so cautious, sketchy. The final guide must be one's own intuition. For the true searcher, I mean. Perhaps I should wear a miter? No—then I couldn't dance. Well? What do you think?

DOMINICK: Them jewels real?

ADRIAN: They'll fetch next to nothing in the open market. Buy Oriental rugs, Dominick. It's the only stylish hedge against inflation. Above all, avoid government bonds. Hasn't Gran'-mère taught you anything?

DOMINICK: No.

ADRIAN: Then you aren't listening. Gran'mère has built the family fortune *pain*-stakingly. You do know about the scimitar dance?

DOMINICK: *(Distracted)* Sure, sure . . .

ADRIAN: I'm learning it in a course at the Y. The teacher reprimands me for relying on the curve, the edge; for neglecting the point. Quite un-Roman, she keeps saying, screwing up that little nose in distaste. Her favorite in the class is a teen-ager, a speed freak. Dazzling on the upswing—and always exactly on point. It seems vulgar to me—the repetitive precision, I mean. In Syria we prefer indirection in all matters. I *will* dance to the rhythm of the curve. Here, I'll demonstrate, so you'll know what to expect. One second. (HE *goes into the bedroom and immediately returns with a curved scimitar in one hand and a small ceramic jug in the other*) The movement is as follows. (HE *does several slow rhythmic steps while swinging the scimitar in seven concentric curves from the top to the bottom of his body*) Seven times. In honor of the seven days which do not fit into monthly or yearly cycles. They are teratites, oddities, exceptions. "Painted Willies," in your archaic jargon. "Lucus naturae" in Baal's eternal phrase. All exceptions warrant honor. The less visible, the more noteworthy. Baal's special favorites are manticores and minotaurs, hippogriffs and dipsas, wiverns and whang-doodles, procks and sidewinders, wampus cats and swamp gaboons, whiffle-birds and tree squeaks. Today is one of the seven days that do not fit. A highly propitious time for ceremonial. We should, of course, have seven white bulls. (*Frowns*) New York is so confining. (*Smiles*) Well, we must make do. That attitude is itself a meritorious oddity. (*Looks at the ceramic jug in his hand*) I shouldn't dance with the pao. It throws off my balance. (HE *sets the jug on the mantle, then places within it the large black onyx skystone.* HE *stands back and looks at the jug, then smiles with pleasure*) Skystone in pao. A wondrous union. I do believe Baal will accept the offering. If only because of his sense of humor.

DOMINICK: Yeah, it's a laugh riot.

ADRIAN: Anscombe will giggle. Or grow angrily covetous. Always mistaking reality and symbol. So unlike Mother. (*Sighs*) Poor thing.

DOMINICK: *You* think that's a real cock?

(ADRIAN looks startled)

(Ligeti music under)

ADRIAN: Heavens no! A real *god*. It is part of Baal, not a substitute for him. *(Bows reverentially before the stone)*

DOMINICK: You're a mixed-up kid awright.

ADRIAN: Only when questioned.

DOMINICK: I think it's time to go to the country.

(FAUSTINA and DANNY enter suddenly. THEY're quarreling. FAUSTINA is carrying a large box. Ligeti music out)

FAUSTINA: . . . imbecile! . . . mira cato de maricón! . . .

DANNY: Me volvera loco!

FAUSTINA: —Chulo!

DANNY: —Comunista!

ADRIAN: Faustina! Danny! Stop it! Stop it!

FAUSTINA: *(To ADRIAN, calmer)* Loco, loco, he make me loco!

DANNY: She wouldn't leave the store! Kept screamin' her dress wasn't ready.

DOMINICK: Another freak show.

(FAUSTINA throws the box in disgust on the couch)

FAUSTINA: El me hiso enridiculo!

ADRIAN: Calma, calma, Faustina. I can't bear petty differences.

FAUSTINA: Ai, calma! Si, qué calma! Qué wild goose chase! *(Sinks melodramatically onto the couch)*

(DANNY applauds rhythmically, as if at a performance)

DANNY: *(To FAUSTINA, mocking)* Brava, brava!

342

FAUSTINA: Ladrón! Informadór! Pickpocket! *(SHE gives up and falls back on the couch)* Ai, me lavo las manos.

ADRIAN: *(To DANNY)* What *happened?!*

(DANNY takes him aside)

DANNY: *(Whispering, gesturing to DOMINICK)* What's he doin' here?

ADRIAN: I *told* you he'd be here. Be pleasant.

DANNY: *(Confused)* Huh?

ADRIAN: What *did* you do to Faustina?

FAUSTINA: *(To DOMINICK, gesturing toward DANNY)* Muy raro, no?

DOMINICK: Yeah sure, whatever you say.

DANNY: Some kid on Forty-second Street tried to pick her up. Thought she was a drag queen.

(The apartment buzzer rings)

FAUSTINA: *(Brightening)* Ah—la fiesta.

DANNY: Fiesta bull *shit!*

FAUSTINA: Ratón! Puto!

ADRIAN: Enough! Let bygones be bygones. *(To FAUSTINA)* Lo que paso, paso, Faustina! Go change clothes. Both of you. Quickly, quickly, pronto, pronto!

(FAUSTINA picks up her box from the couch. SHE and DANNY go into the bedroom)

(DOMINICK rises)

ADRIAN: Everything in its own time.

(FAUSTINA rushes out of the bedroom, gesturing back toward it in dismay. DANNY sticks his head around the corner, grinning broadly)

FAUSTINA: Qué es esto? Qué es lo qué pasa?

DANNY: Cynthia—outasight!

(HE exits again. The apartment buzzer rings without letup. ADRIAN *coaxes* FAUSTINA *back into the bedroom)*

ADRIAN: Faustina, no more. Tonight is the night. Now.

FAUSTINA: *(Overcome)* Oh no, Señor Adrian, no . . .

ADRIAN: It's all right, it's all right. Tenga confianza en mi. Have confidence in me. Confianza, Faustina . . . confianza . . .

(HE succeeds in getting her back into the bedroom, then rushes to the door and opens it. JULIA *and* ANSCOMBE *enter)*

JULIA: *(Disappointed)* Oh, it's you.

ADRIAN: Of course it's me, Gran'mère. I live here.

JULIA: So you do. *(SHE looks at DOMINICK, who shrugs)*

ADRIAN: *(To* ANSCOMBE*)* I hear you were delayed in the country. How is my dear mother?

JULIA: Your dear mother is—as ever.

ADRIAN: As are we all.

JULIA: *(To* DOMINICK*)* What's happened?

DOMINICK: Nothing.

ADRIAN: Now then. Make yourselves comfortable. I have a few last minute items to check, and then we'll begin.

JULIA: Begin what?

ADRIAN: The canceled wedding rites. *(HE takes the pao off the mantel and goes with it toward the kitchen)* A brief libation all around. *(Calls into the bedroom as* HE *passes the door)* We're almost ready.

FAUSTINA: *(From the bedroom, barely audible)* . . . lagrimas! . . . lagrimas . . .

JULIA: Are *they* here?

ADRIAN: You can't cancel a wedding without notifying the brides. Make yourselves comfortable. *(As* HE *disappears into the kitchen,*

HE *holds up the pao)* Ask Dominick to tell you about the pao, Dr. Anscombe. You'll find it amusing. *(Exits)*

JULIA: What's the fool gibbering about now?

DOMINICK: The kid's crackers for sure. *(To* ANSCOMBE*)* Everything go okay with Selena?

ANSCOMBE: *(Distracted)* To perfection. Did Adrian say "pao"?

JULIA: Pao or Mao. God knows what he's up to in that red dress. *Don't* comment on the costume. It will only lead to more carryings on. And delays.

ANSCOMBE: *(Nervously)* A pao is an ancient Chinese ceramic jug.

JULIA: Dominick suspected as much.

ANSCOMBE: In the Imperial Court, eunuchs would carry their testes in a ceramic jug to prove they were castrati.

(ADRIAN comes out of the kitchen, carrying the pao, now brimming with wine)

ADRIAN: Exactly, Dr. Anscombe! They, too, were a credentials-oriented society. I've always said you were a learned man. *(Holds up the pao)* Now then: a toast all around. (HE *hands the pao to* ANSCOMBE, *who looks questioningly at* JULIA*)*

JULIA: *(To* ANSCOMBE, *impatiently)* Oh drink the damn thing!

(ANSCOMBE brings the jug to his lips, but is stopped by ADRIAN's words)

ADRIAN: Gran'mère—such uncharacteristic language! And impatience. First the toast. (HE *goes to the wall near the stereo, turns on the tape deck, dims the lights. Then* HE *calls into the bedroom)* Niños —venga, venga! We're beginning. (HE *kneels in front of the black onyx piece on the mantel)* To Baal. To the eternal promise of sunlight. A los niños. A todos los niños.

(FAUSTINA and DANNY appear in the bedroom door. THEY *stand motionless.* FAUSTINA *is dressed in a purple stola, but cut open at the*

345

sides, ragged, incomplete. DANNY *has on a paper miter two feet high, a jeweled collar, a purple breast plate that ends in silk streamers barely covering his genitals, and purple buskins;* HE *carries a long, curved scimitar)*

ADRIAN: *(Calling)* Cynthia!

(Goes into the bedroom and brings her out. SHE's *wearing a body stocking.* JULIA *jumps out of her chair)*

FAUSTINA: *(Serenely)* A los niños. A todos los niños.

JULIA: What outrageous nonsense are you—!

ADRIAN: *(Cutting her short; with firmness, yet evenness)* Be seated, Gran'mère. *Now.*

CYNTHIA: This isn't what I rehearsed.

(JULIA remains standing)

ADRIAN: *(More firmly)* There's only one way Uncle Paul's instructions will be carried out. *My* way. The results will be everything you wish. The process everything *I* wish.

(JULIA hesitates, then sits)

JULIA: *(To* DOMINICK*)* None of this should have—

DOMINICK: —leave it to me.

ADRIAN: Yes. Leave it to Dominick. And Baal.

CYNTHIA: Which one is Baal?

DANNY: Keep your eye on Dominick.

(ADRIAN crosses his hands in prayer)

ADRIAN: A los niños.
A los niños triste, convulso.
A los niños dulce, descalzo.
Sin lagrimas, sin piel.

346

Mañana

O pasado mañana.

To be taken always into the sky

To participate always in the life of the stars.

To be reborn—and reborn again.

(HE *rises.* FAUSTINA *kisses him*)

FAUSTINA: Precioso, bendito.

DANNY: (*Half whispering; to* ADRIAN) Hey I didn't catch all that. Am I supposta do somethin'?

ADRIAN: Improvise, darling. (HE *goes over to* ANSCOMBE, *takes the pao, drinks from it, then hands it back to* ANSCOMBE) Just a small sip. Baal despises greed. Though not excess.

(ANSCOMBE *sips from the pao, then hands it to* DOMINICK)

DOMINICK: Here's blood in your eye. (HE *sips, grimaces, then holds out the pao to* JULIA) What the hell's in it? Donkey piss?

FAUSTINA: Lagrimas. Solamente lagrimas.

(As JULIA *reaches for the pao, some of the liquid spills on her dress.* SHE *jumps back*)

JULIA: (*To* DOMINICK) Clumsy fool!

ADRIAN: Entirely your fault, Gran'mère. You failed to get a firm grip.

JULIA: Don't stand there. Get some cleaning fluid.

ADRIAN: (*Examining the stain*) A perfect color for you. It matches my tunic. (HE *cocks his ear toward the stereo*) Shush—quiet please. The flamingos are about to come on. This is Dominick's favorite section.

VOICE FROM STEREO: . . . beautiful birds . . . far too beautiful to kill . . . but . . . but . . . but . . . but . . .

347

(ADRIAN goes over to FAUSTINA *and leads her formally by the hand to the couch, where* SHE *sits in solemn regality)*

ADRIAN: *(To* JULIA *and* ANSCOMBE*)* As Dominick already knows, this is a mating call. Authentically inadvertent. *(To* FAUSTINA, *as* SHE *sits)* You look divine. The gown is perfect. Perfecto.

FAUSTINA: Yo sufro, sufro . . .

DANNY: *(To* ADRIAN*)* Psssst! *(Juggling the miter)* This hurts.

ADRIAN: Nonsense, it's paper.

VOICE FROM STEREO: . . . but . . . but . . . but . . . but . . . but . . . but . . . but . . .

(The "buts" gradually blend into the sound of castanets)

DANNY: I'm takin' it off.

DOMINICK: That fuckin' noise.

(The "buts" end; Ives's "Spanish" Variation begins)

CYNTHIA: *(Disgusted)* This is some party.

JULIA: Watch for my signal.

DOMINICK: You watch for *my* signal.

ADRIAN: *(To* DANNY*)* All right, take it off. The castanets have started, anyway. *(Trumpets and cymbals blare out from the tape.* ADRIAN *walks to center stage; formally)* We give you now the ritual dance of the priests of Cybele.

(ADRIAN moves the black onyx stone to center stage, carries CYNTHIA, *her legs tucked under her, to a chair, then sits next to* FAUSTINA *on the couch, holding her hand.* DANNY *begins to dance with the scimitar around the onyx stone)*

ADRIAN: *(Stage whisper)* First the words, Danny. The incantation.

DANNY: Pure stone.

FAUSTINA: De piedra limpia.

DANNY: Hard stone. *(CYNTHIA giggles)*

FAUSTINA: De piedra dura.

DANNY: Bare stone.

FAUSTINA: De piedra desnuda.

ADRIAN: De piedra limpia, dura, desnuda.

> *(DANNY continues to dance around the stone. ADRIAN suddenly rises. HE dims the lights further, then switches the tape. "Ground Control to Major Tom" starts to play. HE takes the scimitar from DANNY, who retreats. FAUSTINA's body begins to rock in a mournful, steady rhythm, her head bent over her chest. ADRIAN faces JULIA, ANSCOMBE, and DOMINICK)*

We approach the patriotic climax. You may rise. Now, Danny, replace the pao on the mantel and—

> *(DANNY suddenly scurries to DOMINICK's side)*

DANNY: *(To DOMINICK)* Hey man, can I go back to the stables?

DOMINICK: You're a little late, kid.

ADRIAN: *(Sad, sweet)* Beautifully ad libbed, dear Hierocles, Priapus's own essence. I would have paid a talent for you, Hierocles. Do you know that? A full talent—three thousand, six hundred dollars. That's more than a farm costs. As Cato complained: values are awry.

VOICE FROM STEREO: *(Under)*
This is Ground Control to Uncle Paul.
This is Ground Control to Uncle Paul.

Soon you'll be atop the Lincoln Mall.
Soon you'll be atop the Lincoln Mall.
Then there'll be no stopping us at all.
Then there'll be no stopping us at all.

ADRIAN: *(To DANNY)* I reward you with— *(Dramatically opens his clenched palm)* —a handful of flies! *(Ligeti music begins)*

349

CYNTHIA: I don't see anything. *(To* FAUSTINA*)* Is Adrian okay?

FAUSTINA: *(Mournful)* Elagabalus . . . Elagabalus . . .

ADRIAN: After six days of systematic slaughter, the Roman troops reduced the population of Carthage from 500,000 to 50,000. The Carthaginians surrendered. Their general, Hasdrubal, pleaded with the Romans for his life.

ANSCOMBE: *(Steps forward into a spot)* The family will not stand for it.

VOICE FROM STEREO: *(Echoing, reverberating)* The family will not stand for it.

ADRIAN: Hasdrubal's wife, denouncing his cowardice, plunged with her sons into the flames.

JULIA: *(Steps forward into spot)* The Senate will not stand for it.

VOICE FROM STEREO: *(Echoing)* The Senate will not stand for it.

ADRIAN: Roman soldiers plowed and sowed the soil with salt, and laid a formal curse on any man who should build upon the site.

DOMINICK: *(Steps forward into spot)* The army will not stand for it.

VOICE FROM STEREO: *(Echoing)* The army will not stand for it.

ADRIAN: Today Tunis marks the original site. *(Ironic)* But there's a Carthage in Missouri. (DANNY *crawls into a spot)*

DANNY: *(Softly)* Hey man, the people will not stand for it.

VOICE FROM STEREO: *(Piercing volume)* THE PEOPLE WILL NOT STAND FOR IT. ELAGABALUS: YOU DANCE TOO MUCH!

(Applause rings out from stereo. Then everything comes to a halt. The spots go out. The tape stops.)

(A sudden spot comes up on ADRIAN. *A knife blade flashes in the light.* ADRIAN *plunges it into his groin)*

FAUSTINA: *(Mournful, piercing)* Elagabalus . . . Elagabalus . . .

(Sound of military drums beating a funeral dirge)

(Dim lights come back up on stage. ADRIAN *lies in a pool of blood.* ALL *except* FAUSTINA *and* DANNY *make their way slowly toward him.* FAUSTINA *continues to rock mournfully on the couch.* DANNY *remains crouched in a corner)*

FAUSTINA:

> *(As in a chant; to* ANSCOMBE *)*
>
> No es linda su patria . . .
>
> *(To* JULIA *)*
>
> No ondula su palmera . . .
>
> *(To* DOMINICK *)*
>
> No vibre su estrella . . .
>
> *(To* AUDIENCE *)*
>
> No es linda su patria.

ANSCOMBE: *(Singsong)*
Suicide.—Certified.—Mortified.
Suicide.—Certified.—Mortified.

JULIA: Every expert in the land will agree: self-mutilation is the one sure sign of madness.

DOMINICK: The kid never knew the meaning of a dollar. Christ, how he struggled.

DANNY: Hey, can I go now?

CYNTHIA: Me, too, hey?

DOMINICK: You'll be told. There's been too much playfulness here.

ADRIAN'S VOICE: *(On stereo)* They say Elagabalus was killed while trying to hide in a latrine. As if I don't know what latrines are for. They dragged my corpse through the streets, then flung it into the Tiber. No ritual burial. And therefore—no rest. Did you know they used to eat lampreys in Colonial Virginia? Put Baal's ring on the fourth finger of my left hand. I will not die an old maid.

(FAUSTINA goes for the ring)

Thousands of years ago, the black stone fell into the garden of a virtuous man, the fulfillment of Baal's promise to shine forever on the Earth.

(FAUSTINA places the ring on his finger)

Ah, now I am bride to you all. Say "hi" to Uncle Paul.

(Purcell's "Music for the Funeral of Queen Mary" comes up. Lights dim out, except on FAUSTINA. SHE plugs in the vacuum and begins to clean the rug)

FAUSTINA: *(Mournful, sobbing)* . . . Elagabalus . . . Elagabalus . . .

(Screen lights up the back of stage. On it, a frozen frame from the porno film "Big Stick" of teen-age girl sucking sensuously on a huge popsicle)

FINAL BLACKOUT